THE BEST OF
FRANCE

PARIS, BRITTANY, CASTLES OF LOIRE and PROVENCE

vmb
PUBLISHERS

Contents

PREFACE by Enrico Lavagno — PAGE 8

SECTION ONE: *PARIS* — PAGE 16

ANCIENT GLORIES, NEW SPLENDORS — PAGE 18

ETERNAL GRANDEUR — PAGE 28

AN OPEN-AIR MUSEUM — PAGE 66

ETERNAL SEDUCTION — PAGE 116

VERSAILLES: GOLD-LEAF, MIRRORS
AND ABSOLUTE POWER — PAGE 126

TEXT BY
Milena Ercole Pozzoli

TRANSLATION BY
Neil Frazer Davenport

SECTION TWO: *BRITTANY* — PAGE 136

INTRODUCTION — PAGE 138

THE MISTS OF TIME — PAGE 146

ARMOR: THE INHERITANCE OF THE SEA — PAGE 168

ARGOAT: THE 'LAND OF WOODS' — PAGE 226

THE AWAKENING OF IDENTITY — PAGE 254

TEXT BY
Thierry Jigourel

TRANSLATION BY
Studio Vecchia, Milan

SECTION THREE: *CASTLES OF THE LOIRE* — PAGE 262

INTRODUCTION — PAGE 264

THE GENTLE SOUTHERN COUNTRYSIDE — PAGE 272

A WORLD PRESERVED IN STONE — PAGE 292

CASTLES AND THE REMEMBRANCE
OF THINGS PAST — PAGE 370

TEXT BY
Milena Ercole Pozzoli

TRANSLATION BY
A.B.A., Milan

SECTION FOUR: *PROVENCE* — PAGE 380

INTRODUCTION — PAGE 382

AN ENDURING LAND (THROUGH MILLENNIUMS) — PAGE 392

IN THE FOOTSTEPS OF ARTISTS — PAGE 414

RIVAL SISTERS: A DIVERSITY OF CHARACTERS — PAGE 420

ALONG THE COAST, FROM PORTS TO BAYS — PAGE 442

STONE VILLAGES AMIDST OLIVE
GROVES AND LAVENDER FIELDS — PAGE 466

FESTIVALS AND TRADITIONS:
SACRED AND PROFANE — PAGE 492

TEXT BY
Silvana Rizzi

TRANSLATION BY
C.T.M., Milan
Richard Pierce

INDEX — PAGE 502

PHOTO CREDITS — PAGE 510

vmb
PUBLISHERS

Vmb Publishers® is a registered trademark property
of Edizioni White Star s.r.l.

THE BEST OF FRANCE
© 2005, 2010 Edizioni White Star s.r.l.
Via Candido Sassone, 24
13100 Vercelli, Italy www.whitestar.it
The best of France
ISBN 978-88-540-1346-9

2 3 4 5 6 14 13 12 11 10

Printed in China

Taken from:

PARIS - Places and History
© 1997 White Star S.p.A.
ISBN 88-8095-137-8

BRITTANY - Places and History
© 2004 White Star S.p.A.
ISBN 88-540-0018-3

CASTLES OF THE LOIRE -
Places and History
© 2002 White Star S.p.A.
ISBN 88-8095-878-X

PROVENCE - Places and History
© 2001 White Star S.p.A.
ISBN 88-8095-695-7

1 Rush-mat houses, such as this one immortalized in a street in the center of Rennes, are a typical element of Breton architecture.

2-3 This evocative aerial photo allows us to admire the old street plan and the principal monuments of Paris. In particular the Ile de la Cité and the Ile Saint-Louis, the historic heart of the city, can clearly be seen.

4-5 Giving onto the Place du Champ Jacquet, these buildings in the city of Rennes are splendid examples of rush-mat houses.

7 A massive keep precedes the main building of the Chateau of Chenonceaux, one of the finest and most singular in the world, built in the 16th century on the River Cher, just before it meets the Loire.

Preface

by Enrico Lavagno

*T*he relationship between form and substance has been a subject for speculation for thousands of years. It might even seem outdated, were it not for the fact that, every now and then, everyday expe-rience makes its idea re-echo like an arcane warning. It is form which gives character to whatever fills it, without which it would be vague, inert material.

And in the case of France, what char-acter! What substance! Enclosed in the solid hexagon of its geometry, France may be inscribed in a circle, the most impeccable of shapes. So ancient, so filled with its rich heritage and culture that it appears almost expanded by history, it is infinitely dense and coherent. It is like being confronted with perfection. If con-trast exists in France, it is only to create new, unpredictable harmonies, things never seen before and never experienced elsewhere. It is a question of fragrances, colors, memories and visions of the future.

Let us try to cut out a rhombus in this hexagon, four vertices offering a repre-sentative sample of this propensity to a very special equilibrium. Paris, Brittany, the Loire Valley and Provence. They are all names which implicitly convey history with all its charm, taking on a fascination which the rest of the world may only imi-tate, even in their names. The very foun-dations of modern Europe may be traced back to these four corners of Europe, the basis of a civilization which has never ceased to evolve.

Take Paris, for example. Here, in the decentered heart of the country, every opposite, every divergent element cohab-its with the utmost naturalness. There is no strident note. We cannot deny that the Eiffel Tower was not liked by all when it was built. Yet it has remained, and even become a symbol, so much so that now we could not image Paris (or France, or even Europe) without it. To-day the Tower is beautiful, very beautiful. And the equally criticised utopias achieved in the Défense or Beaubourg districts, are hyper-modern and abstracted from history to the point that they have become models. Only in Paris could a pyramid of cold material like glass and steel fit perfectly in front of the Louvre. It is a highly singular way to live history and monumentality. Here concepts like "glory" and "majesty" may be applied with all naturalness. Paris glows with grandeur. Certain squares are literally breathtaking, most of what you see is symbolic and majestic. Yet Notre Dame, the Louvre, the immense expanse between Les Invalides and Place Ven-dome, even the Eiffel Tower, cohabit without being diminished by the modesty of the old book stalls along the Seine, the suffocating dust of the brocanterie in the flea markets, the somewhat primitive, chaotic life of Montmartre and Beaubourg. And the result, as everyone throughout the world knows and acknowl-edges, is unique.

But the oldest face of what is present-day France is situated west of the capital, in that Brittany bat-tered by the waves and winds of the Atlantic. In this land of decided features, any invasive attempt has only lost its strength, capturing the fra-grances of the apples and wild flowers to

9 In this unusual shot, the Eiffel Tower is framed between the obelisk from Luxor and one of the many statues that grace the famous Place de la Concorde.

10 top Shades of red, yellow, mauve and straw colors: ochreous minerals like hematite and limonite, washed by the rains into the clay of the subsoil, tinge with unexpected colors the verdant landscape at Roussillon in the Luberon region.

10-11 The port of the charming town of Paimpol (or Pen Poull in Gaelic) rises at the end of the bay of the same name, snugly sheltered from the fury of the Atlantic. During low tide the sea goes out so far that it leaves the dock completely isolated.

scatter them amongst the hills. The pre-Celtic world, the splendid Megalithic age of prehistoric Europe, is here preserved alongside the Celtic heritage in the impressive forms of Carnac or Locmariaquer: a venerable spirit which has withstood centuries of cultural aggression, with the only outcome that it has been strengthened. The venerable oaks have remained the same, to the extent that even Christian religion may, with little pretence and without a shade of embarrassment, be tinged with the nuances of a powerful faith which preceded it for thousands of years. The hands of the clock of history move forward for many centuries along the great, lazy Loire. The mirror of beauty here is water, reflecting the splendor of the Middle Ages which brought more light than shadow, and a Renaissance which, outside Italy, only succeeded in taking root in those hills covered with vineyards of ancient stock. Heroic deeds, endless wars and brilliant conquests have over the centuries produced a fairytale-like landscape, but which could not be more real, made up of granite, dazzling limestone and slate. The France of the great courts has all its jewels here, built to defend the realm from the threat of England and Burgundy. A gentle land in climate and scenery, the Loire Valley also provides an important model, since with its castles it exemplifies the determination needed to make a great united power out of a fought-over, almost defeated land. No effort seems too great to achieve this result. Lastly Provence, the realm of light and poetry, the temple of Mediterranean culture. The Greeks at Marseilles and the Roman colonies at Orange and Arles found on this southern side of the hexagon a land which did not make them miss their homeland. Equally warm and at times harsh, Provence seems to be nourished only with fragrances and colors. And it is the land of passions. Courtly love found its most inspired troubadours here, where the vaguely uncontrolled spirit of the Mediterra-nean makes love appear as the highest good and the worst of curses. The echoes of the past have not been extinguished in Provence, which is proud of its classical and High Medieval heritage. It is a land purple with lavender and yellow with broom, tinged with white in the limestone of the inland areas and on the Alpine peaks, everywhere green with aromatic pines, here and there dotted with a violent red of the sedimentary clay of the calaques. It seems created especially to be sung and painted. Provence: if it were not an overturning of reality, we might describe it as "impressionist" by nature. It is true that the abolition of grey, the result of the development of the paintings of Cézanne and Monet, of Van Gogh and Renoir, would never have been able to take place except in this theater of chromatic euphoria. Compressed within its solid hexagon, the elusive genius of France has over the millennia welcomed contributions and influences from every direction; it has processed them and made something new, unique and perfect. But it is not only a question of substance: it is above all a question of form, or rather, character.

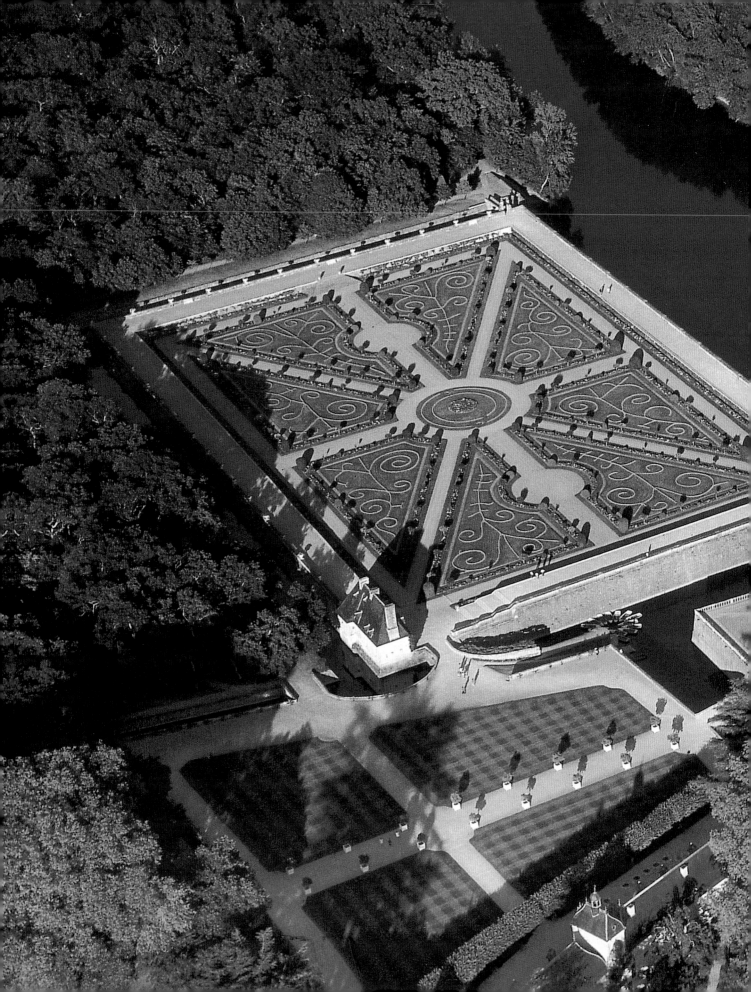

Paris

SECTION ONE

16-17 An aerial view
of the Seine, the
celebrated river
flowing through Paris
along the banks of

which the city's intense
trading activities
were concentrated
up until the end of
the 17th century.

ANCIENT GLORIES, NEW SPLENDORS

There are many things — the obvious and the less obvious, mysterious figures, ghosts of the past and stunning architecture — that each dawn change the face of Paris and ensure that she is, and always will be, one of the world's most talked-about cities. Since time immemorial, almost as if by divine right, there has been no other capital that has had such a dominant influence over the rest of its country and Europe as Paris. Ever since the sixth century, when Clovis chose it as the capital of Gaul, Paris has never wavered from this consecrated path. Knowing how to project continuously her broad and mutating appeal has long been a particular talent. Paris has always been able to renew its creative energy in infinite celebration of its own myth, and is always adept at finding ways of talking about herself, through music, theater, painting, cinema, literature and architecture. The Eiffel Tower was built in celebration of the centenary of the French revolution; Pompidou decided to link his name with that most controversial of urban planning projects, the bizarre Beaubourg. In his turn Mitterrand backed the Grand Arche de la Défense project and celebrated the bicentenary of the founding of the Louvre with the opening to the public of a new wing of the museum pierced by the tip of a glass pyramid, projecting light into the subterranean labyrinth of the Cour Napoléon. Still not satisfied, he also authorised the building of the immense National Library: four skyscrapers standing like vast books of concrete and glass, open to the sky.

Paris is a city of continual challenges and movement, bold in its imposition of the contagious youthfulness of the most excessive of avant-garde pro-

18 and 19 From the top of the Eiffel Tower you can look out at an uninterrupted panorama in all directions. On clear days you can take in the whole city and identify all the most important monuments. In the photograph at the top, the shadow of the famous Iron Lady is cast on the Seine, from the Arc de Triomphe to the Basilica of the Sacré-Coeur. The photo bottom left, on the other hand, shows the white Sacré-Coeur rising from the celebrated slopes of Montmartre. Lastly, in the photo on the right, the golden light of sunrise enhances the amphitheater-like design of the grandiose Palais Chaillot.

jects, whilst at the same time a *grande dame* ever capable of provocation and seduction. However, Paris is above all a state of mind, an imaginary world, a great unspoilt dream, a living legend that conquers with its sudden, tentacular hold over the senses. It is a capital of the world and of the spirit. Fundamentally we visit Paris on the pretext of the new in order to be reassured as to the fact that the old is unchanged, and it is on the subtle boundary between past and present that we find the eternity and uniqueness of this metropolis. In contrast with other capitals that resemble geological strata, Paris blends its past and future: the seventeenth-century quarters and the Défense, the Louvre treasure-chest and the challenge of the glass pyramid, the great boulevards and the heavily criticised Opéra-Bastille. If there is a city in the world that can boast of always having been a cradle of the avantgarde, that city is Paris. Here were born the most violent of political, cultural, artistic and social revolutions, from the Reformation to the Can-Can, from Cubism to the civil unrest of 1968, from fashion to architecture to the cinema. Almost all the writers and painters who count from the mid-nineteenth century onwards have lived and dreamed in Paris; no other city in the world can claim as much.

Brilliant and adventurous lives have been consumed on every street corner, have inhabited Bohemian attics and sumptuous palaces, have wept, laughed, loved, suffered and above all written chapters, exposed kilometers of celluloid, sculpted faces and painted canvases that have become pages in the very history of the city itself. It was here that in just fifty-two days Stendhal wrote *La Chartreuse de Parme*; it was here that Picasso lived and worked; Modigliani found a house

20 The bull's head and the dog of Paul Jouve, the gilding glittering in the sun, adorn the Trocadero fountain.

20-21 This stunning photograph, taken from the Arc de Triomphe shows Paris as the sun sets.

22-23 *When it was erected it was a source of scandal, but a hundred years on, the Eiffel Tower, an attraction built for the 1889 World's Fair, is so much a part of the Parisian landscape as to be the symbolic hub around which the whole city revolves. In this image the Iron Lady appears by a trick of perspective to be rising from the roofs of the city.*

in Rue Delta in Montmartre and later in Montparnasse. In the church of Saint-Roch, Alessandro Manzoni saw the light and decided on his conversion; Casanova lodged in Rue de Tournon, Goldoni died in Rue Dussoubs and Chopin breathed his last in a white palace close to Place Vendôme.

Paris is the city where reality and literature have always met as if in the suspended universe of a dream. Together with the ghosts of authors, the streets are roamed by the spirits of characters that came into the world thanks to their pens, spirits that carry with them a world of pure imagination. They go in and out of houses, they wander the banks of the Seine, linger in the yellow lamplight of Parisian nights and whisper among the lime trees of Saint-Germain-des-Près. They too are an integral part of the atmosphere of Paris, along with a sensation that the city is holding something special in store for you, an adventure, a surprise, a favor, an emotion. From her faded rooftops, dotted with chimneys, from her romantic parks, from the top of the Eiffel Tower or from a stroll along the bridges of the Seine, Paris reveals the myriad facets of her popularity and offers the fullness of her appeal to tourists and residents alike. Whilst Paris retains its mysteries and is the ideal city of folly, she is also a futuristic capital of telecommunications, a city that lives according to frenetic rhythms and exploits every last square centimeter of space, a city of the ephemeral and exorbitant prices. After all, what modern metropolis does not exist through perennial contradictions?

The difference is that Paris possesses the exclusive weapon of total seduction and unconsciously infects us all with its eternal and irrepressible *joie de vivre*.

24-25 Paris, the romantic city par excellence, reveals all its appeal and mystery in this photograph.

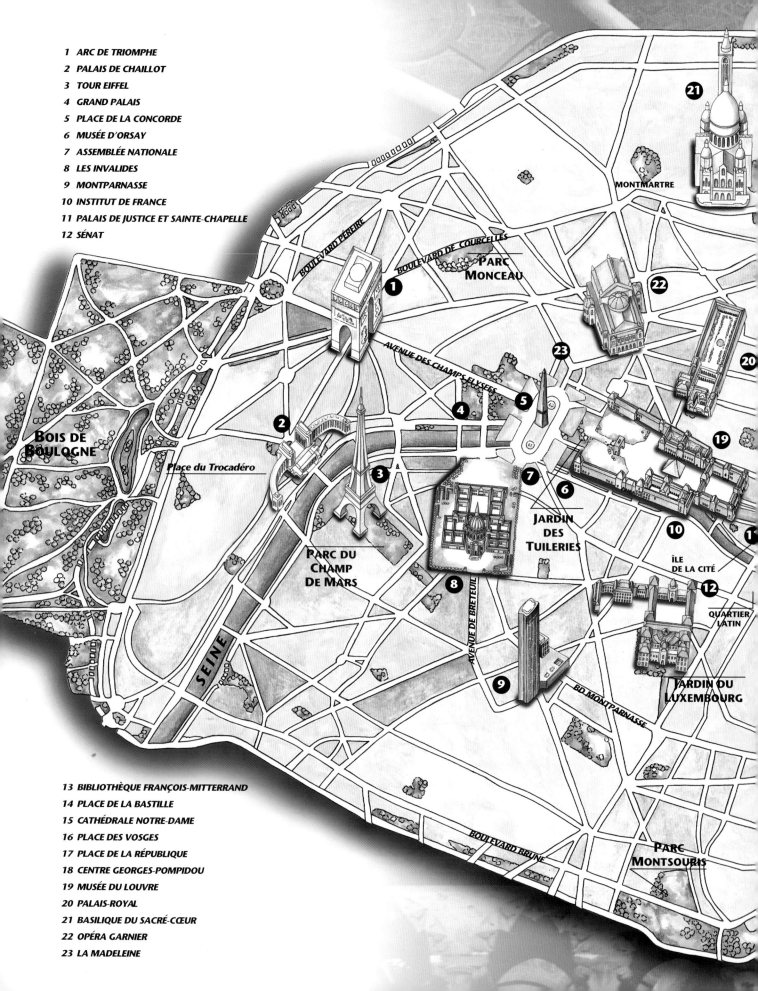

1 ARC DE TRIOMPHE

2 PALAIS DE CHAILLOT

3 TOUR EIFFEL

4 GRAND PALAIS

5 PLACE DE LA CONCORDE

6 MUSÉE D'ORSAY

7 ASSEMBLÉE NATIONALE

8 LES INVALIDES

9 MONTPARNASSE

10 INSTITUT DE FRANCE

11 PALAIS DE JUSTICE ET SAINTE-CHAPELLE

12 SÉNAT

13 BIBLIOTHÈQUE FRANÇOIS-MITTERRAND

14 PLACE DE LA BASTILLE

15 CATHÉDRALE NOTRE-DAME

16 PLACE DES VOSGES

17 PLACE DE LA RÉPUBLIQUE

18 CENTRE GEORGES-POMPIDOU

19 MUSÉE DU LOUVRE

20 PALAIS-ROYAL

21 BASILIQUE DU SACRÉ-CŒUR

22 OPÉRA GARNIER

23 LA MADELEINE

BOULEVARD PEREIRE

BOULEVARD DE COURCELLES

PARC MONCEAU

MONTMARTRE

AVENUE DES CHAMPS-ELYSÉES

BOIS DE BOULOGNE

Place du Trocadéro

PARC DU CHAMP DE MARS

SEINE

AVENUE DE BRETEUIL

JARDIN DES TUILERIES

ÎLE DE LA CITÉ

QUARTIER LATIN

JARDIN DU LUXEMBOURG

BD. MONTPARNASSE

BOULEVARD BRUNE

PARC MONTSOURIS

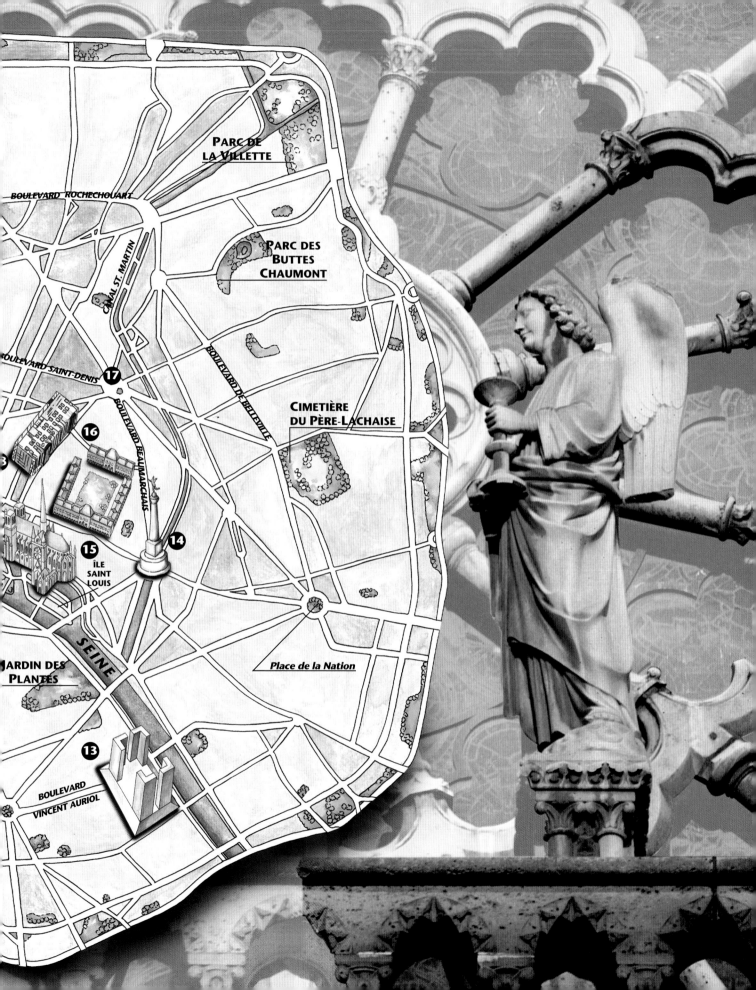

PARC DE
LA VILLETTE

BOULEVARD ROCHECHOUART

PARC DES
BUTTES
CHAUMONT

CANAL ST. MARTIN

BOULEVARD SAINT-DENIS **17**

BOULEVARD DE BELLEVILLE

CIMETIÈRE
DU PÈRE-LACHAISE

BOULEVARD BEAUMARCHAIS

16

14

15

ÎLE
SAINT
LOUIS

SEINE

JARDIN DES
PLANTES

Place de la Nation

13

BOULEVARD
VINCENT AURIOL

ETERNAL GRANDEUR

28-29 Reproduced
in the works of Julius
Caesar and Strabone,
the antique street
plan of Roman
Lutetia shows the
primitive nucleus of
the nascent city
created on the Ile de
la Cité in the Seine.
As can be seen, the
extensive flood plain
was still completely
forested.

Jewels, vases, furnishings, necklaces, axes, daggers, statuettes and many other artefacts have been recovered thanks to archaeological excavations over the last two hundred years that have allowed us to reconstruct the decisive phases in the development of Paris. The legendary Roman *oppidum* has revealed many of its secrets: the location of the principal streets, the foundations of the *forum*, the remains of the *capitolium*, the theater and the arena. In the quarter of Bercy in the 13th arrondissement, the building of an underground car-park brought to light a Neolithic village following the discovery of a number of wooden canoes and 250 bronze age vases; it was excavations along the Rue Pierre-et-Marie-Curie that revealed the secrets of a Gallic-Roman kiln found almost intact, whilst the subsoil of Notre-Dame has given up, at least in part, the pillars of the temple of Tiberius, erected on behalf of the boatsmen's guild in the middle of the first century B.C.

Digs around the Latin quarter have also helped to complete our picture of ancient *Lutetia*, the Gallic-Roman village built on the foundations of the primitive village inhabited by the Parisii tribe. In the year 52 B.C. one of Julius Caesar's centurions arrived to challenge the Gaul Camulogenus close to this settlement, composed of simple huts on an island in the middle of the Seine. A full-scale war was fought that led to the destruction of the Gauls. The Roman settlement of *Lutetia* was then raised on the remains of the ancient village on the cradle-shaped island now known as the Ile de la Cité. The principal axis was oriented along the approximate route of what is today Rue Saint-Jacques and the decuman probably led straight to the boats moored along the banks of the Seine.

28 top left Over
the centuries the birth
of Paris has inspired
engravings, prints,
paintings and bas-
reliefs.
This illustration
shows part of ancient
Lutetia, taken
from an engraving
published in Paris
à travers les siècles,
by the historian
G. de Genouillac.

28 bottom left and
top right The first
inhabitants of what
in time was to become
the legendary Ville
Lumière were the
Parisii, a rough,
primitive people as
seen in these
engravings showing
men and women
engaged in daily
chores.

LUTECE
ou
PREMIER PLAN
DE LA VILLE DE PARIS
Tiré
De Cesar, de Strabon, de l'Empe
Julien, et d'Amnian Marcell,
Par
M. L. C. D. L. M.
1705.

DESCRIPTIO

Cette partie Ville que les Gaulois nommoi
Capitale de la Province des Parisiens,
portoient tout l'état des Gaules.
Elle étoit renfermée dans l'une des îsle
du Nord couvert d'un Marais et d'un
une partie en Prez et le reste
en Bois.
Ses Maisons étoient de forme rond
Terre couvertes de Roseaux ou d
nées.
Camulogene en étoit le Gouv
s'assujetissoit l'orsque les Romains en
l'an du Monde 3998, et avant N

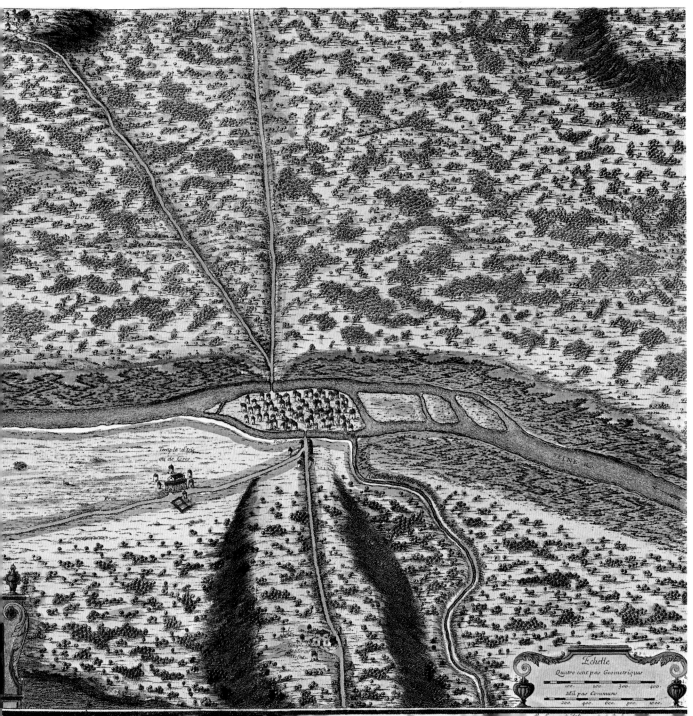

30 top Every epoch
has produced
historical figures
who have contributed
to the history and
legend of Paris.
In 250 the first
bishop Saint-Denis,
hated by the pagan
priests who are
depicted in this
manuscript in the
act of despatching
messengers to Rome
to ask for help
against him, died
a martyr on what
was to become the
famous hill of
Montmartre.

This was to all intents and purposes the birth of Paris. "The gravel beach of that island was its first city wall, the Seine its first moat" wrote Victor Hugo in *Notre-Dame de Paris*. He went on to add, "For a number of centuries Paris remained an island, with two bridges, one to the North, the other to the South and two bridgeheads that served her as both ports and fortresses, the Grand-Châtelet on the right bank and the Petit-Châtelet on the left. Then, from the epoch of the kings of the first dynasty, Paris, feeling constrained on her island on which there was no longer space in which to move, decided to cross the river. Beyond the larger and smaller Châtelets a first turreted wall of stone began to enclose the countryside on either side of the Seine… little by little the tide of houses, thrust out from the heart of the city towards the periphery, broached, eroded and erased that first wall." The sequence of civil wars and the barbarian invasions did little to prevent Rome from extending its control for many centuries over these lands and much of France. In 250 the first bishop Saint-Denis died as a martyr on, as legend would have it, the hill that would later become known as Montmartre, but Christianity nevertheless spread through the small community.

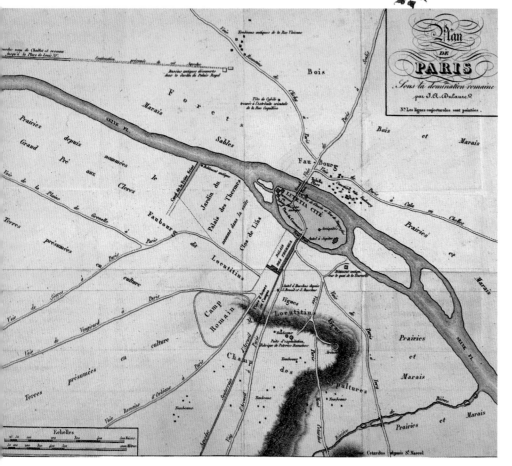

30 bottom Many areas of Paris have provided traces of the ancient Roman oppidum with the principal cardum or axis and the decuman that perhaps led directly to the boats moored along the banks of the river. Archaeological investigations have reconstructed the development of Paris from an insignificant Neolithic village to the glorious Ville Lumière. Every excavation has enabled new pages to be added to the centuries-long story of this fantastic city. From one arrondissement to the next, every open building site offers an opportunity for a fascinating trip through time.

*31 left The first of a
series of barbarian
raids by the tribes
from beyond the Rhine
began in 275. Faced
with this threat Paris
retreated within the
well fortified Cité.
Nevertheless, Attila,
the Scourge of God, as
noted in this
illustration taken
from a 12th-century
painting, besieged the
city in 451.*

*31 right At this point
legend takes over from
history: it is said that
thanks to the divine
intervention implored
by the young
Geneviève, seen here
in an illustration
by Lion Royer from*
Le Petit Journal,
*the fearsome Attila
turned his back on
the city and departed
for the South without
sacking it.*

From 275 onwards the threat of barbarian invasions represented a severe test of
the defences of the *oppidum*. In the
fourth century the already densely populated fortified city was protected by
the fleet of Roman ships moored on the
Seine, a small but well-armed garrison
and massive city walls. For over a century the houses clambered one on top of
the other and the streets became
increasingly narrow, imprisoned within
the ring of tall, solid towers. In the fifth
century, Paris was thus able to put up
stubborn resistance to the siege of Attila
the Hun, backed by the divine intervention of young Geneviève who convinced the besieged population to pray.
As if by a miracle, Attila completed an
about turn and left with his army heading south. *Lutetia*, by now known as
Paris, was safe and Geneviève was later
canonised and proclaimed as the patron
saint of the city. A slim statue in pale
marble depicting her still dominates the
Pont de la Tournelle.

32 top These helmeted and armoured warriors from the era of the alliance between the Franks and the Gauls give an idea of the customs and costumes of Merovingian Paris. Soon after he was declared King, Clovis transferred the capital of his kingdom to the banks of the Seine.

32 center left Victorious at Soissons over the troops of the Roman Empire, Clovis (481-511) became master of Gaul, converted to Roman Catholicism and was proclaimed King of the Franks and crowned as such in Reims cathedral, as can be seen here in an illustration taken from Les Grandes Chroniques de France.

32 center right Taken from Paris à travers les siècles, *this engraving shows Clovis being carried in triumph by his men.*

Late in the fifth century the history of the Salian Franks was unified with that of Roman Gaul. Clovis, victorious at Soissons against the troops of the Roman Empire, became King of Gaul. He married the Christian Clotilda who persuaded him and his army to convert to her religion. He was crowned King of the Franks (from whom the name of the country derives) at Reims in 508 and transferred the capital of his kingdom to the banks of the Seine. In this period Paris was dotted with half-built churches, nine in construction on the left bank and three on the right. Clovis ordered the construction of the church dedicated to the Apostles where he wished to be buried and where some time later the remains of Saint Geneviève were also interred. A son, Childebert, who was to reign for 47 years, commissioned the building on the same bank of the Seine of an immense basilica, the largest in Merovingian Gaul and another that housed the remains of St. Germain, the bishop of Paris late in the sixth century, on the foundations of which the St. Germain-des-Prés abbey was built.

32 bottom This illustration from 1541 depicts the coronation of King Pepin by St. Boniface in 751.

33 top Charlemagne only briefly resided at Paris, preferring Rome or Aix-la-Chapelle to the city on the Seine. In this painting by Julius Schorr von Carlosfeld he is seen entering Paris in triumph.

33 bottom left
In 751, following the deposition of Childeric III, the last Merovingian king, Pepin the Short and then Charlemagne were crowned as King. Charlemagne is seen here in regal dress and with the symbols of power in his hands in a celebrated portrait by Albrecht Durer. The King subsequently left Paris defenceless and late in the 9th century it was sacked on a number of occasions by the Normans. The Cité resisted a long siege, but nothing remained of the Roman Paris of the Rive Gauche.

33 bottom right
This 15th-century engraving shows the Ile de la Cité in the era of Charlemagne. As you can see the city was already notably well developed.

The Merovingians conquered almost all of Roman Gaul, but with the advent of the seventh century, civil disorder, the undisciplined court life, the lack of a political policy, the division of the kingdom and internal strife among the rulers, led to the decay of the dynasty and the rise of Pepin the Short and the Carolingians. In 751 the last Merovingian King Childeric III was deposed by Pepin who himself took the title of King. When his son Charlemagne came to the throne, he established the capitals of his kingdom at Rome and Aix-la-Chapelle and was rarely resident in Paris. Hard times beckoned as the city was abandoned by the last of the Carolingians; during the ninth century it was sacked by Norman adventurers. The outskirts were destroyed and as Paris retreated within the confines of the Cité the last traces of the Roman *oppidum* disappeared.

In 987 Hugh Capet of the Capetian dynasty entered the scene and, as it approached its first millennium, Paris, with its wealthy abbeys, its annual fair and its markets, reassumed its role as capital of the kingdom. Louis VI "the Large" (1108-1137) established his residence in a palace on the Cité, the original island that was increasingly crowded with houses. In 1163 Bishop Maurice de Sully began the construction of Notre-Dame on the site of the old Merovingian church and in 1180 Philip Augustus once again imprisoned the city within a new ring of fortified walls with tall, powerful towers; in order to cope with the assaults of the King of England he built the Louvre fortress that was soon to serve as a royal residence and gave new impulse to the Les Halles de Champeaux, the celebrated Paris market established by Louis the Large and that was to remain in situ for eight centuries. Bianca of Castile, the wife of Philip Augustus, commissioned the building of Sainte-Chapelle. Within a few decades even the new city walls proved unable to allow for the expansion of the city that was by now composed of fourteen parishes. Medieval Paris developed on the right bank of the Seine and was a major center on the great trading and communications routes. Textiles from Flanders arrived along Rue St.-Denis, grain along Rue Saint-Honoré and the fish from Normandy and Brittany arrived in the city along Rue des Poissoniers. The Seine, the most natural and immediate means of communication for all trade, was by now the scene of a constant bustle of barges and boats. "The houses breached the walls of Philip Augustus", wrote Victor Hugo, "and happily scattered across the plain with neither order nor symmetry as if they had escaped from a prison. Once there they dug a garden in the fields and sat at their ease". The origins of the Parisian suburbs lie in this period and are linked to the expansion of the inhabited areas around the first urban parishes such as Saint-Germain l'Auxerrois, Saint-Merry, Saint-Jacques-la-Boucherie and Saint-Nicolas-des-Champs. In contrast, the left bank was almost completely abandoned. The slopes of the Sainte-Geneviève hill became agricultural land owned by the monks of the great abbeys such as the nearby and already flourishing Saint-Germain-des-Prés.

Under St. Louis IX, the aristocracy was weakened by the crusades in the Holy Land and against the Cathars. The university, instituted and recognised by a Papal Bull issued in 1209 by Pope Innocent III, ensured that the city enjoyed international prestige as a center of learning. In 1257 Robert de Sorbon founded the university for the teaching of theology, law, art and medicine that was to take his name. When he came to the throne Charles V ordered the construction of the Bastille and city walls on the right bank to enclose the new quarters. Once again, however, these soon proved inadequate in the face of the continued rapid expansion of the city. Thus it was that by the fifteenth century Paris extended far beyond the concentric rings of fortifications that since the era of Julian the Apostate had attempted to restrain her within their defensive patterns.

36 left St. Louis IX, depicted while visiting Notre-Dame accompanied by his mother Bianca of Castille; according to Jacques Le Goff "he was a sainted knight, a sainted warrior. The King applied the two great rules of Christian war, of right and just war, whilst continuing to serve the interests of the French monarchy." The category to which St. Louis belonged was that of the lay saints. In terms of politics he attempted to be an ideal Christian king whose virtues were manifested through power, wisdom and goodness.

36 right This painting shows St. Louis in front of the church of John the Baptist; in the background can be seen the towers of Paris.

37 Charles V, "The Wise", seen here in a portrait by Orley Bernard was an able financial strategist and skilfully reorganized the army. Having reopened the war with the English he managed to reduce their possessions to a few coastal fortresses. When he was still the Dauphin, however, he had had to tackle the first Parisian revolt led by Etienne Marcel, the spokesman for a discontented populace. Having come to the throne following the execution of Marcel, Charles carried with him the memory of those signals of fracture between sovereign power and the capital and the first thing he did was to leave the Ile de la Cité (top left), order the building of the Bastille and complete the construction of a new city wall on the Right Bank that, following the course of the Seine, was set at a right-angle to the present-day Carrousel. The Louvre (bottom) ceased to be a fortress and began to be meticulously transformed by Charles V into a royal palace. He had the building heightened, enriched with windows, decorated with statues and embellished internally. He placed his rich library in the northwest court and his collection of works of art in the large halls. He also ordered the planting of lush gardens with porticoes and pavilions.

The fourteenth century was a difficult period for Paris. In 1348 it was struck by the Black Death, a plague that decimated the population of 200,000 souls. What was worse was that the struggle for the French throne between the Capetians and the English king Edward III of the Plantagenet dynasty sparked off the Hundred Years War (1337-1453). The war did, however, bring to an end a series of civil disorders provoked by legendary demagogues such as Simon Caboche and Cape-

luche who threw Paris into a climate of terror between 1413 and 1418. On the death of Charles VI, the Dauphin and future King Charles VII fled the peril of rebellion by seeking refuge at Bourges, giving rise to that period of gilded exile that saw the banks of the Loire with their enchanted castles adopted as the "capital" of the kingdom. The English entered Paris in 1420, on the death of Charles VI, and proclaimed Henri VI of England as the King of France despite his tender

38 bottom This 15th-century miniature depicts a battle between knights on horseback during the Hundred Years War. The English occupation, the devastation caused by the war and the economic crisis all had an effect on Paris. In 1348 the city was also struck by the Black Death that decimated the population.

age. Just as victory appeared to be within the English grasp, a country girl, Joan of Arc, reached the French army and implored the Capetian King Charles VII, sheltering at Chinon, to allow her to march at the head of his troops. A miracle then took place. The enemy was routed and Charles VII entered Paris in triumph and was crowned as King. Joan of Arc was burnt to death, accused of witchcraft by the English, who eventually left French soil in 1453.

39 left The English entered Paris in 1420 and upon the death of Charles VI proclaimed Henri VI of England King of France, even though he was still a child. However the indomitable, legendary figure of the Maid of Orléans soon appeared on the horizon. Here she is portrayed while fighting in front of the Saint-Honoré gate. It is said that she was sent by God to restore Charles VII, in hiding at Chinon to avoid the perils of the capital, to the throne of France. Thus Joan of Arc made her way to Chinon, where she arrived on March the 9th, 1429 to be presented to the King. When she found herself in front of the sovereign she said, "My name is Joan, I have been sent by the King of the Heavens to tell you that you will be crowned as the true King of the French in the cathedral of Reims."

39 right In this contemporary miniature, Charles VII is seated upon the French throne, surrounded by members of his court.

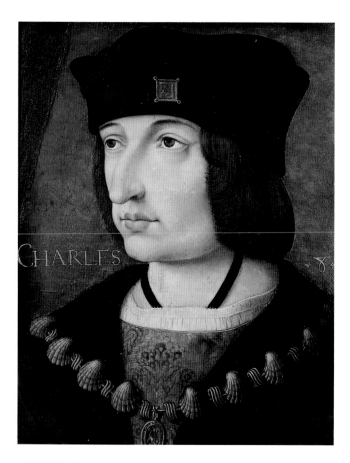

In the fifteenth century, Paris, as Victor Hugo wrote, "was divided into three completely distinct and separate cities, each with its own shape, uniqueness, customs, traditions, privileges and history: the Cité, the Université and the Ville. Each of these three parts was a city, but a city too special to be complete and to be able to do without the other two. They therefore presented three individual faces. The Cité was a city of churches, the Ville of palaces, the Université of colleges... as if to say the island was the province of the bishop, the right bank of the merchants and the left bank of the rector". In the fifteenth century the Seine flowed around five islands, all

40 bottom The Valois line ended with Charles VIII, but it was through him that the Renaissance entered France. As shown in these engravings of the Abbey of Saint-Germain-des-Prés and the Louvre (left) and a palace under construction (right), Paris was already in a fervour of building, well-prepared to receive this new flowering of art.

40 top This contemporary painting shows Charles VIII, who succeeded his father, Louis XI, in 1483, under the regency of his sister Anna of Beaujeu. In 1491, at Langeais castle,

he married the 15 year-old duchess Anna of Brittany, and at the urging of his advisors, in 1494 he travelled through Italy in order to annex Naples, enticed by the offers of exiles from the kingdom.

The expedition was immediately successful, but shortly thereafter, due to the strength of Naples' anti-French league, the King was forced to abandon the city and retreat back up the peninsula to France.

within the Paris city walls. Seen from above, each of these quarters appeared to be an inextricable tangle of twisting alleys from which the ornate Gothic architecture of many churches and palaces thrust its way into the sky.

Under Charles VIII and later Francis I, the great architectural and cultural phenomenon of the Italian Renaissance crossed the Alps and reached the banks of the Seine. Until then Paris had been a homogeneous city, an architectural and historical product of the Medieval. Now that severe unity was blended with the dazzling luxury of the new style, and softened by the introduction of rounded Romanesque arches, Greek columns and acanthus leaf volutes. The period saw the building of the Carnavalet, the Fountain of the Innocents, the Pont-Neuf and the Tuileries. In 1528 Francis I decided to move the court back to Paris following the intermission on the Loire, and to entrust Pierre Lescot with the complete rebuilding of the Louvre.

41 bottom left
This engraving shows Paris during the reign of Francis I. It was a city dominated by turrets and bell-towers that nevertheless reserved considerable space for greenery and nature, and boats rather than carts drawn by horses or oxen served the capital's commerce.

41 bottom right
In the 16th century Paris was a city of remarkable size, as this map dating back to the time of Francis I demonstrates.

41 top In 1528 Francis I, seen here dressed in damask, made his residence in Paris official. Besides expanding the Louvre, a project which he conferred upon the architect Lescot in 1546, the King began construction of a Hôtel de Ville worthy of his
grandiose capital. Francis I, tall and anything but ugly, a fearless warrior, adored by his courtiers and loved by women, found a life-time adversary in Charles V, who had defeated him in the race for the Empire. The two sovereigns would have many opportunities to meet,
but nothing positive that would bring peace to Europe was ever to come out of them. The ambitions of Francis I were in any case satisfied when, during a visit by Charles V to Paris, the city seemed, to the stupefied eyes of the Emperor, a city as large as the world.

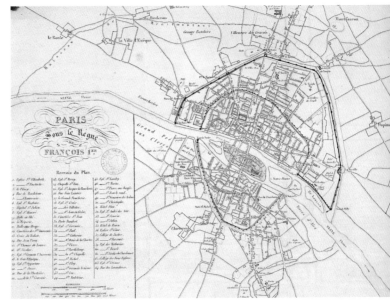

42 top Niece of Lorenzo the Magnificent, daughter of the Duke of Urbino Lorenzo de' Medici and the French Princess Madeleine d'Auvergne, and mother of three kings of France, Catherine de' Medici (in a painting depicting her when she was still young) had one of the most remarkable lives in history. In a century of both splendor and horror, she was educated in Florence, but at a very early age was sent to France to marry Henri of Orléans, the son of Francis I. The King never loved her, openly preferring throughout his life his lover Diana de Poitiers. However, Catherine, in spite of being despised as a foreigner and not of royal blood, was in a certain sense Queen for 30 years, as she was the mother of three Kings of France who succeeded one another. Her life was often in danger, but she confronted every risk with courage.

42-43 One of the finest qualities of Catherine de' Medici was her religious tolerance, but nevertheless, the massacre on the night of St. Bartholomew's Day happened during her reign on August 24th, 1572. This incident, in which thousands of Huguenots (French Protestants) were killed, is depicted here in a famous painting by François Dubois.

43 top right
This engraving immortalises a difficult moment for France on the 12th of May, 1588, when the capital was barricaded and violent clashes took place over religious differences.

43 left This fresco by Giorgio Vasari in the Sala Regia of the Vatican portrays a scene of the Saint Bartholomew's Day Massacre, in particular its justification by Charles IX to the Parliament.

This was the era in which Rabelais, a Franciscan monk, attacked all and sundry from his priory near Tours, monks, the church, princes and politics feeling the weight of his pen. In the meantime Calvin was attracting proselytes for his Reformation. In Paris, the first to be infected by these new ideas were the wealthy merchants, the princes and the intellectuals. The Wars of Religion were not slow to break out, along with political in-fighting. In 1572 the

*43 top right
This engraving immortalises a difficult moment for France on the 12th of May, 1588,*

when the capital was barricaded and violent clashes took place over religious differences.

Huguenots were massacred in Paris on St. Bartholomew's Day permitted by Queen Catherine de' Medici. It was a difficult moment for France and the Huguenot King Henri IV who in order to enter Paris and save his throne was obliged to convert to Roman Catholicism, passing into history with the celebrated phrase "Paris is well worth a Mass" in 1594. Having assumed power he restored the city, causing it to rise from the ruins to the point where Paris represented the ideal city of an urban civilization illuminated by the splendor of the King and his court. We are now at the threshold of the Grand Siècle: Descartes stirred debates among the intellectuals of the entire western world; the first great royal squares were completed: Place Dauphine and Place des Vosges.

*43 bottom right
In order to secure the French crown, Henri IV converted to Catholicism. Once upon the throne, he began a restoration of the ruined city, embellishing it with new works, opening the first large squares and reviving work on the Louvre and the Tuileries. He also inaugurated the Pont-Neuf, encouraged the development of the Marais and the urbanisation of the Ile Saint-Louis. Moreover, he had Place des Vosges set out, initially as a plaza for equestrian competition, but high aristocracy soon arrived to live in the sumptuous red brick buildings surrounding the square.*

44 left The King
of France and
Navarre, Louis XIII
(above), portrayed
in a famous
contemporary
painting, made Paris
a grand capital,
taking the initiative
on many projects,
but above all leaving
Cardinal Richelieu,
here depicted in his
official gowns, free
to construct the
Palais Cardinal,
today the Palais-
Royal.

*44-45 and 44 bottom
By the 17th century
Paris had expanded
in all directions.
This map of the city
and the print dating*

*from that period
clearly demonstrate
this expansion and the
urban agglomeration
locked inside the city's
massive circular walls.*

*45 These engravings
show a number
of aspects of the
expanding city in
continuous growth.
Above one can
admire the
extraordinary view
of the Louvre and
the Seine from the
Pont-Neuf; the
painting in the
center offers a view of
the Louvre, while the
painting below shows
the Seine as seen from
the Ile de la Cité.
In this period the
architect Louis Le
Barbier was creating
a new quarter on the
Rive Gauche between
the University and
the Seine, while
Christophe Marie was
constructing upon the
two little muddy and
uninhabited islands
bordering the Ile de
la Cité.*

After the reign of Louis XIII
(1610-1643), dominated by the controversial figure of the Prime Minister,
Richelieu, the future Louis XIV (1643-
1715) and the author of the famous
phrase "I am the State", came to
throne at just five years of age. He
replaced the old city walls of Paris with
great boulevards, promoted the creation of extensive public parks and built
the grandiose Palace of Versailles to
where, in 1682, the Sun King transferred his court.

The Sun King was succeeded by Louis XV (1715-1774), who also was to live at Versailles and was to devote himself to the embellishment of Paris, by now a city of around 500,000 inhabitants. He united the Faubourg Saint-Honoré with the Faubourg Saint-Germain with the Pont-Royal and had further bridges constructed over the Seine; he also ordered that the ancient cemetery of Saints-Innocents, a source of infection and disease, be demolished and replaced by a great market. In the meantime the Panthéon, the École Militaire and Place de la Concorde were all improved. On the international political front the disastrous Seven Years War (1756-1763) concluded with the loss of the colonies in Canada, the West Indies and India to the English, whilst the capital, in the absence of the King, was increasingly a hotbed of revolutionary ideas.

46 Whilst in 1500 Paris was experiencing a moment of glory and architectural reconstruction, it was also devastated by the Wars of Religion, aggravated by the Fronde activities that turned Louis XIV against the city (the Sun King is portrayed below alongside the drawings for the royal residence spread out on the table). It was under Louis XIV, in spite of his obsession with the dream of the Palace of Versailles, splendidly depicted above, that the city began to assume in part an appearance that we still recognise today. Sixty convents were built in the first decades of the 17th century. Largely thanks to Colbert, the controller of the finances and the superintendent of the monuments of the capital, during the reign of Louis XIV Paris saw the construction of many new buildings such as the Observatory and the Hôtel Royal des Invalides, designed by Hardouin-Mansart. This was the great architect and friend of the King who complied with and interpreted Louis XIV's desire to construct the immense Palace of Versailles.

*47 top and bottom left
Although absorbed by
the Versailles project,
Louis XV (portrayed
below with the sceptre
of power) did not
forget Les Tuileries
(above), to which
continuous
modifications were
made. Great staircases,
galleries and new
apartments were built,
whilst the garden, with
its flower beds and
fountains, where the
noblemen and ladies
would step aside as the
King passed, became
one of the most
felicitous spaces of the
grandiose construction.*

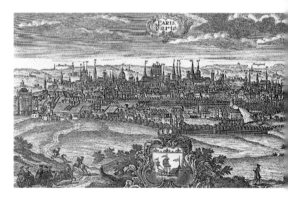

*47 bottom right
17th-century Paris
became ever more
beautiful around
Les Tuileries, as
demonstrated by
these images, which*
*show a glimpse of
the Seine and the
cathedral of Notre-
Dame (above) and
a view of the port
near the Tour Saint-
Jacques (below).*

48 left Historical events have made Louis XVI (portrayed above in his pompous coronation outfit) and Marie Antoinette of Austria, (at bottom, shown in a painting by Elisabeth-Louise Vigée-Lebrun), the most famous sovereigns in French history. She was the youngest and favorite of the 15 children of Emperor Frederick I and Maria Theresa of Austria. When she was only ten years old she was promised as the wife of the Dauphin of France, who was then only twelve.

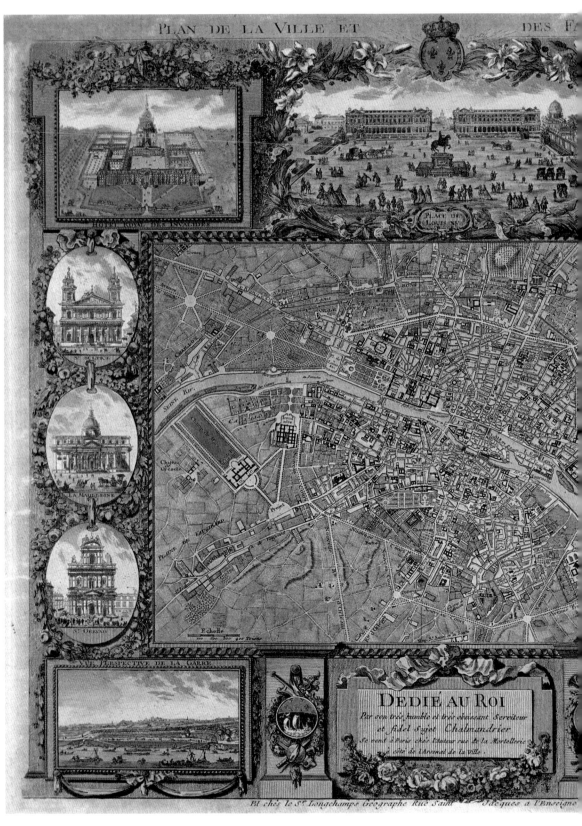

In an atmosphere that was by now hostile to the crown, Louis XVI came to the throne in 1774 with his Austrian wife Marie Antoinette. On the 5th of May, 1789, the States General met at Versailles in a climate of messianic expectation convinced that radical changes were on the horizon. Following the elaborate opening ceremony, and prior to tackling the real problems, the assembly was faced with a major procedural question over whether the motions presented should be voted according to order or per head. The representatives of the Third Estate (the upper and middles classes), numerically superior to the other two orders together (the nobility and the clerics), were in favor of voting per head whilst the others naturally preferred to vote per order as this would ensure them secure victory and confirm their privileges. The question seemed insoluble until the Third Estate suddenly proclaimed its own National Assembly in a surprising and highly significant move. Whilst the intervention of the King proved to be in vain, the privileged orders were obliged to bow to the will of the bourgeoisie and agree terms. On the 9th of July, 1789, the National Assembly was proclaimed as the Constituent Assembly and the States General ceased to exist. The King, however, still hoped to regain control of the situation by dismissing the liberal minister Necker and ordering a strong garrison to be placed around Versailles.

48-49 This map shows the development of Paris between 1785 and 1789.

49 While Marie Antoinette was squandering huge sums, the people were being infected by new revolutionary ideas. On the 5th of May, 1789, the States General met at Versailles (top) in a climate of expectation. Regardless of the fact that the atmosphere was perhaps not the most relaxed, a peaceful resolution to the conflicts was hoped for. However, the first signal of the Revolution had been sounded. The painting below shows the famous Jeu-de-Paume speech on the 20th of June, 1789.

This was the move that triggered the Revolution: on the 14th of July, 1789, the people, exasperated by a sharp rise in the price of bread and inflamed by revolutionary ideas, flooded the streets and squares and besieged the prison, the symbol of royal despotism. The storming of the Bastille had as an immediate consequence the constitution of a new municipal council the Commune, that immediately replaced the old aristocratic administrators with members of the bourgeoisie and decided upon the constitution of an urban militia, known as the National Guard, under La Fayette. A revolutionary wind blew throughout France. Following the Declaration of the Rights of Man the situation developed still further. On the 20th of June, 1791, Louis XVI escaped from the Tuileries where he had been obliged to reside after having left Versailles, and attempted to reach the troops faithful to him in Lorraine. However, after having been recognised at Varennes he was arrested and brought back under escort to Paris. Imprisoned in the Temple Tower, he was put on trial, condemned to death and executed on the 21st of January, 1793. The French Revolution, with all of the events and developments

51 top left The protagonists of the Revolution inspired many artists. This image shows La Fayette at the Champs de Mars on the 14th of July, 1790.

51 bottom left The Musée Carnavalet contains many relics of the French Revolution, such as the symbol of the revolt as represented by the legendary phrase "Liberté Egalité."

51 top right Following the Revolution, the royal family left Versailles and returned to Paris. As prisoners of the Revolution they were held at Les Tuileries and later executed at the Place de la Concorde. In this painting Louis XVI is being accompanied to the gallows on the 21st of January, 1793.

51 bottom right Marat, the French revolutionary who in 1789 began publication of the newspaper L'Ami du peuple, is here being carried in triumph. His articles against the Assembly would have a significant impact upon the course of the revolution. He was one of the most active Montagnards (those who sat on the high benches in the Assembly) and president of the Jacobin club. In this capacity he conducted an open war against the Girondins. He was eventually assasinated by the knife of Charlotte Corday.

following the death of the King, had profound echoes throughout Europe. Goethe predicted as much upon the victory of the Jacobin volunteers over the Austrians and Prussians at Valmy on September 20th, 1792: "From this place and from this day begins a new era in the history of the world."

50 bottom The Proclamation of the Rights of Man was heard as a new gospel that would lead to the liberation and regeneration of all men. The work of disciples of the philosophers, and apparently addressing all the populace, the Declaration of Rights clearly revealed its bourgeois origins, and was full of restrictions and conditions. Civil rights were conceded to all French citizens. Protestants and Jews were granted the right of citizenship, slavery was abolished in France but not in the colonies, and political rights were reserved for a minority.

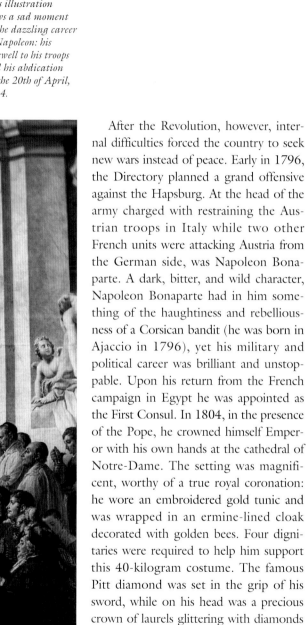

After the Revolution, however, internal difficulties forced the country to seek new wars instead of peace. Early in 1796, the Directory planned a grand offensive against the Hapsburg. At the head of the army charged with restraining the Austrian troops in Italy while two other French units were attacking Austria from the German side, was Napoleon Bonaparte. A dark, bitter, and wild character, Napoleon Bonaparte had in him something of the haughtiness and rebelliousness of a Corsican bandit (he was born in Ajaccio in 1796), yet his military and political career was brilliant and unstoppable. Upon his return from the French campaign in Egypt he was appointed as the First Consul. In 1804, in the presence of the Pope, he crowned himself Emperor with his own hands at the cathedral of Notre-Dame. The setting was magnificent, worthy of a true royal coronation: he wore an embroidered gold tunic and was wrapped in an ermine-lined cloak decorated with golden bees. Four dignitaries were required to help him support this 40-kilogram costume. The famous Pitt diamond was set in the grip of his sword, while on his head was a precious crown of laurels glittering with diamonds — the work of Biennais, the court jeweller, and costing eight thousand francs. This grandiose moment also signalled the beginning of the legend of the great Corsican: the Emperor declared war against half of Europe, defeated the Austrians at Austerlitz, descended into Italy, and then confronted the terrible Russian winter with the dream of deposing the Czar, but failed. Napoleon's epic invasion ended in catastrophe. In March, 1814 the allies conquered Paris: Russians, Prussians, Cossacks and Austrians marched down the Champs-Élysées. Napoleon abdicated and left for the island of Elba. The Congress of Vienna consigned the throne of France to the Bourbons, but in March 1815 Napoleon escaped from Elba, landed in the south of France and marched upon Paris. His "100 days" finished at Waterloo: he was defeated by the English, and then exiled to the remote island of St. Helena in the middle of the Atlantic Ocean, where he died in 1821.

54 top The Revolution left Paris with no significant monuments apart from the grand patriotic space of the Champs de Mars. Sacking and confiscations took place in this period, and vast estates belonging to religious orders or members of the aristocracy were liberated and passed into the hands of new speculators. The Commission of Artists was formed to give new order to the city plan, but with no great results. Napoleon was even more brutal and when he became First Consul he affirmed that "if Paris is to be beautified there is more to demolish than to construct. Why not knock down the whole quarter of the Cité, that vast ruin fit to house only rats?" As Emperor he could realise his dream of making Paris the most beautiful city in the world. He opened Rue Rivoli, and had the market of Les Halles reorganized. Four bridges were built across the Seine, the arch on the Carrousel was constructed and the colossal Arc de Triomphe on the Étoile was begun. The Palais du Luxembourg, seen here, became the home to the Senate under Napoleon.

54 center and bottom Napoleon's grand innovative and revivalist plans for the rebirth of Paris also included the completion of the construction of La Madeleine, center, that resembles a Greek temple. Napoleon housed his veteran soldiers at the Hôtel des Invalides (bottom).

54-55 *The Panthéon, seen here in a famous painting depicting it in the mid-19th century, houses the tombs of the most illustrious figures of France.*

55 top *These two illustrations present two celebrated Paris churches. Saint-Sulpice (left), which after Notre-Dame is the largest church in Paris, and Saint-Etienne-du-Mont (right), a singular church in which the Gothic styling is already showing signs of the innovative new wind of the Renaissance.*

56 top Under Louis XVIII, portrayed here in his sumptuous coronation gowns (left), and during a party given in his honor at the Odéon theater in 1819 (right), nobody was concerned with changing or enriching the face of Paris.

56-57 At the behest
of Napoleon and in
honor of the victory
of the Grande Armée,
a column based on
Trajan's column
drawn from Rome
was erected in the
Place Vendôme. Cast
from the bronze of
melted cannons taken
from the enemies at
Austerlitz, the
column is a
continuous spiral of
historical bas-reliefs.

57 top left Like his
predecessor Louis
XVIII, Charles X
did little in the way of
providing Paris with
new architectural
works.

57 top right
The construction
of the Arc de
Triomphe, begun by
Napoleon Bonaparte
in 1806, was completed
during the reign
of Charles X.

57 bottom right
On 25th of October,
1836, a great obelisk
from Luxor was
erected in Place de la
Concorde as this
contemporary print
illustrates.

The Revolution had sacked and confiscated, but had not built any great monuments except for the patriotic expanse of the Champs-de-Mars parade ground, the stage for national celebrations and military exercises. After the sober, precious Louis XVI style, and the Neo-classicism of the Directory with its richer architectural features, the glory of Napoleon Bonaparte came to be celebrated in the first decades of the nineteenth century in monumental works. The marble Arc de Triomphe was erected at the end of the Champs Élysées, the Rue de Rivoli was relaid and at the center of the Place Vendôme a column cast in bronze from enemy cannons captured at Austerlitz was inaugurated on August 15th, 1810. A symbol of the glorious Napoleonic era, it was decorated with a bas-relief depicting the feats of the Grand Armée.

The nineteenth century advanced with political instability under the new rulers Louis XVIII (1815-1824), and his successor Charles X. The Romantics, with their long hair, red vests, and flowing shirts, challenged the conservatives with the dreams of liberty brought forth in their work.

The heroic symbol of this period was *Hernani* by Victor Hugo, which opened one memorable evening on the stage of the Théâtre Français.

58 top and 58-59 Baron Haussmann, portrayed below whilst receiving from Napoleon III the decree annexing the suburban communes to Paris, was responsible for the conception of the 19th-century city. Gutting and levelling whole quarters, building others from scratch, laying out very broad streets to meet the new demands of urban traffic, within a few years he imposed upon medieval, baroque, romantic Paris a new modern, imperial vision of the capital, the plan of which can be seen reproduced above.

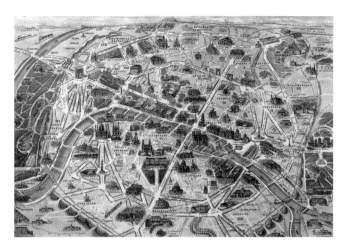

In February, 1848, the Second Republic was proclaimed (the first having had a short life during the Revolution of 1792), with the unanimous election of Louis Napoleon Bonaparte as its leader. Four years later he would assume the title of Emperor of the French with the name Napoleon III. The Second Empire, which concluded in 1870, was a period of relative liberalism: the field of art saw the explosion of Impressionism; literature flourished with works of protest and rebellion; while Paris itself was subjected to the daring urban transformations of Baron Georges Haussman, who for 40 years left Parisians to walk through the mud of construction sites that were to provide the city with the most beautiful streets in the world. However, the city suffered serious damage during the disasterous Franco-Prussian war and in the subsequent months when the French regular army besieged the capital in a cruel attempt to put down the insurrection that broke out following the surrender.

60 With a series of state interventions Napoleon attempted to meet the demands of a country in the process of transformation. This was the period in which roads, canals and railway networks expanded and the great avenues, squares and sumptuous buildings were created. Napoleon III's policy was designed to revive the spirit of revolutionary France, but the war of 1870 consumed this euphoria and laid the basis for the fall of the imperial regime. The revolt exploded in Paris on 18th of March, 1871: the Commune was constituted as a revolutionary government. The illustrations on this page depict the salient events of those days: at the top, the revolutionaries and the manifesto of the Commune; in the center, the assembled representatives of the Commune; bottom, the disturbances in the capital.

The Third Republic came about following the violent struggles between the National Assembly (still controlled by the monarchy) and the revolutionary government, known as the Commune, installed in Paris on March 18th, 1871. In just a few short weeks, this new revolutionary regime succeeded in demonstrating the validity of applied socialism, an event which later would serve as an exemplar for Karl Marx. The restoration of peace coincided with the birth of Impressionism, the art movement led by Monet, Renoir, Pissarro, Cézanne and Manet. The first exhibition was held in the studio of the photographer Nadar, but it was not until 1877 that the term *Impressionistes* was officially acknowledged.

61 top and center These two contemporary illustrations depict a sad moment in the history of Paris: the Prussians besieged and bombarded the capital at the end of the terrible Franco-Prussian war.

61 bottom After the fall of the Empire, the Third Republic was proclaimed and this contemporary print illustrates the general euphoria the event provoked.

62 top left and center left The Belle Époque was a period of frenetic creativity: Art Nouveau was all the rage — the work of A. Mucha (top left) was a clear synthesis of the airy canons of the style — and an evening at the Folies-Bergère was not to be missed (center left).

62 center right This unusual photo has captured a moment in the construction of the celebrated Statue of Liberty, presented to the United States by France.

At the end of the century, Paris blossomed in the fields of art, music and the theater. Paris became the stage for the birth of modernity: the *Belle Époque* dawned, Art Nouveau burst onto the scene, the first Metro lines were laid and gas lighting was adopted. The unmistakable outline of the Eiffel Tower climbed into the sky. In the first decade of the new century, Braque and Picasso overturned the old artistic canons with Cubism, inagurating an extraordinary period of creativity that was to see artists such as Fernand Léger and Marcel Duchamp. All of Europe was however heading towards one of the most tragic periods of its history.

62 bottom This photo shows a typical Paris Metro station. Work on the system under the direction of Fulgence Bienvenüe began late in 1898. The road entrances were conceived in the style of the age, 141 of them being designed by Hector Guimard, father of French Art Nouveau.

62 top right and 62-63 The 1889 World's Fair in Paris, of which here we can see the main entrance (bottom) and an exhibition hall (top right), had as its dominating symbol the Eiffel Tower (top left), designed by the French engineer from whom it takes its name. As it climbed into the capital's sky, the celebrated Iron Lady aroused fierce controversy with its detractors signing petitions of disgust and condemnation of the bizarre construction. Many intellectuals entered the debate, claiming that the beauty of Paris would be ruined by that "ugly factory chimney".

64 These photos illustrate some of the key moments in the recent history of Paris, in particular the occupying German army marching victoriously through the Arc de Triomphe (top). The photo at bottom right portrays General De Gaulle against the backdrop of the legendary Arc de Triomphe. The photo at bottom left depicts the Parisian joy on the occasion of the allies' entrance into Paris.

During the First World War the city was saved from an invasion of the German troops, but in the course of the second conflict the German army marched beneath the Arc de Triomphe. The city folded in on itself.

Following the capitulation, General Charles De Gaulle launched an appeal from the studios of the BBC asking the French people to continue the resistance against the Germans. Finally, the allies landed in Normandy and Nazi Germany was defeated.

The Fourth Republic saw a series of unstable governments that hindered economic recovery. The war in Indochina concluded in defeat for France, while on the horizon loomed the dramatic prospect of war with Algeria. The Fifth Republic was born in 1958 with the election of General De Gaulle as President, brought back to power in order to avoid a coup d'état. This relaunched France on the international scene. In 1962 De Gaulle signed the Evian Accords, which put an end to the war in Algeria.

65 top A century seems to have passed since that May in 1968 when the flames of revolt once again lighted the Ville Lumière. The student rebellions of that year marked a momentous change in the way in which the social classes and the authorities interacted. For better or for worse, neither Paris nor the world would ever be the same again.

In the now legendary May of 1968, the claims of students and workers were heard on barricaded squares, signalling a significant moment in the city's history. Once order had been restored, a number of concessions were made, including a reform of the education system. In the presidential elections of 1969, De Gaulle was overtaken by Georges Pompidou, who was in turn succeeded by Valéry Giscard d'Estaing in 1974, and François Mitterrand in 1981. Leader of the socialist party, Mitterrand was re-elected for a second term, but was then defeated by Jacques Chirac in the elections of 1995. These last Presidents were also the moving spirits behind new developments affecting Paris's urban future. Pompidou bequeathed his name to the bizarre Beaubourg, "the blue refinery," as it was defined by its detractors. Giscard d'Estaing approved the plans for the Musée d'Orsay, the Cité des Sciences et des Tecniques at La Villette, and the Institut du Monde Arabe. However, the most ambitious projects were those of François Mitterrand: the Grand Louvre, the Arche de la Défense, the Opéra-Bastille and the Grande Bibliotèque, built "to preserve the historical memory of France", and, above all, in order to surprise the world and exalt once again the eternal *grandeur* of the *Ville Lumière*.

66 top and 67 top
The Ile de la Cité is
the cradle of ancient
Lutetia, *the historic*
heart of the city.
The island contains
not only remains
of the Roman
oppidum *and some*
of the city's most
important
monuments such
as Notre-Dame and
Sainte Chapelle,
but also two of
the most romantic
and exclusive corners:
the Square Galant
and the intimate
Place Dauphine,
constructed at the
behest of Henri IV
to the design approved
by Sully, in honor
of the Dauphin of
France, the future
Louis XIII.

66-67 The Seine
and the Eiffel Tower
are two symbols of
the Ville Lumière.
In spite of being
defined as an old
factory chimney by
its detractors, the
celebrated tower
continues to be one
of the capital's most
popular monuments.
Work began on the
tower in January,
1887 and was
completed two years,
two months and five
days later, just in
time for the
inauguration of the
World's Fair of 1889
of which it was
intended to be
the symbol.

*67 right The Ile
Saint-Louis, whilst
linked to the Ile de
la Cité, is a world
apart, isolated and
deaf to the noise and
bustle that surround
it. Thanks to this
exclusiveness the
island has always
been inhabited by
celebrities such as
Georges Pompidou
who had a home on
Quai de Béthune,
Baron Guy de
Rothschild and the
actress Michèle
Morgan. In the 14th
century, the island
served only as pasture
for livestock. In the
17th century the
land was reclaimed
and divided into lots.
The streets that now
criss-cross the island
are lined with
beautiful 17-century
buildings, a number
of exclusive boutiques
and small bistros.*

P aris was born on two small
islands in the Seine: a world
apart from the rest of the city,
a world containing some of
the capital's most significant
monuments. Here on the Ile de la
Cité are the roots of Celtic *Lutetia*, a
village founded by a group of fisherman of the Parisii tribe in 200 B.C.
The Ile Saint-Louis seems to have
been frozen in the Grand Siècle, a era
of elegant houses and silent streets, an
oasis of peace and austere aristocracy.
Crossing the Pont-Neuf, the oldest
bridge in Paris, initiated by Henri III
late in the sixteenth century and
opened by Henri IV in 1607 (the
nineteenth-century statue depicting
him mounted on his horse separates
the tip of the island from the Place
Dauphine) you enter the living political
and religious history of Paris.

68 top left
The southern facade of the Palais de Justice faces onto the Quai des Orfèvres where in the 12th and 13th centuries craft workshops and jewellers flourished. This photo shows the main entrance to the Palais de Justice, separated from the street by an imposing Louis XVI-style 18th-century gate.

68 bottom left In the Conciergerie, the state prison during the Reign of Terror, are to be found the Salle des Pas-Perdus and the Chambre Dorée where in 1793 the sittings of the Revolutionary Tribunal led to the summary trials that sent guilty and innocent victims alike to the guillotine.

68 top right
More recently the celebrated writer Georges Simenon identified the Palais de Justice with the imaginary "PJ", the legendary French judicial police of the detective Maigret.

68-69 and 69 top Sainte-Chapelle, a jewel of Gothic art, exalts the mysticism of an epoch with its airy, soaring structure and the multi-colored transparencies of its windows, as these photos show.

The Palais de Justice features the city's oldest public clock, one which has struck the hours for six centuries thanks to the precision mechanism designed by the German watchmaker Henri Vic in 1370. This building became the seat of the Paris Parliament when Charles V shifted the royal residence to the Louvre and afterwards became the Palais de Justice during the French Revolution. The stark walls of the Conciergerie and the adjoining, sinister prison still evoke the tragic moments when those condemned to death during the Terror left from here, in long white shirts, to be guillotined in Place de la Concorde. From the turbulent years of the Revolution to the mysticism of La Sainte-Chapelle. The precious chapel enclosed within the walls of the Palais de Justice is a masterpiece of Gothic art, built at the beginning of the thirteenth century at the behest of the sainted Louis IX, King of France, to house priceless relics of the Crown of Thorns and the Holy Cross from Byzantium. It boasts large stained glass windows that leave almost no room for the stonework: these windows are a triumph of bright red and blue and narrate scenes from Genesis, the Old Testament, and the life of Christ.

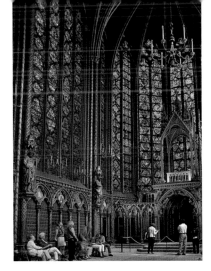

70 *This photo shows the beautiful west facade of the cathedral of Notre-Dame with the three-part vertical structure accentuated by the portals. Restoration work on Notre-Dame was begun in 1845 and completed in 1864 by the architect Eugène Emmanuel Viollet-le-Duc.*

The most precious monument of the Ile de la Cité is the Cathedral of Notre-Dame, towering and immense on the Place du Parvis-Notre-Dame, a clearing created by Haussmann at the time of Napoleon III to exalt the building's celebrated facade and that conceals the vestiges of the primitive Gallic *Lutetia*. "Every wall, every stone of this venerable monument is a page not only from the history of France," wrote Victor Hugo, "but also of science and art. Among all the old churches of Paris, this central, mother-church is a kind of chimera: it has the head of this, the limbs of that, and the torso of another, something from everything. Each flux of time has brought its own alluvial deposit, every race has made its own contribution to the monument, each individual has added a stone. Like great mountains, great buildings are also the works of centuries." In 1163 Bishop Maurice de Sully invited Pope Alexander III himself to lay the foundation stone of the cathedral, during the reign of Louis VIII. Thus on the foundations of the primitive church of St. Stephen, a new basilica was erected, reflecting that anxiety over the infinite that animated the consciences of men of the thirteenth century. The construction of Notre-Dame lasted roughly two hundred years and finished midway through the fourteenth century. All the history of France has passed through these imposing naves, including the French Revolution which "consecrated" the Cathedral to the cult of the God of Reason, plundering and sullying it in the process. A walk around the outside of Notre-Dame reveals the masterful interplay of architectural elements: rampant arches, spires, peaks, windows, doors, rose-windows, and a magical population of monsters and demons emerging from magnificent doorways or springing out from pilasters garlanded with acanthus. The view from the top of the tower of Notre-Dame is a panorama of light and air over all of Paris and the nearby Ile Saint-Louis. Linked to the Ile de la Cité by the Pont Saint-Louis, this island is quiet and relatively undisturbed by tourism, a tongue of land laid gently down in the Seine, and the residence of many of the capital's leading figures. This island features a succession of old seventeenth-century patrician residences such as the Hôtel de Lauzun, which housed the poet Charles Baudelaire and the bohemian artistic and literary circles of his time.

71 top left
The Gallery of the Kings, only part of which can be seen here, contains 19th-century copies of 28 statues of the French Kings; the originals were destroyed during the Revolution.

71 bottom left
In front of the western rose-window can be seen the Virgin Mary and to either side representations of the virtues and vices.

71 right *The portals of Notre-Dame are heavily decorated with fine sculptures. In this photo you can see two details of the Door of the Virgin, the sculptures for which were executed in the 13th century.*

72-73 The flourishing of the Gothic style in France between the 11th and the 15th centuries can be seen in many cathedrals from the era throughout the country. Among the most famous of these is undoubtedly the cathedral of Notre-Dame, the most venerated Parisian church, begun in 1163 at the behest of St. Louis IX and completed over the next 150 years. In its grandiosity it was intended to rival the nearby Saint-Denis. The cathedral earned literary immortality in the famous novel by Victor Hugo as the setting for the unhappy stories of Esmeralda

and Quasimodo, and under its roof a number of significant chapters in the history of France have been written. Here Mary Stuart was married, Joan of Arc was proclaimed a saint, Abelard met Heloïse, Henri VI of England was crowned as the child King of France, Napoleon crowned himself Emperor of the French in 1804 and in 1944 General De Gaulle announced the end of the German occupation of Paris. The cathedral was devastated and stripped of its treasures during the French Revolution. In the autumn of 1793 the vandals destroyed many of the statues and the building was consecrated to the God of Reason. Only in 1795 was Notre-Dame reconsigned to the Church, purified and in 1802 once again held Catholic services. Through a small door close to the north tower you can climb to the top of the cathedral to enjoy the stunning panorama.

The Petit-Pont is Paris's shortest bridge and at one time everyone, save the usual fraudsters, paid a toll to cross it. At the far end of the bridge from the Ile de la Cité lies the legendary Left Bank, a community of churches and convents before becoming famous for its bars and bistros, Saint-Germain and the Latin Quarter. Above the mansard roofs of the imposing mansions rise the curves of historic domes. Some are sublime, such as that covering the Institut de France. This is the most beautiful

dome in the country, standing over the building in which the five National Academies meet in plenary assembly each October. Some are noble, such as that of the Hôpital du Val de Grâce, built in the sixteenth century to thank God for having provided France with an heir to the Crown, the future Louis XIV. Some domes are imposing, such as that of the Panthéon in the Latin Quarter, a tribute to the nation's heroes. Since 1791 many illustrious

figures, intellectuals and famous literati such as Mirabeau, Voltaire, Rousseau, Marat, Victor Hugo and Emile Zola have been laid to rest below the vaults of this solemn building (which is based upon a Greek cross plan). Marie Curie, who died in 1934, is the only woman to be included in this celebrated company. From the top of the dome hangs the famous Foucault's Pendulum (perhaps to be relocated once again), which in 1851 was used by the celebrated French physicist to demonstrate the rotation of the planet. The "dome of knowledge" is that of the Sorbonne, the celebrated Parisian university founded by Robert de Sorbon, a rector and confidant of the king. In 1528 de Sorbon obtained the authorization to found the Collège de Sorbon for poor students and teachers desiring to further their studies in theology. To aid the realization of a *Universitas Studiorum*, Louis IX and Cardinal Richelieu (who is buried at the Sorbonne in a marble coffin) ordered the construction of a new building by the architect Le Mercier, of which only the chapel remains today. Between 1885 and 1901 the entire complex was rebuilt, and today it occupies a vast portion of the Latin Quarter. Just a step away are the Luxembourg Gardens: "there is nothing more charming," wrote Léon Daudet, "nor anything more inviting of idleness and daydream, or to young lovers, who, on sweet spring mornings or beautiful summer evenings, slip into the shadows of hundred-year old trees."

74-75 and 75 top right The Panthéon, "the enforced gift of the Church and the Kings to the Republic" as it has been defined, stands on the Sainte-Geneviève hill and houses the tombs of some of France's most illustrious figures. The facade was inspired by ancient Greek architecture and the magnificent dome rises proudly above it.

75 top left This photo shows the superb 17th-century architecture of the Institut de France, a building financed by Mazarin and designed by Louis le Vau. In the east wing of the building is the library dedicated to the distinguished statesman and housing precious volumes.

76 *Historic figures*
such as Diderot,
Beaudelaire and
Alfred de Musset
have enjoyed strolling
along the avenues
of the Luxembourg
Gardens. The latter
defined the gardens
as "a delightful place,

a solitary haven
open day and night
for the student with
his books under his
arm, for the dreamer
and his indolence
and for the lover with
his beloved who meet
here as if in
Paradise".

The Luxembourg Gardens encircle the Palais du Luxembourg (today occupied by the senate of the Republic of France), the Florentine island constructed to remind Maria de' Medici of the Palazzo Pitti in Florence. At all hours of the day students stop to rest on the terraces of the bars or in the windows of the bistros in the Latin Quarter, so named because in medieval times the official language used by professors and students was Latin, and also because this community — bounded by the Luxembourg Gardens, the Seine, and the Boulevard St-Michel — is built upon the ancient plan of the Gallic *Lutetia*. Not far from here, in fact, the shadow of Caesar is still cast on the Arènes de Lutèce, an amphitheater probably constructed sometime in the first century AD, the heart of ancient *Lutetia* and unearthed in 1869 during an excavation of the Rue Monge, and on the Cluny Baths, where, amidst green fields and thick forests, the Romans would relax at the end of a fatiguing day.

The Musée National du Moyen-Age and the Cluny Baths contain the remains of three large rooms: the *frigidarium*, the *tepidarium*, and the *calidarium*. Backing onto the baths and built late in the fifteenth century is the Hôtel des Abbés de Cluny, itself the custodian of a collection of rare masterpieces of medieval art, including the six tapestries based upon the theme of the "Dame à la licorne", masterpieces of Flemish textile art.

76-77 The Luxembourg
Gardens officially
belong to the Senate as
they surround the
grandiose building of
the same name in which
the senators assemble. In
reality however they are
the refuge of the students
from the nearby
universities and all
those looking for
peace and tranquility
amidst their luxuriant
greenery.

77 top The Luxembourg
Gardens were created
in 1617 by Boyeau de
la Bareaudière, the
first authority on
French-style gardens.
The numerous statues
set along the avenues
were mostly erected
during the reign of
Louis Philippe in the
19th century.

The Left Bank is also rich in famous churches: Saint-Severin in the Flemish Gothic style, "delicate and small in a poor corner of Paris," is how the writer Huysmans described it, where it's said that even Dante came to pray during his supposed trip to Paris; Saint-Julien-le-Pauvre, in the heart of the university life of the city, encircled by the tight alleys of a most picturesque Paris (near the church, at Place Viviani, there is a curiosity: here grows the oldest tree in Paris, a false acacia or Robinia, planted in 1601 by the botanist J. Robin, from whom the species takes its name); Saint-Etienne-du-Mont, just a stone's throw away from the Panthéon, noted for the decoration of its splendid Renaissance *jubé* as well as for the remains of St. Geneviève, the patron saint of Paris, buried here today in a chapel not far from those of Pascale and Racine. Finally, of course, the most famous of all the churches of Paris and also the oldest: Saint-Germain-des-Prés, the abbey founded in 543 by King Childebert in the open countryside, of the vast plain where the Parisii were defeated by the Roman legionnaires. The interior features three naves, beautiful capitals on the choir stalls and frescoed walls, and up high, the sharp spires of a Romanesque bell-tower preside over one of the liveliest squares on the Left Bank, not far from Saint-Sulpice, the largest church in Paris after Notre-Dame. At the end of the Boulevard St. Germain, along the Quai Saint-Bernard, sparkles the curved facade of the Institute du Monde Arabe, built in 1987 by the architect Jean Nouvel: ten stories upon which aluminium diaphragms, inspired by the Alhambra of Granada, open and close according to the light of the sun, in a continuous dialogue between Arab architecture and modern technology. Beyond this is an oasis of peace: the Jardin des Plantes, the grandiose botanical gardens surrounding the Musée National d'Histoire Naturelle. This was a royal garden of medicinal herbs during the reign of Louis XIII, and was opened to the public in 1640. A modern restoration commissioned by Mitterrand sits happily with the metalwork of the Galerie de l'Évolution leaving intact the exciting view of the long rows of stuffed giraffes, rhinoceroses, hippopotamuses, zebras, antelope, and elephants that seem to go on forever. From Saint-Germain-des-Prés, the Rue de Rennes meets Montparnasse and its most striking symbol: the Tour Montparnasse, a giant steel and glass structure that has been piercing the sky since 1973. The tower is 210 meters tall, with 59 storeys that are climbed in an instant in an incredibly fast elevator, and it commands a breathtaking view of Paris. From here it may seem almost impossible to tie the threads of this small hill's past and the myths woven around it by Apollinaire and the artists who at the beginning of the twentieth century elected the area the "navel of the world," to the current urban agglomeration and the busy swarming of the populace at its feet. There remains the Musée Bourdelle on the Rue Antoine-Bourdelle to evoke something of the spirit that animated Montparnasse at the beginning of the twentieth century. The studio of the celebrated sculptor, and favorite pupil of Rodin, houses more than five hundred works of art that were created within its walls between 1884 and 1929, the year of the artist's death.

78-79 In the twilight Paris is illuminated like some fantastic stage set. Out of the shadows emerge the most distinguished monuments, cars trace bands of light along the grand boulevards, Rue de Rennes being seen here, and the city unfurls its joie de vivre *in anticipation of the adventures of the night to come. This photo shows the floodlit façades of the most celebrated churches of the Rive Gauche, Saint-Germain-des-Prés on the left and Saint-Sulpice on the right.*

80-81 Against the backdrop of the stunning panorama to be seen from the top of the Eiffel Tower stands the imposing Tour Montparnasse, a steel and concrete building constructed in 1973.

83 bottom left
The famous painting
by Eduoard Manet
entitled Déjeuner
sur l'herbe was
executed in 1863
and was subsequently
presented at the
Salon des Refusés
created during
the reign of
Napoleon III.

83 top right In this
masterpiece by
Claude Monet
entitled The Woman
with the Umbrella
one can admire the
luminosity and
breadth of the
Impressionist style.

83 bottom right
The painter Auguste
Renoir was a
prominent figure
in the cultural and
worldly fervour that
characterised Paris
in the late nineteenth
century. This is his
Portrait of Margot,
oil on canvas, 1878.

The historic Gare d'Orsay, the cathedral-like railway station from the end of the nineteenth century, anchored to the left bank of the Seine in front of the Louvre, is today one of Paris's most prestigious museums. It has been given over to the works of major artists who were working between the middle of the nineteenth century and the beginning of the First World War. Erected in 1871 to connect the capital to Nantes, Toulouse, and Bordeaux, this railway station was later condemned to demolition like Les Halles. Fortunately it was spared the clamour aroused by the absurd demolition of the latter and handed over to the winners of a competition to find the best project for its revival. This huge building, made of iron and stone from Buxi, was converted into the Musée d'Orsay by the Italian architect Gae Aulenti in 1986 and is now one of the largest and most visited museums of the capital. The immense central nave, where the steam locomotives used to belch smoke, has been transformed into a labyrinth of clear light and suspended walls like theater backdrops, which leave visitors free to wander, rather than imposing a particular path. The museum has assembled the works of many of the most fascinating artists of the nineteenth century: Ingres and Delacroix; the acclaimed Impressionists once housed in the old Jeu de Paume museum: Degas, Monet, Manet, Pissarro, Renoir, Cézanne, Van Gogh, Gauguin, Seurat, Toulouse-Lautrec, and Matisse; the realists Daumier, Millet, Corot, and Courbet; academy painters; the furniture of Gallé; and the works of Camille Claudel.

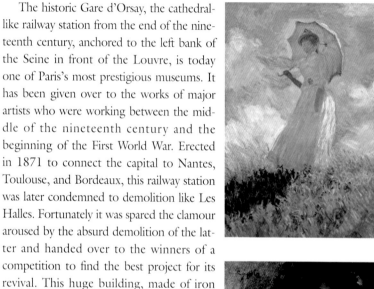

82 A turn-of-the-century railway station, the Gare d'Orsay was designed by Victor Laloux. Thanks to a complete restoration, the building now houses one of the most prestigious and popular Parisian

museums. This photo shows the broad glazed vaults where steam trains once belched smoke and where today you can admire some of the most famous works by artists from the period between 1848 and the First World War.

83 top left The Card Players by Paul Cézanne was painted between 1890 and 1895. In the opinion of many critics the angular treatment of the figures, particularly the player on the left, and of the table, anticipates Cubism.

85 top Camille Pissarro, 1830-1903, succeeded in bringing to the canvas the magical, mysterious atmosphere of Paris, as in this painting entitled La Seine et Le Louvre.

85 center left This extremely well known 1889 painting by Van Gogh, La Chambre de Van Gogh en Arles, *reveals all the strength and* the bold handling of paint typical of the great Dutch artist.

85 center right Paul Gauguin, 1848-1903, was initially an Impressionist painter, but subsequently developed a very personal pictorial style. Here we can admire his 1892 painting Joyeusetés.

85 bottom left Edgar Degas successfully captured the grace and lightness of a group of classical ballerinas waiting to perform in his Danseuses bleues of 1893.

85 bottom right Henri de Toulouse-Lautrec immortalised La Clownesss Cha-u-Kao du Moulin Rouge in 1895.

84 When Napoleon III came to power in 1852 there was an explosion in of creativity in all fields of life and the arts. Poets flourished and painters began to pay a greater attention to reality, giving rise to the successful period of Realism and Impressionism. Other celebrated works conserved in the Musée d'Orsay were created in these fertile years, including this work by Van Gogh depicting L'église d'Auverse-sur-Oise executed in 1890.

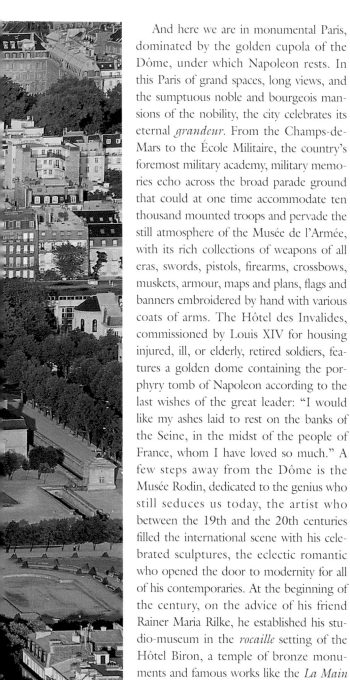

And here we are in monumental Paris, dominated by the golden cupola of the Dôme, under which Napoleon rests. In this Paris of grand spaces, long views, and the sumptuous noble and bourgeois mansions of the nobility, the city celebrates its eternal *grandeur*. From the Champs-de-Mars to the École Militaire, the country's foremost military academy, military memories echo across the broad parade ground that could at one time accommodate ten thousand mounted troops and pervade the still atmosphere of the Musée de l'Armée, with its rich collections of weapons of all eras, swords, pistols, firearms, crossbows, muskets, armour, maps and plans, flags and banners embroidered by hand with various coats of arms. The Hôtel des Invalides, commissioned by Louis XIV for housing injured, ill, or elderly, retired soldiers, features a golden dome containing the porphyry tomb of Napoleon according to the last wishes of the great leader: "I would like my ashes laid to rest on the banks of the Seine, in the midst of the people of France, whom I have loved so much." A few steps away from the Dôme is the Musée Rodin, dedicated to the genius who still seduces us today, the artist who between the 19th and the 20th centuries filled the international scene with his celebrated sculptures, the eclectic romantic who opened the door to modernity for all of his contemporaries. At the beginning of the century, on the advice of his friend Rainer Maria Rilke, he established his studio-museum in the *rocaille* setting of the Hôtel Biron, a temple of bronze monuments and famous works like the *La Main de Dieu* and the celebrated *Kiss*.

It is now only a step to the celebrated Eiffel Tower. 7,300 tonnes of iron went into the construction of this "ridiculous factory fireplace," "the gigantic skewer, good for poking the clouds" (as it was described at the time it was built), a grey structure rising wildly from its solid foundations on the Champ-de-Mars. On 12th of June, 1886, the engineer Gustave Eiffel won the city of Paris's competition: the World's Fair of 1889 chose this "grande dame of iron" as its symbol from amongst 107 proposals. The workers began con-

Tower's feet, the Pont d'Iéna crosses over the Seine and arrives at the hill of Chaillot, high against the right bank of the river and home to the semicircular Palais de Chaillot, constructed for the 1937 Paris exhibition. The building contains the Musée de la Marine, which will take you to the high seas, the Musée de l'Homme, with its history of the world in reverse, and the Musée du Cinema Henri Langlois, where the ghosts of Rudolph Valentino, Marilyn Monroe, Greta Garbo, and Federico Fellini are brought back to life.

88 and 89 The Eiffel Tower was from the very outset a "monster" that could be seen from all four corners of Paris as it soared high above all the city's greatest monuments. Today the bizarre construction, the fruit of laborious calculations, is no longed regarded with desecrating irony, but rather as the most acrobatic and glorious symbol of the city. It required a gestation period of two years during which time it grew to a height of 276 meters, the antenna topping out at 318 meters. The 18,030 cast iron sections and two and a half million rivets weigh a total of 10,000 tonnes. Should you wish to climb to the top on foot then 1,665 steps await you.

struction at the beginning of July, 1887, and soon all heads were turning upwards to stare at the marvel of the century — such a strange, crude construction that day by day climbed higher towards the sky like some crazed, gangly giant who had taken the era's claim that progress was made of metal much too literally. The official inauguration was held in May, 1889. Since then, six million visitors per year (one hundred and sixty million in total!) have climbed to the top to take in the breathtaking expanse of Paris. At the

Great flights of steps run down the sides of the hill, and intrepid youths execute crazy skateboard stunts in the square. We are still in the Paris of grand spaces and long views that lead to the Étoile and to that colossal symbol of the city, the Arc de Triomphe, a solemn anthem to glorious victory. Upon his return from the Battle of Austerlitz in 1806, Napoleon commissioned this immense and pharaonic monument to celebrate his men's triumphant military campaign. The view in one direction from the top of the arch takes in the major artery that leads to the Grande Arche de la Défense, Otto von Spreckelsen's cube covered in white Carrara marble and inaugurated in the bicentenary of the French Revolution. In the other direction the Champs-Élyseés leads to the Place de la Concorde, and Les Tuileries. A military parade marches down this street every July 14th, with much fanfare and fluttering of tricolor flags. This old vie Royale was initially laid out only up to the Étoile, in order to extend the Les Tuileries gardens and to create a grandiose prospect for the king's pleasure, and in the eighteenth century it was simply a walk through pastures and fields; in the first years of the nineteenth century it already hosted a few buildings; and by the second Empire it featured great hotels and luxurious estates. Today, boutiques, cafés, cinemas, airline offices, and the celebrated Lido are among the attractions of the most famous street in the world. The Champs-Élysées triumphantly reaches the Louvre, leaving on the right along the Seine the *rocaille* exuberance of the Pont Alexandre III and the scenic view of the Petit Palais and the Grand Palais. The latter are testimony to the era in which Paris, capital of science and technology, gathered together the nations of the world every ten years to celebrate the marriage of Progress and Reason.

92 top In these photos can be seen a number of views of the futuristic Quartier de la Défense, also known as "Wall Street-sur-Seine" *in acknowledgement of the financial importance assumed over recent years by this area in the western suburbs of the city.*

92-93 La Grande Arche de la Défense stands out in the western suburbs of the city in all its spectacular and clean-cut futuristic glory. The gigantic cube of white Carrara marble, over 100 meters tall, could comfortably contain the entire cathedral of Notre-Dame.

93 A symbol of challenge and modernity, La Grande Arche de la Défense, the work of the Danish architect Von Spreckelsen, was backed by President Mitterrand as the home of the International Foundation for Human Rights and as a monumental work commemorating the bicentenerary of the French Revolution.

94 and 95 Stone lions, allegorical statues, grandiose lamp-posts, copies of those on the Trinity bridge in St. Petersburg, lend a magical, absolute beauty to the Pont Alexandre III that links the Esplanade des Invalides with the Champs Élyseés. The bridge was named after the Tzar of Russia Alexander III to mark the 1893 alliance between France and Russia and has a single span around 100 meters long.
These photos exalt the wealth of the decorations and the stature of the lamp-posts illuminating the bridge as dusk falls.

Enlarged and partially reorganized at the behest of Mitterrand, the grandiose Louvre houses the largest collection of art in the world. To stroll among the statues of the Cour Marly in the Richelieu wing; to step back in time in front of the winged bulls of Korsabad, the *Venus de Milo*, and the *Winged Victory of Samothrace*; to plunge into the High Renaissance of Michelangelo, Raphael and Leonardo, then into the sixteenth century

Dutch still-lifes and the bucolic landscapes of Poussin and Watteau; and to admire the stunning, seemingly endless sequence of masterpieces in the Grande Galerie requires time, effort, and more than just one visit.

Following the Mitterrand revolution, the entrance to the museum on the Rue de Rivoli has become a remarkable sight, with the inverted glass pyramid of architect Jeoh Ming Pei, drawing light from the larger, external pyramid serving as the principle entrance to the Louvre at the center of the Cour Napoléon. Seen from below, the magical play of light and glass reflects the clouds and the silhouettes of tourists who seem to be suspended in mid-air, actors in a surreal world, while the Parisian sky penetrates the hazy transparency of the glass, and sheds its silvery light upon the inverted pyramid below.

96 and 97 The new Louvre created in the heart of the city, seen here in an aerial view, throws a new light on immortal masterpieces such as the Winged Victory of Samothrace, *top right, and the* Venus de Milo, *bottom left.*

98 The entrance
to the New Louvre
is located below
the glass pyramid
designed by
the Chinese-American
architect Jeoh Ming

Pei and built in the
center of the Cour
Napoléon, but the
museum can also
be reached via Rue
de Rivoli via the
Carrousel du Louvre.

99 The spacious, well-lit halls of the Louvre contain masterpieces from all eras and from all over the world. The world's greatest museum can in fact boast works of art dating back as far as 5,000 years B.C. as well as contemporary pieces.

100-101
The Mitterrand era changed the face of Paris. Among the grands travaux *initiated by the celebrated President was the transformation of the Louvre complex,* *beginning with the inauguration of the pyramid in the middle of the Cour Napoléon and continuing with the opening of the Richelieu wing and the reorganisation of the Denon wing.*

103 Here the work is surrounded by Jan Vermeer's The Lace-maker, *Raphael's portrait of Baldassare* Castiglione, *Eugène Delacroix's* Liberty leading the people *and Camille Corot's* Dame en bleu.

102 Among the innumerable masterpieces to be found within the Louvre, the sweetly enigmatic smile of Leonardo da Vinci's Mona Lisa *stands out.*

At the end of the Cour Napoléon, the Arc de Triomphe du Carrousel, with its eight columns of pink marble, frames the celebrated view of the Champs-Élyseés. Bucolic in the shade in the Tuileries gardens, yet regal in the vast arena of the Place de la Concorde, this is the setting for well known celebrations, funeral processions and military parades. The obelisk, from the temple of Luxor, was placed in the middle of this square in the autumn of 1836, at the site where, from 1793 to

1795, the inexorable guillotine brought thousands of people, including the minute, austere figure of Marie Antoinette, to meet their maker. Kings and queens also haunt the nearby church of Saint-Germain l'Auxerrois in the Place du Louvre which was once the parish church of the French sovereigns, patronised by Francis I, Henri IV, and Louis XIV, and dedicated to Saint-Germain, bishop of Auxerre.

106-107 The Centre Pompidou rises in the heart of the city, and with its brightly colored tubes, exposed steel tie-rods and external escalator enclosed in a transparent Plexiglas tube, its challenging character has been a source of controversy ever since it was built. It has nevertheless become the city's most popular cultural attraction.

106 top The futuristic Center Pompidou faces onto the singular Igor-Stravinsky plaza, characterised by the multi-colored animated fountain designed by Niki de Saint-Phalle and Jean Tinguely.

106 bottom Each day the broad open space alongside the Beauborg provides a stage for numerous street artists who perform for hurrying Parisians and fascinated tourists.

The nearby Musée des Arts Decoratifs and the Musée des Arts de la Mode take us on a trip through time, with their packed rooms of antique furnishings: Louis XV furniture, tapestries, jewels, fabrics, ceramics, glass, toys, rugs, objects from daily life, lace, and sumptuous clothing belonging to famous figures of the past. Nearby in the Jardin des Tuileries, the Musée de l'Orangerie displays the impalpable softness of Claude Monet's *Waterlilies*, the solitary still-lifes of Cézanne, Renoir's *Les Fillettes au Piano*, a number of *Odalisques* by Matisse and, between a Picasso and a Modigliani, the unmistakable Parisian scenes of Utrillo. The strangest, most controversial, modern, and daring museum of Paris comes into sight suddenly at the corner of the Rue Rambuteau. This is the Centre Pompidou, the famous Beaubourg, with its improbable weaving of colored and transparent pipes and all those steel rods. This building is the original creation of architects Renzo Piano, Gianfranco Franchini, and Richard Rogers, and it has frequently been likened to a colored refinery, a "modern idol of leaded Plexiglas, like a space station in the heart of the city." Visited annually by seven million people, the Beaubourg is an ultra-modern, polyvalent cultural center which includes a huge library of texts on figurative art and the Musée National d'Art Moderne.

107 top "A unique original effort to unite and render accessible the various elements of modern culture in a single complex". This was the principal aim behind the most talked about and unusual of Paris's museums, inaugurated in 1977 and seen here in a stunning aerial photo.

108 and 109 The Centre National d'Art et de Culture Georges-Pompidou, better known as the Pompidou Centre or the Beauborg, contains the Museum of Modern Art in which you can admire works by the greatest artists of the century, almost all of them masterpieces that once hung in the Museum of Modern Art created in 1937 and the National Centre for Contemporary Art created in 1967. The collections are to be found on the fourth floor of the Pompidou Centre: it is here that you will find works such as The Muse *by Pablo Picasso (large photo right),* Lolotte *by Amedeo Modigliani (top right), Georges Braque's* Young Girl and guitar *(top left) and Giorgio de Chirico's* Premonitory portrait of Apollinaire *(bottom). Alongside the works of these artists there are also those of the Fauve painters such as Pierre Bonnard and Henri Matisse, the Cubists including Picasso, Fernand Léger and Braque and the major movements from the First World War to the 1960s.*

110 top Following a long period of neglect the Marais has been revived to experience a moment of explosive rejuvenation. It is now the most fashionable area of the capital, the quarter with the most museums, aristocratic buildings and trendy boutiques. Some of the streets have retained something of their original atmosphere, in others the old shops and commercial stores have given way to art galleries and the most sophisticated fashion houses of the moment. In this photo you can see a number of the sumptuous buildings facing onto Place des Vosges.

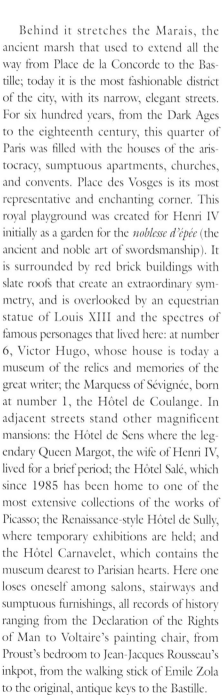

Behind it stretches the Marais, the ancient marsh that used to extend all the way from Place de la Concorde to the Bastille; today it is the most fashionable district of the city, with its narrow, elegant streets. For six hundred years, from the Dark Ages to the eighteenth century, this quarter of Paris was filled with the houses of the aristocracy, sumptuous apartments, churches, and convents. Place des Vosges is its most representative and enchanting corner. This royal playground was created for Henri IV initially as a garden for the *noblesse d'épée* (the ancient and noble art of swordsmanship). It is surrounded by red brick buildings with slate roofs that create an extraordinary symmetry, and is overlooked by an equestrian statue of Louis XIII and the spectres of famous personages that lived here: at number 6, Victor Hugo, whose house is today a museum of the relics and memories of the great writer; the Marquess of Sévignée, born at number 1, the Hôtel de Coulange. In adjacent streets stand other magnificent mansions: the Hôtel de Sens where the legendary Queen Margot, the wife of Henri IV, lived for a brief period; the Hôtel Salé, which since 1985 has been home to one of the most extensive collections of the works of Picasso; the Renaissance-style Hôtel de Sully, where temporary exhibitions are held; and the Hôtel Carnavelet, which contains the museum dearest to Parisian hearts. Here one loses oneself among salons, stairways and sumptuous furnishings, all records of history ranging from the Declaration of the Rights of Man to Voltaire's painting chair, from Proust's bedroom to Jean-Jacques Rousseau's inkpot, from the walking stick of Emile Zola to the original, antique keys to the Bastille.

One may go to the Place de la Bastille to admire the July Column erected in memory of the victims of the revolution of 1830, and the Opéra-Bastille, the great modern palace of concrete, marble and wood, the creation of Carlo Ott who has subverted the ancient concept of the theater. "No longer horseshoe halls, no longer gilded candy bowls in which sound spins as if it were inside the body of a cello," writes Alessandro Baricco, "but megahalls, enormous spaces, gigantic stages, thousands of seats, and multiple galleries." The right bank at the Place de la Concorde has become the epitome of luxury and supreme elegance. Gold and jewellery glitter in the shop windows of Place Vendôme, the architectural jewel created by Jules Harduin-Mansart for Louis XIV. At the end of Rue de la Paix is the ostentatious and Neo-baroque Opéra Garnier from the period of the Second Empire, and the Rue du Faubourg-Saint-Honoré which boasts the most exclusive shops. But you can already see the unmistakable profile of the Sacré-Coeur in the distance. At some point we all inevitably arrive here: this hill with its long flight of steps overlooking the roofs of the city, is where the Paris of myths still lives.

In a tree-lined square, garrisoned with artists ready to paint your portrait, with the brilliant whiteness of the church of the Sacré-Coeur, the blazing lights of the Pigalle, and the worn walls of the Bonne Franquette, it is still possible to imagine those roaring years in which Montmartre and brought forth its memorable contributions to art, and the outbursts of those restless, aimless youths of the most legendary bohemia.

114 top and 115 top Montmartre was the focus for a remarkable period in the history of the arts. An entire generation of artists contributed to the creation of its reputation: from Degas to Cézanne, from Delacroix to Monet and Van Gogh all of whom lived, suffered, painted and exalted here. However, few traces remain

of their presence. The early Bohème of Renoir and Lautrec was to be found at the top or the foot of the hill and 20 years later the likes of Picasso, Juan Gris, Van Dongen and Modigliani arrived to make their contribution to the legend of the quarter. Today the narrow streets swarm with people, mime artists, hawkers and buskers.

114 bottom There are numerous painters, especially in Place du Tertre, who attempt to revive the distant memories of a Montmartre that is no more.

114-115
The majestic white basilica of the Sacré-Coeur that dominates the hill of Montmartre was the fruit of a vow made by two businessmen, Alexandre Legentil and Rohault de Fleury at the beginning of the Franco-Prussian war of 1870: if France was to emerge victorious from the bloody conflict they would erect a church dedicated to the Sacred Heart of Christ. The work, under the direction of Guilbert — the city architect of the era — did not begin until 1875 and the church was not consecrated until 1919, following the victorious outcome of the First World War.

116 center left
The Train Bleu
is the restaurant
at the Gare de Lyon,
the station from which
trains to the South
depart. For this
reason, in the great
stuccoed halls with
their gilded cornices,
19th-century frescoes
depict the most
famous tourist
destinations on the
Mediterranean
Riviera.

116 bottom left
and right
The cafés of Paris
are not mere refuges
of conversation and
relaxation, some
of them, like the
Deux-Magots seen
in the photo bottom
right, have in fact
contributed to the
Parisian legend.

116 top left The Café de Flore is considered to be the symbol of a certain Paris; the Flore was, in fact, a permanent home for Jean-Paul Sartre and Simone de Beauvoir during the era of the Existentialists.

Divine Paris, an "immense shed of marvels, a theater within the great theater of the world": where to begin to share in the intimacy and spirit, emotions and charms, secrets and memories of this great capital of dreams? In the museums or during a walk along the Seine; in front of the latest, most controversial piece of architecture, or in a chic café on the Champs Élysées? Among the crowds on the boulevards or beneath the trees of the lonely Vert Galant? Walking, walking and more walking is the key to establishing an open dialogue with this city, which at every corner changes face and dimension, stirring one's memories and promising surprise. There is the Paris of history or the Paris of shopping, of art or of the joys of life, of wild nights or cosy bistros, the Paris of merchants or intellectuals, of the glittering shop windows or of the most improbable future, the Paris of long boulevards and the Paris of modernity. Within the great well of the city's golden history, dreams and fantasies, each of us finds our own beloved, unforgettable Paris, that mythical Paris we yearn to experience. Along the banks of the Seine, the serene and lofty river of poets and artists which divides the city into two worlds, the *bouquinistes* of the Rive Gauche, the oldest tenants of the Pont-Neuf, have been selling books and pamphlets since the seventeenth century. At night their goods are locked into cases of green-painted wood, an ancient custom which continues to this day, and one reproduced on countless postcards. In the gloomy half-light of Notre-Dame, pierced only by a few iridescent rays breaking through the stained glass windows, the ghosts of history may be perceived. Here Mary Stuart was married, Joan of Arc was proclaimed a

117 Strolling along the Champs Élysées you will find cafés offering an opportunity to rest in the leafy shade of the trees lining the boulevard.

118 top left The display windows of Cartier, the celebrated Parisian jeweller, look out onto Rue de la Paix, the attractive street built for Napoleon in 1806, inaugurated in 1814 and named in commemoration of the peace treaty.

118 bottom left The Galeries Lafayette, close to the Opéra, is one of the most famous Parisian department stores. It started out quietly as a small boutique at the corner of La Fayette and Chausée-d'Antin and was expanded early in the 20th century.

118 right The interior of the Galeries Lafayette still features the balustrades attributed to Majorelle and an imposing glazed dome. Today the great store occupies a surface area of 120,000 square meters and is composed of three large inter-connected buildings.

saint, Abelard met the demure Eloise, and Napoleon crowned himself Emperor of France, wrapped in a pale brocade cloak embroidered with tiny golden bees. Little shops and restaurants, and Berthillon, the famous and historic ice-cream shop making the best ice-cream in Paris, all help to enliven the nearby Rue Saint-Louis-en l'Ile, an intimate street far removed from the Paris of broad spaces and conspicuous modernity. Saint-Germain-des-Prés is just a step away, on the left bank of the Seine, home to cafés in which pages of the legend of a certain Paris were once written, the Flore,

the Deux-Magots, and the brasserie Lipp. Here the ideas that stirred the hearts and souls of a generation were born. The powerful and rebellious atmosphere of the golden Sixties once thrived here, and Jean-Paul Sartre and Simone de Beauvoir were permanent fixtures at the Café de Flore, and with them their existentialist followers, unshaven in black turtleneck sweaters and wearing duffel coats rather than bourgeois overcoats. In the caves of this neighbourhood, the classic settings of this tumultuous world, Yves Montand and Juliette Gréco, dressed in black turtlenecks, were taking their first steps in what later became glorious careers. Today, the most stylish shopping streets branch off from the axis of the Boulevard Saint-Germain-des-Prés; luxury flirts with bohemia on Rue du Bac, Rue de Grenelle, and Rue de Sèvres, and fashion triumphs.

A world of fine antiques can be found a few blocks away along the

119 The passages *and the* galeries *are secret covered alleys that link two or more of the streets in a particular quarter. They were a very fashionable architectural feature early in the 20th century, partly because gas-lamps made them particularly attractive at night. These photos show the Passage Verdeau with its entrance at Number 6 Rue de la Grange-Batelière (top left) and the Galerie Vivienne, created in 1823.*

*121 top left
Montmartre has lost
the personalities
responsible for
creating the legend
of the celebrated* butte
*(hill), but as the poet
Gérard de Nerval
once wrote, little has
changed, "there are
still windmills,
cabaret and
greengrocers, rural
paradises and silent
alleys flanked by
overgrown gardens".
It was on this hill that*

*Saint-Denis, the first
bishop of* Lutetia, *was
decapitated (hence the
name* mons martyrum
*transformed into
Montmartre). Here in
the 12th century was
built a Benedictine
abbey, Dames de
Montmartre,
surrounded by fields
and vineyards, that
was razed to the
ground during the
Revolution. In the top
left can be seen the
sign of a tea room.*

*120 Two tourists
observing the façade
of Au Lapin Agile,
an unusually rustic
night-spot built
in 1910 and
for many years
the home of literary
circles.*

*120-121 This night
view allows us to
observe the still sails
of Paris's most
famous windmill,
the Moulin Rouge,
today a destination
for tourists in search
of a taste of the
wilder, more carefree
side of Parisian life.*

Quai Voltaire, the mythical *carré d'or* with all the unspoilt appeal of old Paris; the area bounded by the Rue de l'Université and Rue des Saints-Pères boasts nearly a hundred art shops. Montparnasse is in full sail at the end of Rue de Rennes, its bright, soaring mainmast represented by the vertiginous tower of glass and cement. This is an area bustling with life, that at night cloaks itself in the red lights of the more risqué shows, as well as the myriad lamps of the bistros (including the renowned Coupole and Dôme, the former favorites of the likes of Mirò, Picasso, Hemingway and Chagall). However that world of energetic *filles de joie*, young models with painted flowers on their calves and watches saucily attached to their garters,

is far away. Remote is the world of *Kiki of Montparnasse*, the quarter's symbol immortalised in the photographs of Man Ray. His nude portraits of her have found their way into museums all over the world. At the beginning of the century Montparnasse took the place of Montmartre, another legendary temple of a bygone Paris: the bohemian Paris of a hundred years ago colored with love, avant-garde art and contradictions. In 1887 Degas, Cézanne, Monet, and many other artists lived upon the hill dominated by the Sacré-Coeur basilica. They were all friends and met at the Place du Tertre and danced together at country fairs in front of the Moulin de la Galette. In the same era, at the window of his room on Rue Lepic, Vincent van Gogh painted the roofs of Montmartre. Today Montmartre exists in flux between memory and consumerism, old quarters and new restaurants, false and authentic artists, the Moulin Rouge and Pigalle, and the heritage of those memories left upon the stubby hill — the *butte*, that has the Place de Tertre as its fulcrum — by a generation of legendary artists. You climb upwards, as if on a pilgrimage, to search for a world of memories, to gaze from above upon the grey roofs of Paris and the immobile sails of the Moulin Rouge, the mythical haunt of Montmartre's prime.

You then descend again and begin another tour, a hunt for another facet of Paris, to be found in the havens of

taste, custom and tradition.

A trip to Paris is inconceivable without an excursion to its shops, boutiques, and most famous stores. In the sumptuous lounge of Faubourg Saint-Honoré or in the windows of the *triangle d'or*, reigns the world of haute couture and the most prestigious fashion houses. On the élite Place Vendôme, or scenographic Rue de la Paix, the window

displays ooze luxury and extreme elegance.

Behind the Opéra, you will find the colorful bustle of the most famous department stores. These are located along the grandiose boulevards designed by Baron Haussmann under Napoleon III — a new, modern and imperial city built atop the flattened remains of the romantic and baroque medieval Paris.

The appeal of the old Marais, the city's Jewish quarter and today the most fashionable district in Paris, has been retained intact in its maze of narrow streets and rash of trend-setting boutiques grouped around the Place des Vosges, the most romantic and celebrated of the city's squares. Here one finds fascinating little museums devoted to the secret treasures of past lives (the Museum of romantic life, the Edith Piaf Museum, dedicated to the fragile and magnetic French *chanteuse*, and the Museum of merry-go-rounds and theater design). There is also the alluring weekend market of Saint-Ouen, the largest flea market in the world, where you can roam for hours amongst the secrets of time past.

But Paris would not be Paris if, at sunset, the lights of a romantic restaurant, the colorful buzz of a brasserie, the sequins and spangles of the irresistible Folies-Bergère, or the artful rite of the eternal can-can did not take center stage.

123 top It was the Pont-Neuf, the jewel of town-planning built at the behest of Henri IV, that housed the first booksellers, the bouquinistes, who still today represent one of the best-loved postcard images of Paris. Along the banks of the Seine, close to the Pont-Neuf and the Cathedral of Notre-Dame they display second-hand books and old prints and postcards which they lock into typical green-painted wooden containers hung on the parapets along the river at night.

*124 top The broad
expanse of the Champ
de Mars is all the
more evocative at
night when skilful
lighting emphasises
the great spaces
and the solid structure
of the École Militaire.
On the left of the photo
you can see the gilded
dome of the Hôtel
des Invalides.*

*124 bottom
These aerial photos
reflect the great
harmony and
monumentality
of Paris and allow
the historic quarters
to be identified.*

*124-125
This spectacular
nocturnal photo shows
the Bastille, the center
of a new revolution
in a quarter with a
wealth of craft
workshops, cafés and
bistros that have
grown up around the
controversial Opéra-
Bastille. At the center
of the square, where a
50-meter column
now rises, once stood
the famous fortress-
prison of the Ancien
Régime stormed on
14th of July, 1789, at
the very start of the
French Revolution.*

125 top
The unmistakable
sign of the Paris
Metro at Porte
Dauphine, known
as the Libellule,
is a splendid
example, the last
remaining,
of the creative genius
of Hector Guimard,
the father of French
Art Nouveau who
early this century
designed these
remarkable entrances
for the underground
railway system.

VERSAILLES: GOLD-LEAF, MIRRORS AND ABSOLUTE POWER

126 top Reflected in the central pool, the main body of the Palace of Versailles is revealed in all its glory.

*126 bottom
The Temple of Love, created for Marie Antoinette, is enclosed in the dense vegetation of the park of Versailles.*

*126-127
The architecture of the entire Versailles complex was intended to be the highest expression of regal opulence. It was built for Louis XIV who fell in love with the design of the architect Le Vau to the extent that when the palace was almost completed he transferred his*

Beyond the gilded gateway opens the door to an epoch marked by the glories of the French monarchy at its height. The forest of mirrors, the immense staircases, the silk-lined salons, damask curtains and gigantic crystal chandeliers have witnessed processions of courtiers, princes, high

prelates and ambassadors, come to pay homage to the Sun King. Far away under the arch of the Salon de la Paix, the King sat solemnly on a throne three meters tall, set on a carpet of gold. The Marquess of Sévigné described the palace of Versailles as "a regal beauty unique in the world."

At every step the palace reminds you of the infinite power wielded by Louis XIV and his successors. In 1623 the joy of hunting, of the woods, and fresh, fragrant air, and the satisfaction of an overflowing game bag, led Louis XIII to build, in this place, a *pavillon de chasse*, later transformed into a larger edifice, the *petit château de cartes* of stone and brick, traces of which can still be seen in the facade of the Cour de Marbre, which has remained almost completely intact to this day. In 1661 Louis XIV, reluctant to demolish his father's favorite hunting lodge, decided to transform it into a much larger complex with the help of the architect Le Vau. The work begun then was to last until the end of his reign. At the beginning the King used the small castle as a secret refuge for his romantic dalliances with the beautiful Louise de la Vallière, and created a fairy-tale park around the hunting lodge, where he modelled nature after his dreams. And thus one summer night a stupefied court was invited to the unforgettable *Fête des plaisirs de l'île enchantée*, a great party in honor of the King's mistress which even Molière attended.

127 top *Hundreds of statues are scattered throughout the immense park at Versailles. The gilded statues of Latona Basin (left) and the Apollon (right) are particularly stunning as they adorn the celebrated fountains and the pools in the great garden.*

128 Louis XIV was obsessed with the Palace of Versailles and dedicated himself to the building throughout his reign. The apartments and the great halls such as the Salon de Diane (right) or the Opéra Royal (left) with the gallery decorated by Pajou reflect the continuous search for decorative splendor and opulence.

Extensions were then begun, and Versailles was transformed into a magnificent baroque palace, the King's finest achievement, his most eternal and admired invention. In 1666, after the death of his mother, Anna of Austria, Louis XIV began to consider Versailles more seriously as the principal residence for the sovereign and his court, a dream that was realised in 1682. This great complex, about twenty kilometers from Paris, became the most extraordinary *ville royale* in the world. Ten thousand courtiers (including five thousand noblemen) were fed in the court dining rooms every day. They surrounded the King, serving him with dignity and honor. From 1683 the King opened the doors of his apartments to his court, hosting dances, games, and spectacles for their amusement. If in 1661 the little village of Versailles was just a handful of houses in the country, by 1713 it was a town of forty-five thousand inhabitants; and the *ville nouvelle*, as it was known at

the time, was connected to Paris by an incessant coming and going of horses, carriages, and carts. The immense estate that enclosed the palace in a great green lung was surrounded by a wall around forty kilometers long, with twenty-four monumental gates (of which only five remain today). Only a small part of the primitive park remains but it is still magnificent.

It was Louis XIV's constant preoccupation throughout his reign. He found the ideal interpreter and accomplice for his most fantastic projects in Le Nôtre, the celebrated architect of the gardens. Le Nôtre conceived for the king not a garden, but rather a baroque city, full of surprises, in which the most fertile imaginations were free to express themselves in the creation of the world's most extravagant parties... To realise this idea of a green city, Le Nôtre modelled nature as though it were a theater, resorting to every type of visual trick, great screens of trees and numerous little woods growing in every corner enclosing mythological statues, playful fountains, or unexpected labyrinths. He flooded the Grand Canal, upon which Venetian gondolas and a flotilla of miniature warships glided. The court remained at Versailles until 1789, when the Revolution forced Louis XVI to return to Paris. In the face the rebellion, on the dramatic night of 6th of October of that year he descended through a spectacular secret passage in the palace to rejoin his queen Marie Antoinette, who had already escaped by another route. Versailles was ransacked and soon fell into

129 The photos on this page offer further glimpses of the interior of the palace and bear witness to the magnificence of the decorations completed for Louis XIV, his successor Louis XV, the only King to have spent his life and the years of his reign at Versailles, and Louis XVI. In the royal chapel, dedicated to St. Louis (center) the harmony of the Neoclassical colonnade stands out.

The staircase that leads to the apartments of the Queen (bottom right), features beautiful inlaid marble whilst the Galerie des Batailles (top right), created in 1836 in the old apartments of the southern wing, is an important picture gallery containing works depicting the great battles that belong to the Musée de l'Histoire de France, established in the 19th century.

130 left Pure gold is the key motif in the splendors of the royal palace. In this photo you can see a detail of the decoration of the panelling designed by Richard Mique in 1783 for the Queen's cabinet doré.

130 top These photos depicting some of the interiors of the Palace of Versailles, provide clear evidence of the boundless luxury of the King's apartments and in particular the Salon de l'Oeil de Boeuf (left) and Marie Antoinette's chamber (right).

ruins, as did the park and all its marvels, until 1837 when the Chamber of Deputies declared Versailles a museum. Thanks to the American patron Rockefeller, a restoration of the complex was undertaken after the First World War, and was continued by the French government after 1952. Thus, today, the halls and salons can recount their magical history rendered all the more exceptional by some quite breathtaking figures: a surface area of 800 hectares, 330,000 plants, 375 windows facing onto the enormous garden whilst at the service of this "factory of marvels" are 70 gardeners, 200 guards, 12 firemen, and 400 members of the general staff. The palace receives nearly 5 million visitors per year.

Having passed through the perimeter wall, the immense construction unfolds in all its splendor. Rigorous order was imposed at Versailles: the princes and other dignitaries lived in the north and the south wings, facing the garden, while the courtiers had their apartments by the village.

The royal apartments were found on the first floor of the main building — the King to the north, and the Queen to the south. They were reached by two marble staircases, that of the ambassadors which no longer exists and that of the Queen. Behind the Cour des Ministres, bounded by balustrades and featuring an equestrian statue of Louis XIV and memories of Montgolfier and Pilâtre de Rozier's early ballooning experiments, lies the Royal Court, which only the carriages of the royal family and ministers reached. Then comes the Cour de Marbre, with its traces of the original castle of Louis XIII, and the King's bed chamber at the center. The Opéra, a building constructed for the wedding of Louis XVI and Marie Antoinette of Austria in just one year (1770), is the architect Gabriel's masterpiece. The long western facade of the palace, which one reaches via the Cour Royale, extends a full 580 meters. Inside are rooms dedicated to Louis XIII and Louis XIV, with portraits of kings, queens, court favorites and famous personages. There is the grand apartment of the monarch, composed of six ceremonial rooms, and the Hall of Mirrors — Versailles at its most theat-

133 top left The small apartments had a private character and it was here that Louis XIV kept and admired the masterpieces in his art collection such as the Mona Lisa. The photo shows the Cabinet de la Pendule that owes its name to the astronomical clock that can be seen in the background.

133 top right The official life of the court took place in the great apartments, here can be seen the Salon du Mercure. Beginning with the Salon du Hercule, each apartment is dedicated to a Greek divinity.

132 This miniature theater was built for Marie Antoinette towards the end of the 18th century and is to be found in the gardens of the Grand Trianon.

rical — the genial creation of Mansart from 1678 to 1686, with paintings by Le Brun. Today the seventeen panels mirrored with mercury, illuminated by as many windows, reflect the figures of visitors, but at the time of the Sun King they reflected a roomful of precious furniture of pure silver set against the walls of the long gallery. Other apartments with the bedchambers of the various kings that lived in

132-133 Louis XVI had the Grand Trianon, a sumptuous palace in stone and pink marble, built in 1687 as a refuge from the strict court protocol. This photo shows the Salon des Glaces, the hall in which the King received his ministers and the members of the royal family.

the palace and salons filled with treasures, silk tapestries and famous paintings lead to the offices of Louis XV, masterpieces of French decorative art and cabinet-making. The queen's apartments follow, with the room of the queen's guard, the coronation hall, the apartment of the Dauphine and Dauphin, and then, after this long exaltation of power and luxury, you finally emerge into the silence of the immense park.

The fountains run only from May to September on scheduled Sundays, and attract up to 20,000 visitors a day to marvel at the play of the myriad water features, and to take part in the great night parties that re-evoke, at Neptune's Pool, the spectacular celebrations at the time of the Sun King. To the right of the Grand Canal, inside the park, is the Grand Trianon, the work of Le Vau, erected on whole hectares of former pastures and villages which were destroyed to make room for the *bon plaisir du roi*. The Grand Trianon stunned contemporary observers: "a nothing, just a small thing crouched between flowers, jasmine, oranges, intimate and splendid," gracefully ethereal. This ceramic *rêverie*, entirely covered in white and blue porcelain, was also a secluded refuge where the king and the queen could repose in intimacy. Today the ceramic has been replaced by white and pink marble, re-establishing the Grand Trianon as a masterpiece of refinement. The *hameau de la reine* was constructed here on the banks of an artificial lake for Marie Antoinette — this was an operetta village, a life-size puppet theater, inspired by Jean-Jacques Rousseau's call for a return to nature. Nestling in the greenery not far away is the Petit Trianon, five sumptuously furnished rooms and a beautiful English-style garden, with magnificent exotic and rare trees. This was a favorite of Marie Antoinette, but also the last residence of Madame de Pompadour, the King's famously influential lover.

134-135 *This is the most symbolic, grandiose and spectacular view of the Palace of Versailles, the Galerie des Glaces illuminated by 17 great windows throwing light onto an equal number of arched mirrors. Scenes depicting episodes from the life of Louis XIV, here seen as an ancient hero, were painted on the ceiling by Le Brun.*

Brittany

SECTION TWO

*138 bottom
In Lamballe, the
ancient capital of the
duchy of Penthièvre,
in the square that
once hosted the pillory,
appears the so-called
Maison du Bourreau,
a building erected
between the end of the
14th and the
beginning of the 15th
centuries.*

*138-139 Betton, in
Ille et Vilaine, rises on
a site occupied by
Celts since the Iron
Age. In the
photograph, beyond
the canal, you see the
Neo-Romanesque
church, construction
of which began
in 1870.*

With an area of approximately 14,000 sq. miles [35,000 sq. km] square kilometers and a population which exceeded 4,000,000 in 2000 and with its long history of independence and subsequent autonomy, Brittany has reason to hope that it will one day be recognized as a "region of Europe" in and of itself. In Ireland, Scotland and Wales, the Bretons' Celtic cousins have already succeeded in receiving certain recognition.

As was forcefully stated by the great 19th-century historian Arthur Le Moyne de la Borderie, Brittany is much more than one of the many regions of France, much more than one of those shapeless, confused jumbles created by not overly attentive technocrats. It is a people! It is a nation forged from the strongest steel, with a will tempered by over twenty centuries of struggle against adversities and cravings of neighbors with the teeth of wolves and the appetite of ogres.

Brittany is composed of nine dioceses,

four using the Breton language and five using Welsh. Although they suffered a great deal during the French Revolution, they are the most important points of reference for Bretons, the depositories of the memory of the people of the isle of Brittany who came to colonize a land which, at the dawn of the Middle Ages, still bore the name Armorica. It was here, in these magical lands on the margin of Europe, lands that best incarnated the great European dream, that the legend was born, taking its form as what, at one time, was defined with respect and envy as "the matter of Brittany." Here in the ancient, venerable forest of Broceliande, Lancelot, the most handsome, the most able, the most courageous, the most extraordinary knight of the Round Table, loved Guinevere. And the cunning Vivian imprisoned her friend and lover Merlin, the "fortress of the sea," in a crystal prison. And it was here that Tristan de Loonois died and that *Ahès Dahud*, the very tall, very blond daughter of Gradlon, the princess with the aquamarine eyes and the seaweed hair, built a city on the billows forbidden to the proselytes of the monotheistic religion.

Brittany is that dream of rocks encircled by grayish-blue water where, in the winter, storms follow one upon the other. It is where, in the Bay of the Departed, the "*vag noz*," the "night boat," slides slowly over the waves, disseminating terror, brimful of the *crierien*, the drowned souls to whom nature has denied a worthy burial.

139 top The Merle River runs beside the imposing bastions of Vannes, one of the most notable fortification complexes in France.

"Brittany is a universe," affirmed the Bretón poet Saint-Pol-Roux. This "balcony on the sea" is a mixture of diverse landscapes.

"Brittany: woods within, sea without," echoed the sweet poet Brizeau in the 19th century, charmed by the ruins and the delightful dizziness of their origins. These worlds, by themselves, summarize the profound, perennial and fundamental dualism of a land divided in men's eyes into two entirely different entities with a climate that is milder on the coast and harsher and less sunny inland, with human activity, the fishing of Armor and the agriculture of Argoat and, above all, with the vegetation. Was this not already succinctly expressed in 1533 by Charles Estienne in his *Guide des chemins de France.* " ... The duchy of Brittany, from ancient times called Armorica, is shaped like a horseshoe, the edges of which are more or less the sea and, for this reason, are called in the vernacular Armoros, which is to say "land of the sea." The bottom or hollow of this figure is on *terra firma* with moors and its common name is *ar goet* ..."

Brittany, in the end, is a legacy from which comes the need — or rather the imperative — for the transmission of an important, even essential part of the identity of our continent.

And though it is true that the Breton conscience is still little known in the great political movements that agitate other nations without countries, the people of the region, freed now of their old complexes and proud of their re-found voice, of their rich music and their roots, finally dare to

look into the future with serenity.

And this is the Brittany, always a little rebellious, as Victor Hugo said, which dares and thinks, the Brittany that we wanted you to see. Or rather, glimpse, since describing an entire country in few pages is a very large challenge.

The *Tro Breizh,* the tour of Brittany, to which we invite you, is the result of a choice, naturally a subjective one. It is the result of the enthusiasm of the author who

wished to emphasize certain aspects, the most authentic ones, rather than describing everything systematically, ending by offering a collection of postcard stereotypes. What this work loses in completeness, it undoubtedly gains in sincerity. May this excursion into the "holy ground" of Brittany, to paraphrase Gwenc'hlan Le Scouézec, give you the desire to continue your voyage which, like all voyages in the Celtic world, can be nothing more than an initiation. This book has no other aim. *Digemer mat e Breizh!*

Granville
Normandy
Cap Fréhel
Saint-Malo
Cancale
Mont Saint Michel
Dinard
Dinan
Rance
Fougères
Vitré
Meu
Vilaine
Forest of Paimpont
Rennes
Josselin
Vilaine
Châteaubriant
Redon
Erdre
Loire-Atlantique
La Baule-Escoublac
Loire
Saint-Nazaire
Nantes
Ile de Noirmoutier

146 top This series of ceramic forms from the 3rd millenium B.C., displayed in the Museum of St.-Germain-en-Laye, come from the site of Conguel, at the tip of the Quiberon peninsula.

146 bottom Archeological finds from the end of the Eneolithic era include bronze and gold objects, for example, this splendid half-moon discovered in Saint-Potan.

H aven't many historians, even the most eminent ones, perhaps begun the history of Brittany with the arrival or even the settlement of the Celts? This is no doubt due to the fact that its pre-historic era is still immersed in a fog so dense that even the mists of Avalon vanish in comparison. In this way, however, our most remote ancestors are reduced to a mere walk-on role! They become shadows with no other name than a "pre" or a "proto" with which we render unconvincing homage to figures that vanish into the obscurity of time.

Looked at more closely, Brittany's memory is constructed of numerous superimposed and intersecting layers.

And though we know very little of the humans known as Teviec, who lived in the final phase of the last Ice Age, finding refuge from external attacks on the inaccessible rocky peaks, we know somewhat more about their successors who left extraordinary testimony of what were the most ancient European civilizations.

It was, indeed, in this region that the Neolithic civilization, which first appeared in the Balkan-Danube area, fully developed. It is in Brittany that its most evocative, even disturbing vestiges are found. Carnac, Locmariaquer, Barnenez are names as weighty as granite. Thus it was in a post-Romantic Europe, the recesses of whose territory was ransacked by armies of Celtic-loving "antiquarians," that the need was felt to baptize these dream stones that materialized from the lands of the Breizh with terms drawn from the language of Merlin, such as *menhir,* the tall rock; *dolmen,* the table of rock; *cromlech'h,* the circle of rock.

The people who probably arrived in waves from the steppes of southern Russia developed a matriarchal as well as sedentary society dedicated to agriculture. They left us megaliths among which the most ancient, the *cairns* and the *mounds,* primitive cupolas dating back to the 4th millenium B.C., were acquired from the Celtic culture together with the names of Ana and Cernunos.

These Neolithic populations were swept away but not annihilated by the Indo-Europeans, shepherds, warriors and worshippers of masculine, solar deities, who gradually spread throughout the territories of Europe between 4400 and 2800 B.C.

147 On the island of Gavrinis in the Gulf of Morbihan, a gigantic cairn or tumulus, was discovered by chance in 1832. It is one of the most splendid examples of the megalithic civilization that developed in Brittany in the 4th millenium B.C. The internal stone-faces are decorated with curvilinear motifs that call to mind those of Newgrange in Ireland.

148 Spirals and circles decorate these two pieces of pottery from the so-called Hallstatt period, a name given to the artistic/artisan production in the transition period between the Bronze Age and the Iron Age, between the 8th and the 5th centuries B.C. Pottery of Celtic origin abounds in homes as well as cemeteries. The variety of shapes and decorative motifs, for the most part abstract, allows for dating the pieces and identifying their geographic origins. Armorica produced not only many examples of stamped pottery but also magnificent vases with free-hand engraved decorations.

The Celtic tribes of the second Iron Age, who belatedly arrived on these western promontories, profoundly influenced the local toponymy to the point that the words they introduced still resound in the names of cities such as Nantes, Vannes or Rennes, respectively Namnetes, Veneti and Riedones.

Around the independent Armorica, which probably included a part of Normandy and Maine, the actual territory of Brittany was divided into five nations, which, generally speaking, were Riedones to the east, Namnetes to the south-east, Veneti to the south, Osismes to the west and Coriosolites to the north.

Surprising monuments have come down from that age which an inexpert eye might confuse with the *menhirs* and which truly seem to have been made by the delightful Obelix! Round and low, slender, conical or cylindrical, smooth or grooved, these monuments called *lec'hioù* or Gallic stelae, are a testimony to the intense spiritual life of our forefathers. Dated between 450 and 250 B.C., they mark cemeteries where bodies or ashes were interred, two burial methods that were used concomitantly in Armorica. Ten of them can be found along the roads of Leon, isolated or in pairs, Christianized or not. Among these the most evocative undoubtedly is that of Sainte Anne, which dominates the beach of Trégastel. Sculpted with squiggles and vegetal designs, it is wisely attached to the complex of the Church of Plougastel-St-Germain. Until not very long ago, the girls of the village encircled this monument during the big procession (the *pardons*) in a ceremony which, in actual fact, had little to do with the Christian rites.

150

150 This 15th-century French miniature, which is filled with errors and anachronisms, depicts the naval battle between the Venetis' fleet, composed of true fortresses of the sea, and the galleys of Brutus, Caesar's nephew, off the coast of what is now Morbihan. The battle, which was turning in favor of the Armoricans, became a bloodbath when the wind fell.

151 In 56 B.C., Julius Caesar, the future dictator, seized on the pretext of the Venetis' detention of two Roman officials, to declare a vicious, bloody war on them.

Unfortunately, the independent Celtic civilization ended suddenly towards the middle of the 1st century B.C.

Caesar looked unfavorably upon the Atlantic commercial routes divided between the Armoricans and the Phoenicians. The Venetis' monopoly over the tin extracted in the Cassiterides Islands, which numerous authors identify with the Scilly Isles, the Sorligues of the French, irritated Rome.

Then, in the summer of 56 B.C., war broke out! The Gauls took refuge on inaccessible rocky spurs from which they were able to flee by sea whenever the Romans were sure that they could encircle them. After exasperating months spent in a vain attempt to entrap the indomitable Gauls, the future dictator decided to defeat them on the ocean. This was no easy task since the ships of the Venetis, compared to the fragile galleys of the sons of the she-wolf, were truly floating fortresses. That was true, but as such they were also very heavy. Fast under strong winds, they become cumbersome and not easily maneuverable in light winds. At the end of the summer, according to Caesar, misfortune or the gods, plagued the Venetis, their Armorican allies and the Bretons themselves. Off the shores of the Peninsula of Quiberon — and not in the Gulf of Morbihan, as 19th-century historians maintained — a naval battle raged. The Armoricans were winning. But the wind fell: Brutus' sailors surrounded the Venetis' ships.

With the aid of ingenious devices, they cut up halyards and shrouds and boarded the fortresses from the keels … of clay. It was a bloodbath, a massacre to which Caesar contributed with his "leg-endary generosity," as Hirtius, his faithful secretary, would say. It ended with the extermination of the enemy leaders and the sale at auction of nearly half of the Venetis population.

But the courageous Armoricans were not, however, annihilated, and many of them found refuge on the island of Britain, in particular in the territory of the modern Wales, where they founded the counties of Gwyned and Gwent.

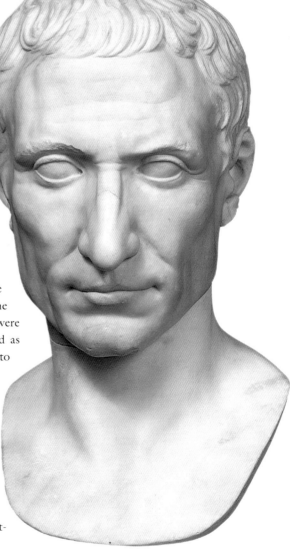

Subsequently a *Pax Romana* was established comparable, in certain ways, especially at the beginning, to a funereal peace. The crushed Armorica was annexed to Gallia Lugdunensis with which it would share its destiny for four long centuries. But is this truly romanticizing? If some authentic Roman cities emerged from the Armorican woods, such as Vorgium, now Carhaix, the entirety of the countryside remained, in all probability, Celtic-speaking. Can we believe Abbé Henri Poisson when he peremptorily said "the Armoricans were nothing other than Celts disguised as Romans"? Now, as then, it is useful to distrust pre-packaged ideas and theories. But since Roman poet Ausonius assures us that, in his family, living in Bordeaux, the Celtic language was spoken in the 2nd century A.D. and that it was still used in the region of Arverne well into the 4th century, there is reason to suppose that it long remained the idiom in use in the western promontories.

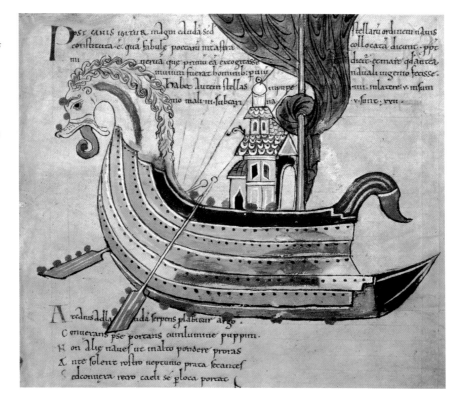

Beginning in the 4th century, new blood and energy came from the island of Britain to an Armorica by then tired, subjected to the pirates raiding from the northern seas, generically amalgamated under the name *Saozon*, the Saxons. The agony of the empire began with the attacks of the barbarians. In gestation was the new world from which modern Brittany sprang. We have long been pleased to promote the image drawn from traditional iconography, showing Britons fleeing from the Anglo-Saxon hordes in their leather coracles, belatedly coming to populate a nearly deserted Armorica.

According to La Borderie, "In this phase, the human presence in the Armorican peninsula was altogether accidental. The territory was infested with brambles, undergrowth and its ferocious inhabitants."

The reality is undoubtedly less definite. The Britons, who shared the same geopolitical environment as the Armoricans, often crossed the Channel to land in an Armorica that was not in fact totally depopulated, as La Borderie sustains.

They arrived there, at least initially, much more as protectors than as fugitives. In short, originally from the western regions, those who fled surrendered most probably to the pressure of the raids of the Scottish pirates or of the northern Picts rather than those of the Angles or the Saxons.

For our patriotic historian: "Without the Britannic immigration, the Armorican peninsula would have been a Latin-speaking region, a province of the Frankish kingdom, a languishing, uncultured, desolated country devoted to paganism." In this apocalyptic description, if you wish to credit these hagiographic accounts, probably only the latter statement is credible.

The Britons who disembarked en masse starting in the 5th century recreated the kingdom on the other side of the Channel, importing a new religion to the inhabitants of Armorica, who were still predominantly pagans. Together with their political leaders, the *tierns,* their priests, Malo, Indut, Brioc and Tudual, they created bishoprics, the *plou* and the

tre, administrative and religious subdivisions that have been handed down to present times.

Here and there saints reputed to be such by the collective imagination, fought shouting and exploding fire-breathing dragons, as did Efflam, presumed cousin of King Arthur, on the shores of the Bay of Lannion. At their side, Gwenc'hlan, "the last druid," hurled his curses against the "foreign" princes and Christian priests who, having put out his eyes, threw him into an unending darkness. In the Bay of Douarnenez, the vulgar invaders assaulted the city of Ys. Unbeknown to Saint Gwendole and his father Gradlon, in search of strength and advice from the priestesses of the Isle of Sein, a beautiful, rebellious princess fled from the city, defying the power of the new spiritual masters of the country. From the mists of its origins a new country emerged, permeated by a dual historical memory, British and Armorican, and by a dual religiosity, Christian-Celtic and Druid.

soldiers who had rebelled against Rome. In the swamps of Bains-sur-Oust, they inflicted heavy defeat on Charles who fled villainously, abandoning his troops and the booty of war.

Important from the military aspect, the victory of Ballon was equally so from the psychological and political viewpoint. Freed from the threat of the Franks, Nominoë lost no time in organizing a true political Breton nation, run exclusively by people from there. According to Yann Fouéré, "In terms of its historical consequences, Nominoë's victory over the Franks is, in many ways comparable to that of the Scot Robert Bruce at Bannockburn over the Anglo-Saxon forces. Thanks to Nominoë and Robert Bruce, Brittany and Scotland were the only two Celtic nations to have a state organization in the modern sense of the term during the Middle Ages."

Beginning in the second half of the 6th century, migration intensified. While on the island, the Britons of Ambrosius Aurelianus were subjected to Saxon assaults, which had by then assumed the proportions of a true invasion, Armorica first became Litavia and then Brittany. According to Léon Fleuriot, "In short, in a century, the number of Britons who established themselves in Armorica grew progressively until they had acquired political power ..., initially as *foederati* of the Romans, and found themselves the rulers of the country."

In the High Middle Ages, the country was divided politically into three distinct realms: Domninée to the north, Cornouaille to the southwest and Bro Waroc to the south. In the clashing of sharpened swords, the assassins amounted to parricides. Brittany was still searching for its limits and the menace of the Franks was already on the horizon.

After innumerable attempts at annexation and a series of more or less fruitful incursions, in 818, Louis the Pious, the Carolingian emperor, succeeded in defeating the troops of King Morvan, who led the resistance from Poher. Brittany lost its independence. At least that is what the Franks thought. Then Nominoë Nevenoe, called Tad ar Vro (literally "father of the country"), the son of a noble, rich Breton family, was named governor. At the death of Louis, he freed the people of the obligations imposed and rejected restrictions and privileges imposed by the new ruler Charles, known as the Bald. Wishing to crush the "rebels" using decisive methods, after the signing of the Treaty of Verdun, which confirmed his reconciliation with his brothers, Charles undertook an expedition to Brittany. In November 845 — and not in June, as La Borderie and all the nationalistic school together with him insisted — at the head of an army, undoubtedly inferior to what Bertrand d'Argentré stated, he invaded Breton territory.

Unfortunately for him, the Bretons were awaiting him. Using light cavalry and throwing weapons, they avoided man-to man combat, re-introducing a strategy inherited from the *bagaudes*, peasants and

154 top Little Brittany has always been coveted by its powerful French neighbor, which constantly attempted to conquer it. In 497 Clovis, portrayed here in a 14th-century French manuscript, succeeded, annexing the region to the Franco-Carolingian kingdom.

154 bottom Louis the Pious, portrayed here in a 14th-century miniature, defeated the famous King Morvan in 818. In the same, disastrous year, he imposed Benedictine rule on the Abbey of Landevennec, which had, up till then, followed Celtic ritual customs.

155 In November
845, Charles the Bald
attempted to annex
Brittany. But the
heavy French cavalry
was massacred in the
marshes of Redon by a
highly mobile Breton
army, equipped with
spears and riding on the
backs of small, fast
horses. During the night,
the sovereign villainously
cut and ran.

Nominoë, the *Tad ar Vro,* pushing the war into the heart of France, met his death at Vendôme in 851, but his work was carried on by his son Erispoé, who annexed the counties of Rennes and Nantes, later receiving the royal symbols. His successor Salomon conquered Avranchin, Cotentin and a part of Anjou.

For Father Chardronnet, "At Salomon's death, the Breton kingdom was at its apogee, which was, nonetheless, fragile." The Norman menace that hung as much over Armorica as Ireland ensured that the "more fragile" Brittany became the prey of these men from the north which devastated it under the scornful gaze of its French neighbors.

But, in 937, Alain, known as Barbe-Torte, inflicted painful defeats on the Vikings, first at Dol and then at Plourivo, initiating a period of stability to the west

of Couesnon. But though having averted this danger from the north, the Breton sovereigns, who by then bore the title of dukes, had no respite in preserving the independence of the country. For several centuries they employed a shrewd policy of balance of power between their two powerful neighbors, the English and the French, who looked with interest on the little state, jealous of its independence and the influence that it hastened to acquire. Unfortunately the death of Duke Jean III left the duchy with no direct heirs, at the mercy of the rivalry between his brother Jean de Montfort and his niece Jeanne de Penthième. The two contenders appealed to the two foreign powers, Jeanne to France and Jean to England, once again placing the independence of Brittany at risk. After a forced exile in Britain, during which the French king, Charles V, brazenly announced the confiscation of the county of Brittany, Jean de Montfort triumphantly returned to Dinard on August 3, 1379, recalled by his vassals in this moment of danger. He was heartily welcome by the population, the memory of which was nourished by *Barzaz Breiz.* "Neventi vad d'ar Vretoned! Ha mallozruz d'ar C'hallaoued. Dinn, dinn, daon! D'ann emgann! D'ann emgann ho, dinn, dinn, daon, d'ann emgann a eann!" "Good news for the Bretons! And curses on the French. Our lord Jean is returning .... Din, don, dan, to battle, din, don, dan, I'm going to battle!" Once more freedom was preserved! Just in time. Beginning with the reign of Jean IV and that of his son Jean V, who succeeded him in 1399, the Breton navy underwent extraordinary expansion, reaching the point of rivaling that of the Low Countries.

While the Duke of Brittany, who still refused to render obeisance and fidelity to the king of France, flourished a crown as royal symbol, his powerful neighbor was preparing plans for attack.

157 bottom In the mid-1400s, English reinforcements disembarked in aid of Breton troops. During the entire period of their independence, the duchies of Brittany maintained a skilful diplomatic balance between their two powerful neighbors, England and France. The Breton army, defeated at Saint-Aubin du Cormier in 1488, included a contingent of 300 English archers.

Louis XI who ruled France from 1461 to 1483, continued to corrupt the great Breton nobility. And he succeeded to the point that it was those of the most noble birth, the Rieux, d'Avangour and other Rohan families that, in 1487, fomented a plot against their duke, François II, imploring the help of the French.

After a siege, the Breton army was defeated on July 28, 1488 near Saint Aubin du Cormier.

With the treaty signed on August 14th in Verger Castle, François II was forced by King Charles VIII to swear submission to him and to promise not to marry his daughters without royal consent.

When the duke died of heartbreak on September 9th of the same year, his daughter Anne freed herself from those

contractual bonds. While Charles was once again attacking Brittany, she married Emperor Maximilian of Austria by proxy. Unfortunately, under siege in the city of Rennes and threatened by an implacable war, Anne, with her husband involved in fighting the Ottomans, was forced to yield to the requests of her torturer who, among other things, succeeded in annulling her marriage.

Charles died in 1499, after cracking his skull on the beam of a low doorway, and Anne was obliged to marry his successor, Louis XII, a totally self-serving marriage which, however, guaranteed Brittany a wide margin of freedom! But Anne was called to God in January 1514. Her daughter, Claude, who would have married Charles of Luxembourg, the fu-

ture Holy Roman Emperor Charles V, was obliged to wed François de Angoulême, who rose to the Franch throne in 1515. It was the end of independence for the duchy because, while the Edict of Plessis Macé signed in Vannes in 1532 conceded, on the one hand, a certain number of rights to Brittany, among which was the withholding of taxes to France, on the other hand, it transformed a marriage of convenience into a perpetual territorial annexation.

160 Initially favourably received, the Revolution displeased Bretons because its leaders refused to abolish the tithe and the expiration of farming contracts. The ban on having sacred processions, the suppression of the rights of the duchy, the hoarding of "national property" by the bourgeoisie and, above all, the draft of 300,000 men, inflamed the countryside.

However, until 1789, Brittany, with the intermediation of its parliament and especially of its States, which had legislative duties, resisted all attempts by the king of France aimed at limiting its autonomy.

Two revolts, a popular one in 1674, called the "Stamped Paper" or "Red Berets," and another in 1719, that of Cellamare or Pontcalleck, of aristocratic inspiration, attempted to restore Brittany's ancestral rights, but they were suffocated in blood.

Tensions between representatives of the duchy and the central government were present, frequent and nearly permanent. But at the very least, the States succeeded in having the clauses of the 1532 treaty respected ... until the fateful night of August 4, 1789 when the representatives of the Third Estate (the bourgeoisie) present at the Estates-General in Paris sacrificed the "privileges" of the "province" at the altar of ideology and an abstract nation, without even consulting the other estates which would, among other things, be suppressed the following year.

The end of autonomy, more than the execution of Louis XVI, and the continued attacks on religious freedom, together with the threat of conscription — the famous "draft of 300,000 men" — triggered the conflagration in a country by then already seething.

In March 1793, Brittany revolted, animated by a strong sense of injustice and laced, (because of intellectuals like the Marquis de la Rouerie), with federalist leanings. The revolt of the Chouans (local insurgents) led by courageous representatives of the people, conquered the countryside, conducting a war of attacks and ambushes until Napoleon finally captured the last Chouan leader, George Cadoual, and ordered his execution in 1804.

The Restoration in 1815 gave no recognition to this peasant army, always suspected of rebellion, hastening, instead, to consecrate a Bonapartist centralism and to ratify the suppression of the ancient provinces, something that the French kings had long desired.

Brittany no longer existed. It no longer had "documents." It was not even on the map. It had no name. It was nearly lost to memory. It was dismembered into five "departments", lacking in sense, history and social significance.

160-161 In 1795, the
ineptitude of Count
Hervily wrecked the
landing of pro-Chouan
reinforcement at
Quiberon though the
Bretons kept control over
the countryside, this
setback demonstrated the
impossibility of
communication between
them and a nobility
which only hoped to
regain privileges.

In the ambitions of Parisian power, very soon it was not even to have a language any longer, persecuted by all the regimes that followed one another over the course of the 19th century which was obsessed by the ideal of cultural uniformity.

Its population, whose annexation had forbidden it outlets to traditional seas, had no choice but suffering or forced immigration to the capital where many young girls ended up as streetwalkers.

The common people bowed down while the bourgeois "elite" integrated themselves with enthusiasm and servility.

But Paris distrusted the Bretons, rightly reputed to be less integrated than other peoples. Despite a bitter and ruthless struggle against the language suspected of threatening "the unity and indivisibility" of the "national" territory, on the whole the Bretons continued to use the last Celtic language on the continent.

In 1870, when the Prussians were threatening Paris, the young Republican government resorted to the draft. General De Keratry, a young aristocrat from Cornwall and ex-prefect of the Paris police, recruited a Breton army. Some 80.000 volunteers were given the task of stopping the German advance. Unfortunately Léon Gambetta, who combined the functions of President of the Council and Minister of War, obsessed by the specter of the "chouans" decided to abandon them in the camp of Conlie, near Mans with no cots for sleeping, no weapons and no food.

The Breton soldiers, victims of the cold and of typhus, died like flies in the tragic winter of 1870-1871. It was an army of ghosts, racked by fever and desperation, which on January 11th was sent to certain defeat in the "battle" of the Tuileries. It is understandable that this massacre, premeditated by the French government, deeply shocked the Bretons: M. Bidard de la Noé, mayor of Rennes, along with General De Keratry, Arthur Le Moyne de la Borderie and Count Le Gonidée de Tresson decided to resume Cadoual's struggle.

The poet of Morlaix, Tristan Corbière, dedicated the splendid *Pastorale de Conlie* to this tragedy, a song of enormous emotional charge in which he manifests his disdain for what his people endured.

The Brittany that lives, thinks and nourishes itself with the grand dreams of chivalric King Arthur is not dead.

In the wake of Théodore Hersat de la Villemarqué's 1838 publication of Barzaz Bretz, the "Kalevala" of the Bretons, a generation of authors, poets and writers worked on "Brittany material," laying the premises for the future. Meanwhile a sort of modern and romantic inter-Celtic movement arose.

At the end of the nineteenth century, a timid reawakening of political claims appeared with the creation of the URB (Union Régionaliste Bretonne) in 1898. It was animated by symbolic figures such as Régis de l'Estourbeillon, deputy of Vannes, about whom the folklore expert Anatole Le Braz, author of the renowned *Légende de mort chez les Bretons armoricains,* had written.

On the spiritual front, in 1900 at Guingamp, Taldir Jaffrenou, Yves Berthou and another twenty men of letters, after receiving the bardic investiture from their Gallic cousins, founded the Goursez of druids, bards and prophets of the peninsula of Brittany.

162-163 Prussian troops march on the Champs-Elysées in Paris after the surrender of the city. In January 1871, the French command sent the volunteers of the Breton Army, reduced by the inferno of Conlie, against the enemy units.

163 The Marquis Régis de l'Estourbeillon, deputy from Vannes, was the heart of the U.R.B. (Union Régionaliste Bretonne).

But, alas, the movement had just seen the light when the terrible First World War, 1914-18, began. It turned into a massacre for the Breton troops largely enlisted in the infantry and systematically sent to the front lines. If certain patriots like Louis-Napoléon Le Roux, the "Breton *Sinn-Feiner*," secretary to Padraig Pearse, head of the Provisional Government in 1916, preferred exile in Ireland rather than fighting and dying for the "invader," the "regionalist" intellectuals faithfully served France, nourishing the hope that when the "the war for peoples' rights" was over, their sacrifice would be repaid with a certain cultural, political and administrative freedom. Unfortunately, the delegation led by Commander Jacob and the Marquis de L'Estourbeillon, was not even admitted to the Peace Conference in 1919. The Bretons had, once again, fought another's war, a war in the interests of the others, for the right of others to decide for themselves, a right which, for the victors in 1918, was evidently not applied to Bretons or to their brothers in Ireland.

However, while once again Ireland arose against the abhorred Sassenach, a handful of young people, radicalising the positions of the *Emsav*, the Breton movement, created the *Unvaniezh Yaouankiz Breizh*, whose newspaper *Breizh Atao,* inspired by the Irish exam-

164-165 Between August 3, the date on which the American tanks overran Rance, and August 25, 1944, the day on which they entered Concarneau, the Allies freed all the Breton territory. The German pockets of resistance in Lorient and Saint-Nazaire, however, stood firm until May 1945.

165 top This photograph, from June 1943, shows in what condition the city of Rennes found itself. It was the victim of tremendous bombardment near its station, which, in broad daylight on May 29, 1943, caused the death of 210 and the injury of 250. Brittany paid a heavy price for the war. The bombing of Nantes, on September 16th and 23rd, caused the deaths of 772 people and injuries to 1,775. The port cities of Saint-Malo, Saint-Nazaire, Brest and Lorient were almost completely razed to the ground.

165 bottom At Saint-Briac, in the interior of Saint-Malo, Bretons welcomed the Americans exultantly. But the hard times had not yet ended; ration coupons remained in use until 1947!

ple, did not delay in supporting national independence.

The attempt in 1940 by a minority to obtain from Nazi Germany the support that the Irish had asked for from the Kaiser in 1916 immediately gave the French government to repress all the Breton movements both cultural and political in the summer of 1944. But when the storm passed, under the form of musical and "folkloric" activities, Brittany began again to live, to breathe, to hope.

In 1947, Polig Monjarret created the first *bagad*, the Breton version of the *pipe band*, giving birth to a movement which, by mid-century, had acquired notable importance. In fact, in 1957, returning from Ireland, where a significant part of the *emsaverien* had found refuge, Dr. Yann Fouéré founded the MOB (Mouvement pour l'Organisation de la Bretagne), which claimed on the political level the rights that Joseph Martray and the CELIB (Comité d'étude et des intérêts bretons) claimed on the economic level. Indeed the Brittany of the 1950s, underdeveloped, hindered from autonomously administrating itself, victim of a downright social hemorrhage, seemed almost like a third-world country.

The "agricultural revolution" of the 1960s and 1970s made Brittany the leader of the European region in agricultural food production, making it possible for part of the population to remain and blocking the migratory flow, even though the Parisian ideological and technocratic rigidity still aroused mistrust and revolt.

*166 bottom
Immediately after the war, there was an extraordinary musical revival, embodied, in particular, by the* bagadoù, *musical groups formed of some* binioù vraz, *or large bagpipes, eight* bombardes *and numerous Scottish drums. In 1947, the musician Polig Monjarret created the* clique *or band of the railwaymen of Carhaix, which, within a very short period of time, had many admirers.*

166-167 Breton agriculture went from the so-called archaic stage of the "Glorious 30s" to that of modern, intensive agriculture, inundating European markets with milk, cauliflower and artichokes. Now biological cultivation and a new farming culture are beginning to make themselves felt.

Both to impede the ill-timed land centralisation and to slacken the centralist hold, the FLB (Front de Libération de la Bretagne) appeared in 1966, gathering in its ranks representatives of all the social-professional categories. The symbolic attacks this clandestine organisation carried out had the aim of attracting the world attention to the fate reserved for the country of King Arthur and obtaining compensation from the French state.

Three decades later, the result seems somewhat modest.

If Brittany appears to be definitively past the condition of underdevelopment derided by the Parisians, the Breton "model" of intensive agriculture is increasingly criticized both within and without the region.

Brittany, indeed, has again found its name and a semblance of recognition of the administrative kind, especially after the Deferre law of 1982, which decreed election of the Regional Council through universal suffrage. And there are grounds for thinking that, if Prime Minister Raffarin's reform sees the light of day, the region will obtain broad responsibilities, bringing it closer to other European regions.

As for the population, which has been freed from the old inferiority complexes thanks to the cultural and musical renaissance that followed the Alan Stivell phenomenon, they dream again of a stronger and more autonomous Brittany, fully reembracing the ancient claims of the *Emsav*.

167 right After the inauguration of the first Diwan associative school in Ploudalmézeau in 1977, teaching of the Breton language has moved forward. In 2002 Breton language schools had 7,682 students.

167 bottom "Brittany is Life" declares this banner around which are gathered, among others, the TV journalist Roger Gicquel, the singer Alan Stivell and the president of the Conseil Culturel de Bretagne, Jean-Louis Latour.

ARMOR: THE INHERITANCE OF THE SEA

168 top The high tides that can be seen in Brittany's waters, creating absolutely spectacular effects, are among the highest in the world, and ocean currents are particularly strong.

Armor, the sea. Can you imagine a fate more connected with that liquid immensity, its songs, its roaring waves, its nightmares than that in which 1250 miles [2000 km] of uneven coast stretches towards the chimerical Avalon as much as towards the very real Americas?

This land is confused with the ocean to such an extent that it even takes its name — ar mor, Armorica ... "the land surrounded by the sea." Everything is written in this name in which the echo of the waves that break against the rocks resounds, the name for an ancient and terraqueous world that, in the West, celebrates the perpetually renewed marriage between land and sea. A border world in which aquatic creatures, Ahès Dahud, followers of the goddess Morrigan and magical inhabitants of the abyss, organize wild witches' sabbaths, sometimes real disasters for the sailors encountered them. In all ages, the destiny of Breizh has been intimately, profoundly, viscerally, ontologically mixed with the ocean. This ocean, contrary to what the neighboring French believed, did not form a border but, rather, a formidable connection! On the other hand, wasn't the reign of Arthur perhaps two-headed, at least in the dreams of the Bretons and their literature?

Sailors' land from time immemorial, land from which, according to the ancient chronicles, the Irish monk Brendan started his second transatlantic journey to the Antilles in the 4th century. A land from which the fishermen of Trégor and Goëlo advanced as far as the coasts of the New World to fish for cod in the Middle Ages.

In the sixteenth century the descendents of Merlin and Vivian, in their 80- or 100-ton caravels sailed all the known seas, selling the wines of Bordeaux in Flanders, the fabrics of Lèon or the woad of Toulouse in England. This was the epoch in which the port of Penmarc'h armed a fleet of over three hundred ships which sailed all over Europe, an epoch in which Jacques Cartier of Saint-Malo found the source of the St. Lawrence River in Canada and in which the cartography laboratory of Guillaume Brousconi in Conquet supplied the most important navigators.

In the centuries that followed, if the annexation to France ended by depriving Brittany of part of its traditional outlets, its people did not stop advancing toward far-off horizons. Privateers such as Dugay-Trouin and Surcoff pursued the English enemy for the King of France, making that defiance the stuff of legend.

The heirs of these giants of the sea are nowadays called Riguidel, Kersauzon, Alain Gautier or Tabarly, one of the most capable skippers of all times, who was lost in the Irish Sea in 1997 aboard his mythical *Pen Duick IV*. It is not an accident that the major transatlantic sailing competitions, such as the famous Route du Rhum, depart from this peninsula which seems like "a balcony extended into the sea" (Xavier Grall).

168-169 *The sea has always shaped Bretons' lives and imagination. This photograph shows the Bay of Quiberon where, in June 1795, a considerable contingent of immigrants attempted to join the Chouans led by Cadoual for the purpose of restoring the monarchy and the freedom of the country.*

169 top *For many people, Brittany has become a synonym for recreation. The country of Eric Tabarly, Jacques Cartier and Dugay-Trouin continues to attract sailing enthusiasts, whether they use the older cotton sails or modern ones made of highly technological materials.*

170 top When he comes back into port, the fisherman sorts the shellfish by size. In order to preserve this important resource, very strict laws require shellfish of less than 4 inches (10.2 cm) to be thrown back into the sea.

170 center A man installs a dredge which will allow him to gather molluscs from the seabed, separating them from the sand and mud.

170 bottom After harvesting, the molluscs are packed into sacks to be sent to auction, to be sold to the highest bidder.

170-171 Of the 17,000 people enrolled in the list of French fishermen, as many as 10,000 are Bretons. Those of the Bay of Saint-Brieue specialise in netting capesante, molluscs which once were little appreciated and which now instead find favor with chefs and gourmets.

But the ocean not only represents the search for individual affirmation; it is also the humble, daily adventure of anonymous heroes who rise before dawn to go to work on the immense watery expanse.

And though the days are over when the fishermen left from Paimpol, Binic or Saint Malo, pushing into the icy inferno of the northern Atlantic to fill their nets with cod, the great ocean still supports thousands of Breton families.

Looking more closely, out of about 17,000 French sailors, more than one-half are Bretons! The Armorican fishing haul on average amounts to 45% of the national total, and 50% of the manpower involved in the art of fishing are Bretons.

Aware of the immense potential wealth of the oceans, the Bretons launched new activities generating considerable added value, such as thalassotherapy or harvesting algae. The latter, with an annual production of 70,000 tons, already involves 3,000 laborers in the production cycle.

171 top left The fishermen come back into port. Once the season for netting mollusks has ended, the spars visible on the stern of the boat can be used for trawling.

171 top right With the winch, the fishermen lower one of the two dredges that will allow them to take as much as 1320 lbs (600 kilos) of molluscs in half an hour.

172 bottom A large French military port, Brest preserves some pleasant medieval vestiges. One of these is its 15th-16th century castle, now home to the maritime prefecture and the Naval Museum. Another is its 16th-century Tanguy Tower, shown in this photograph, on a sheer cliff over the military port, which now holds an interesting Museum of History.

172-173 The Albert Louppe bridge, inaugurated in 1930 by Gaston Doumergue, then President of the Republic, connects the austere Léon with the smiling Cornouaille. Since 1994, the connection has been doubled with the opening of the Pont de l'Iroise.

173 top, left and right Inaugurated in 1990, Océanopolis, at the entry to the tourist port

of Moulin Blanc, is a vibrant homage to Lir, the Celtic god of the sea. A place for discovery, tourism, pedagogy and scientific research, it attracts about 600,000 visitors a year. With 1 million gallons salt water and its 320 employees during the summer season, this imposing complex consists of three pavilions, one for each of the climatic zones — temperate, tropical and polar.

The sea surely represents the future, a precursor of which is the Océanopolis Center which opened in Brest in 1990 and attracts more than a million visitors a year. Yet it also represents the memory of an entire populace. What would the sea have become if it had only been populated by monsters with outboard motors or if the last exemplars of the traditional wooden sailboats had ended their existence rotting in naval cemeteries? But so that this extraordinary patrimony would not be irremediably lost when

172 top Brest pays particular attention to its legacy of wood, hemp and cotton. Every four years, this city, an urban version of the more compact, intimate Douarnenez, hosts thousands of sailors from all parts of the world.

formica supplanted oak in the construction of beds and sideboards, a tiny group of enthusiasts, supported by the magazine Chasse Marée, decided to organize nautical events devoted to classical boats. What great strides have been made from the Pors Beac'h gatherings at Logonna Daoulas in 1980 to the extraordinary sea-fest in Brest and Douarnenez in 1996 which attracted over a million enthusiasts of wooden hulls! Indeed the

movement was not limited to the organization of events; it also gave birth to the awareness that safe-guarding the maritime tradition is as important as handing down music played on instruments such as the Breton bagpipes *(biniou)* or the Celtic harp. Now from the Fête des Vieux Grèements (Festival of Classical Boats) in Ploumanach to the *Chants de Marins* (Sailors' Songs) festival in Paimpol, an entire patrimony is being recovered. In the Bay of Lannion, a traditional trawling net has been reconstructed. In Brest harbor, there is the *Recouvrance,* a faithful replica of a schooner from the beginning of the nineteenth century. In Odet, the lugger *Corentin* can be admired. Great is the wonder when, in the sparkling light of a summer morning, one of these venerable boats appears on the open sea with its dark cotton sails!

Ar mor, the sea. Imagine a land set on an unusually changeable coastline, in a shoreline from which the tide recedes, revealing a border world with the scent of iodine and of other worlds!

The coastline extends into infinity. The skies can change ten times a day with the *gwalarn,* which wails from the north-west, and the *reter,* which compete for the horizon. It isn't surprising that Plutarch pinpointed the landing stage for the *Tir na n'Og* precisely here, the place in which the courageous meet to have drinking sprees, where the cider and the mead run like rivers and where maidens have soft, welcoming thighs that offer repose to the warrior.

174 bottom Port-Anne on the coast of Vannes, pays respectful homage to Saint Anne, patroness of Bretons and, through her, to Deva Ana, the great Mother of the Celts and the gods, who continues to be venerated under the vestments of the Christian saint.

174-175 "Brittany is a universe" affirmed the

Provençal poet Saint-Pol Roux, who made his home in Camaret. It was also he who defined Crozon as a muse "with a bonnet of indefinite outline" because of the enormous number of inlets and promontories.

175 top left At Pointe des Poulains, Belle-Île en Mer has cliffs that are among the highest in Brittany. To fully

appreciate this wild, tortured coast, you have to see it swept by the waves during the equinoctial storms.

175 top right The southern coast of Brittany is a more gentle, colorful universe, less hostile than that in the north. It is an ideal area for nautical recreation, swimming and long walks.

174 top Considered by Plutarch as the departure point for the afterlife, Brittany remained such for centuries. The spectral vag-noz, *the boat laden with the souls of the drowned waiting to be judged, crosses the Bay of the Departed.*

Three bodies of water contend over the territory, making of this *penn ar bed,* the "head of the world," a crossroads and an extraordinary place of exchange. To the north is the Channel, to the west the Iroise or Celtic Sea and to the south the immensity of the Atlantic. An almost indecent variety of landscapes!

The north is an almost uninterrupted succession of high cliffs scarred by the Bay of Saint Brieuc, a deep cove in the bodice of Breizh. The eastern part presents points and capes and a cross-shaped peninsula, a kind of giant sea monster snoozing between the harbor of Brest and the Bay of Douarnenez. The south is a symphony of delightful small estuaries, a rosary of small harbors surrounded by cluster pines in which multi-colored boats float.

"Brittany is a universe" eruditely proclaimed the Provençal Saint Pol Roux, who knew what he was talking about. And it's true. And it's also true for Breizh, which begins here, at the edges of the immense bay of Mont Saint Michel, which, according to the old saying, "Couesnon in his folly placed in Normandy." An immense desert of sand and water in which the scent of the giants gently wafts. Wasn't the Mont perhaps called Gargan before being providentially Christianized, and doesn't the Isle of Tombelaine still remember the time when its name was "Tombe Belen"?

This is the region of excesses, an area in which, the inhabitants of the place assure us, the sea rises at the speed of a galloping horse! This suggestive image was quickly desecrated by the scientists who nonetheless recognize that, with a rise of over 53 feet (15 m), the tides of this area are the most accentuated on the planet after those of the Bay of Fundy (New Brunswick), Canada.

Cancale is famous for its oyster dishes and its *bisquines,* large albatrosses made of wood and cloth that enthusiasts of traditional sailing built in such great numbers that they could race with their Granville neighbors.

176 and 177 Mont Saint-Michel was, without a doubt, the ancient site of a Druid cult. The Ilot de Tombelaine, on which it rises, corresponds to the ancient Tun-Belen, "altura (sacred to God) Belen." It is an ode to the sacred that unwinds through a universe of immense proportions. Almost entirely located in Breton territory, despite the fact that the Mont itself is in Normandy, the Bay experiences tides among the most notable in the world, second only to those in the Bay of Fundy in Canada. The water recedes for over 12.5 miles (20 km), revealing a desert of sand where only those who know its secrets can venture.

178 top left and right
As early as the 4th
century the Gallo-
Roman poet Ausonius
sang the praises of
Breton oysters. Their
fame has not
diminished over the
centuries — and the
annual production of
the dozen or so
principal farms
reaches 15,000 tons.

During low tide, the
oyster farmer (left)
with a tractor goes to
the farm on the estran
facing the bay. The
oysters are then put
into highly resistant
plastic bags (right),
with capacities up to
27 lbs (12 kilos), set on
wide, iron shelves, and
sold at three or four
years of age.

178-179 Direct sales
make it possible for
the oyster farmer to
double his earnings.
Oysters are sold on
the basis of their size.
The average, labeled
M3, which weigh
between 2.7 and
3.0 oz. (65 and
84 grams), are
generally the most
valued.

179 top Cancale
continues to be the
undisputed Mecca of
mother-of-pearl
oysters. Its fame goes
back to the 16th
century and now a
large number of
gourmets gather there
under the banner of
the Confrérie des
Hôtes de la Baie de
Cancale.

179 bottom In this
stock basin where they
are tidily arranged in
boxes, oysters can stay
for weeks, waiting to
be sold.

180 Destroyed by General Patton's bombardments, the city of Saint-Malo, with its wealthy dwellings, was faithfully — or nearly so — reconstructed right after the war. However, the bell tower of the cathedral was completed only in 1972.

181 left The city within the walls preserves the atmosphere of other times when the sailors made the famous "silk way" resound with their laughter. These iron fishermen symbolise the city's historical connections with the New World.

181 top right On the bottom of the ports of Dinan and Saint-Malo, the waters of the Rance are barred by a powerful dam that runs for a good 830 yds (750 meters).

181 center right, the photograph top François-René de Chateaubriand, originally from Combourg, wished to be buried on the island of Grand-Bé. For the Celts, this island is a place of initiation and rebirth, a visible fragment of the afterlife.

181 center right, the photograph bottom As the poet Xavier Grall forcefully wrote, in Brittany it is not rare for "the sea to defy the coast." The daily destiny of Bretons who live on the sea does not spare the proud descendents of pirates.

181 bottom right Over the years Saint-Malo has succeeded in making cultural, intelligent tourism prosper.

At the mouth of the Rance, guarded by the Solidor tower erected in 1382 by the highly suspect Duke Jean IV, rises Saint Malo whose motto "Malouins first, Bretons perhaps, French, if anything remains" reiterates dreams of independence. These dreams took shape at the end of the 16th century, marked by crime and blood, when, following the example of Venice, Saint-Malo proclaimed itself a republic. The leading port in France in the 18th century, the city still exudes the air of faraway places and the memory of sailors such as Dugay-Trouin, Surcouf, Mahe de la Bourdonnais, who initiated commercial activities in the East Indies, and Jacques Cartier, who explored north of the Indies — the West Indies. Now the sumptuous

India cloth and even the acrid odor of the cod unloaded in enormous quantities on the docks of the port until the 1950s are nothing but a memory. Some 80% destroyed by the raining of General Patton's bombs in 1944, the walled city was never again constructed exactly as it had been. Yet the walk along the walls in front of the Grand Bé, where the last dwelling place of François-René Châteaubriand rises, is something unforgettable.

182 top left and right Behind its powerful bastions, the wealthy dwellings, rebuilt between 1947 and 1855, are a vibrant testimony to Saint-Malo's golden age when, in the 17th century, the city's ship owners developed flourishing trade with the Indies and the Americas.

182-183 Behind the bastions fortified by Vauban, behind the ancient walls of the beautiful city wed to the ocean, are told memorable adventures on the high seas.

183 top Saint-Malo and Portsmouth, UK are connected by Brittany Ferries, an efficient service founded by Alexis Gournevece, a local entrepreneur, in 1972.

On the other shore of the Rance estuary, in the Dinard seaside resort, time stopped in the crazy years in which colonies of wealthy Englishmen and American millionaires went to dance the Charleston between a cocktail and a dip in the sea, wearing striped bathing suits. The 1929 crisis saw this mirage vanish while Camille le Mercier d'Erm, founder of the first P.N.B. (Breton Nationalist Party), insisted on maintaining the autochthonous presence.

Cap Fréhel is a long finger of shale and porphyry which takes on a blood-red color, skimmed by the light of the sunset. A cliff 230 feet (70 m) high jealously guards the mouth of the Rance and does it so well that, one fine day, the Gouyon-Matignon family decided to build this improbable citadel which juts out into the sea, a sort of surrealistic castle extrapolated from a Bernard Louédin painting. The film director Richard Fleisher was not mistaken in setting some of the scenes from his film *The Vikings* here, in particular the duel on the tower between Tony Curtis and Kirk Douglas, perfect in the role of that character. It was also here that Philippe de Broca shot the last scene of his excellent *Chouans* in which a lively Sophie Marceau plays an exuberant, aristocratic young woman in love and Lambert Wilson plays a military leader disturbed by abstract ideas.

185 top right *Dunes
are environmentally
delicate areas. To
protect the plant
species that grow there,
the Conservatoire du
Littoral has often been
obliged to limit access
to the dunes.*

Flaubert was too sententious in peremptorily stating in his travel diary, a literary genre in which 20th-century writers excelled, "Saint-Brieuc: zero!" If it is true that the large village promoted to departmental chief town from the Revolution is boring in the monotony of a bay invaded by greenish algae, which are a nightmare for coast-dwellers, the extremities of the small bay enclose places of great interest. This is the case with Dahouëto to the east, the docking port of the launch *Pauline*, which found glory thanks to a song by Guillemer. O di Binic to the west still looks back on the propitious days of cod fishing when, in its port, floated the colorful boats specialized in fishing for Saint Jacques oysters.

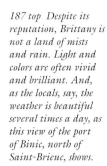

187 top Despite its reputation, Brittany is not a land of mists and rain. Light and colors are often vivid and brilliant. And, as the locals say, the weather is beautiful several times a day, as this view of the port of Binic, north of Saint-Brieuc, shows.

It is more to the west, past the Bréher cliff, that the magic begins. Paimpol never boasted of a cliff except in the mediocre song of that Montmartre fun-maker Théodore Botrel, who needed a rhyme. A short distance from Paimpol, however, the heavy stones of the Abbey of Beauport still preserve the memory of deep-sea fishing when, in the Middle Ages, the abbey imposed taxes on the cod caught in the north Atlantic off the shores of the New World. In good weather, the abbey comes alive to the rhythm of story-telling recitals and Celtic harp concerts.

On the route for the scattered archipelago of Bréhat, a stop at Ploubazlanec is an almost obligatory ritual. Here you find the cemetery of the sailors who died off the shores of Iceland in an epic tale that more closely resembles a punishment. A cemetery? The shadow of a cemetery. Names, thousands of names written with white paint on wooden tablets painted black — the names of all those boys of the land who, between 1853 and 1935, paid a heavy tribute to the great devourer.

190 top Brittany, as free-time culture would demand, is also a paradise for dilettantes, who fish standing on the estran or from small boats, nearly all of which nowadays have plastic hulls.

190 center During the good season, the southern part of the island of Bréhat, more inhabited and less wild, is often flooded by the rays of the sun. This is the kingdom of the agapanthus, the geranium and the hortensia — a true feast for the eyes right from the beginning of spring.*

190 bottom A region influenced by very strong tides, Brittany has understood how to take advantage of this.

During the Middle Ages, it boasted of the largest concentration of mills activated by the movement of the waves. In 1993, the commune of Bréhat entrusted the Birlmot Mill Association with the task of restoring the then neglected but magnificent building erected on the side of the Kerpont canal.

190-191 The name Paimpol is permanently connected with cod fishing, which had its moments of glory — and tragedy — between 1850 and 1930 when, during the summer period, adventurous schooners left the shore to capture fish off the shores of Iceland.

191 top Though more small-scale and diversified than on the southern coast, fishing continues to be very important in the northern part of the region. With an annual catch of 10,000 tons, of which crabs are a significant part, the fishing port of Paimpol is the most important in northern Brittany, second only to that of Brest.

Off the point of Arcouest extend the long pink lace rocks of Bréhant, a town whose sons were once destined to become sailors and which now has been massively converted to tourism. Though in winter almost all the shutters facing the large ocean are bolted, in the spring, the beautiful island begins to smile, murmur and rejoice again. It comes alive to such an extent that the only motor vehicles that can circulate are the small tractors of the islanders. In May, to the delight of the senses, the pastel blue of the agapanthus, the yellow of the mimosa, the pink of hortensia and the brilliant red of the geraniums are mixed together.

It is not surprising that inspired anchorites, such as Maodez arriving from (Great) Britain in his leather coracle, chose this little paradise to build their first monasteries.

Passing Lézardieux, you can ascend the Trieux estuary by boat or by the train that goes from Guingamp to Paimpol up to the Castle of the Roche-Jagut, a proud Breton mansion of the 15th century. It was purchased in 1958 by the Coasts Department, which dropped the adjective "north" to become "of Armor." Here you enter into the deep Trégor.

*192 top and center
Guingamp, on the
border between Argoat
and Armor, is a large
city with medieval
charm. The main
square, with its famous
Plomée fountain, is
one of the most
sumptuous in
Brittany.*

*192 bottom The
austerity of the stone is
exalted by the
enchanting contrast
with the colored frames
of this typical dwelling
on the Côte d'Armor.*

*192-193 The Roche-
Jagu castle in Ploezal,
built on a bend of the
Trieux in the 15th
century, is the emblem
of Breton castles.
Property of the Conseil
Géneral, the building
is open to the public in
the summer. Exhibits of
a good level on various
subjects, from the
bagpipes of Europe to
the history of Brittany,
can be admired there.*

And here, in Pleubian communal territory is the Talbert peninsula, an odd finger of gray pebbles almost 3 miles (5 km) long pointing towards England and swept by storms nine months out of twelve. Then there is the extraordinary maelstrom of Penvenan, Buguélès and Plougrescant. Rocks, an infinity of rocks, skimming the water as far as the eye can see, rocks that make this coast a nightmare for sea-faring people. Going farther, between Perros-Guirec, which awakened at the beginning of the last century

covered with flowering villas, and Trébeurden stretches the Côte Granite Rose. Here you can see almost surrealistic sculptures made from gigantic blocks that flame in the light of the setting sun next to the Ploumanach lighthouse or the neo-Gothic folly of Costaérès, where the Polish writer Henryk Sienkiewicz, a Noble prize winner for literature, withdrew at the beginning of the last century to write his *Quo Vadis*. We find ourselves in the heart of Trégor, the "Attica" of Brittany, the land of the bards, the land of Gwenc'hlan, "the last druid" who cast his spells — and his curses —from the top of the Roc'h Allaz precipitously down into the Bay of Saint Efflam. It is the land of the blind Hervé, canonized by *vox populi*, patron of bards and eponym of the little chapel that crowns the Menez Bré, the highest peak in the diocese.

*194 left To the casual
visitor, the heavy
granite masses that
run along the coast
between Perros-Guirec
and Tréburden can
appear to be
precariously balanced,*
*but they strenuously
resist the wind and
salt water. The locals
have practically
adopted them and
have baptised them
with the oddest
names.*

BOULANGERIE

196 top left In the port of Tréguier, the drakkers led by the fearful Viking leader Hasting have now given place to peaceful recreational sailboats.

196 top right On rue Colvestre, a road that leads from the Cathedral of Saint-Tudwal to the Arch Theater, stone

buildings from the 17th and 18th centuries and rush-mat houses line the street. To better appreciate the fascination of this beautiful city, visit it in the summer, for the famous Tréguier Wednesdays, when the smells of sardines and barbecued pork spread through the streets.

Anatole le Braz, author of *La légend de la mort chez les Bretons armoricains* loved to withdraw into his small cabin in Penvenan. And it was in a rush-mat house in the old Tréguier, episcopal seat until the Revolution, that the philosopher Ernest Renan was born. These places resound with the history of entire generations. Don't the Ancients say that it may have been on the Isle of Aval, that scarf of sand off the shore of Pleumeur Bodou, that King Arthur sank into sleep, watched over by his step-sister and lover Morgana? And in the sound of the waves on the Lieue de Grève, which casts its magic spell near Mont Saint Michel, don't attentive ears perhaps hear the faraway echo of the fight between the Irish Efflam and the horrendous dragon which terrorized the land?

196-197 The episcopal city of Tréguier which, it is said, was founded in 532 by Saint Tudwal, one of the seven saints who founded Brittany, underwent significant economic, cultural and religious development between the 13th century and the French Revolution. Place du Martay and the rush-mat houses that watch over the statue of the philosopher Ernest Renan are a legacy of the city's golden years.

197 top right Ernest Renan, along with Yves Helori de Kermatin, is Tréguier's most important native son. He was born in 1823 in a splendid rush-mat house on the street that now bears his name and died in Paris in 1892. He is the author of the immortal Recollections of My Youth, *a work that faithfully portrays the soul of his people.*

197 bottom left and right The Cathedral of Saint-Tudwal, built between 1339 and the end of the 15th century, houses the tombs of Saint-Yves and Duke Jean IV. It is one of the most lavish churches in Brittany. Its cloisters, in particular, are a marvelous example of Flamboyant Gothic architecture.

198 top The coasts of Brittany are still a paradise for marine birds, at least for those whose populations were not decimated by the oil spills that darkened the coast.

198 bottom Rocks abound on the northern coast of Brittany and only the most expert sailors can venture into these insidious waters. This photograph shows the entire Seven Islands archipelago.

198-199 The solan goose, this albatross of the northern seas, with a wing span of 6 feet (1.8 m), is one of the bird-symbols of the Seven Islands Reserve, a few miles to the north of the Perros-Guiree beach.

199 top left The Seven Islands Ornithological Reserve also hosts several dozen gray seals — the only

colony in Brittany along with that of the Molène archipelago — which like to lie on the rocks covered by goemon algae during the low tides.

199 top right Rouzic Island, closed to visitors, is the only French sanctuary of the solan geese, which, in the springtime, come by the thousands to build their nests.

Only fifteen minutes to the north of Perros-Guiree is the Seven Islands archipelago, at one time the hide-out of pirates and monks, now super-controlled and classified as an ornithological reserve since 1912.

With the single exception of the Île aux Moines, the archipelago, now forbidden to human visitors, is the uncontested domain of the penguin torda, the guillemot, the Dougall tern, the solan goose, the albatross from the northern seas, the crow and the puffin, which succeeded in surviving the slaughter provoked by Parisian "hunters" at the beginning of the twentieth century and the subsequent black tides, among which the most terrible was that of *Torry Canyon* in 1967. With a bit of good fortune, you may happen to see some of large gray seals from the local colony stretched out on the rocks.

200 top Enez Louet, "the grey island," north-east of the vast inlet that forms the Bay of Morlaix, is a familiar shape to those who are accustomed to walking on the coast. Behind it is Taureau Castle, built in 1552 to protect the city from the raids of the detested Saozon (the English). It served as a prison in the 19th century and as a sailing school in the 20th. A clear sign of the times!

200-201 Near Primel Point, the western end of the Bay of Morlaix which dominates the inlet of the Deben and the lobster harbor of Primel-Trégastel, enormous granite masses have pink reflections that recall those of Ploumanac'h. The route beyond the village of Saint-Jean du Doigt, either on foot or by car, offers absolutely unforgettable scenery.

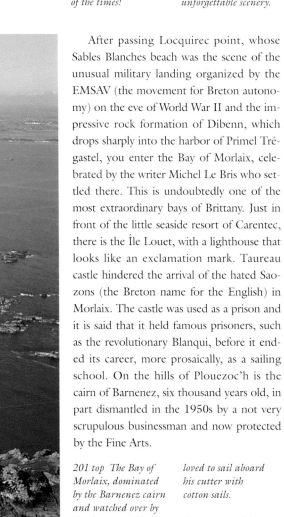

After passing Locquirec point, whose Sables Blanches beach was the scene of the unusual military landing organized by the EMSAV (the movement for Breton autonomy) on the eve of World War II and the impressive rock formation of Dibenn, which drops sharply into the harbor of Primel Trégastel, you enter the Bay of Morlaix, celebrated by the writer Michel Le Bris who settled there. This is undoubtedly one of the most extraordinary bays of Brittany. Just in front of the little seaside resort of Carentec, there is the Île Louet, with a lighthouse that looks like an exclamation mark. Taureau castle hindered the arrival of the hated Saozons (the Breton name for the English) in Morlaix. The castle was used as a prison and it is said that it held famous prisoners, such as the revolutionary Blanqui, before it ended its career, more prosaically, as a sailing school. On the hills of Plouezoc'h is the cairn of Barnenez, six thousand years old, in part dismantled in the 1950s by a not very scrupulous businessman and now protected by the Fine Arts.

201 top The Bay of Morlaix, dominated by the Barnenez cairn and watched over by the elegant, noble residences of the ship owners and the pirate captains of the 18th century, is one of the most extraordinary ones in northern Brittany. It was in these waters that the poet Tristan Corbière, author of the immortal collection Amours Jaunes, *loved to sail aboard his cutter with cotton sails.*

201 center and bottom At Trégastel, the island of Renote is separated from the mainland only when the tide is at its highest. In this world of earth and water, where granite and the light prevail, it is difficult to distinguish between land and sea.

Léon's coasts are undoubtedly less remarkable than those of Trégor. As for their inhabitants, if you want to believe what their neighbors to the east say sarcastically about these "cauliflower sellers" and other "Prussians of Brittany," they may be less extraordinary but that does not make them less authentic. For example, the Île de Batz, which faces Roscoff, "the old pirate hideout," dear to the poet Tristan Corbière, allows a population of 650 souls to live thanks to fishing, gathering seaweed and especially producing vegetables, among which are excellent organic potatoes.

Léon is a marvelous land of *abers*, aber Wrac'h, aber Benoît, aber Ildut, which make the coast from Portsall to Brignogan resemble the Norway of your dreams. Its inhabitants, however, assure you that it is only malevolence that attributes to this "Bro Pagan" (pagan land) a reputation as a pirate hideaway, even though the annals of the Abbey of Saint Mathieu, located on the cape of the same name, attest to the fact that the monks had the right to a tenth of what was found in wreckages.

How many recollections are hidden in the mists of a memory that is sometime unsound and often sad. Now that the great fear of the black tides, such as that of the *Amoco Cadiz*, which in 1978 spread crude oil over 250 miles (400 km) of the coast, is over, people are going back to the sea to live. Now, however, it is the gathering of seaweed, which makes up 80% of the French yield, that is a reason for pride for these pagans.

203 top The economy
of the island of Batz,
along with fishing, has
given ample space to
the production of early
produce.

203 bottom The
western coast of Léon
is marked by deep,
spectacular inlets
called aber, a name
found in the spoken

languages in
Brittany, Wales and
Caledonia. A residue
of ancient glacial
valleys, they are the
fjords of Brittany.

204 The Hotel Kastell-an-Daol, in the microcosm of Molène, is a world apart, a place not to be missed. One has to have spent an evening in the restaurant managed by Erwan Masson and a night cradled by the lapping of the waves on the pier to have a sense of a marine paradise.

205 top This house respects the building canons of Ouessant toward the end of the 19th century. It is a building of about 40 x 20 feet (12 x 6 m), with two rooms on the ground floor, the penn brao or nice part and the penn-kuizin or the kitchen. In contrast to what occurs on the continent, the furniture on the island of Ouessant, often made with wood taken from shipwrecks, is harmoniously painted in blue and white.

205 bottom left The wild coast that forms the western side of the Île d'Ouessant between

the Pointe de Pern and the Creac'h lighthouse is a mesmerizing environment which offers a unique spectacle during winter storms. The emotion is such that one almost expects to see the magical creatures of the abyss emerge.

205 bottom center The Creac'h lighthouse on the western coast of Ouessant, completed in 1863, was the most powerful in the world at the beginning of the last century. Its large cyclopean eye now has the task of watching over one of the most crowded routes, a true highway of the sea.

205 bottom right The Molène archipelago, with its painted wooden houses, vaguely brings to mind Iceland or the Färoës. Stone, however, is the dominant material in its traditional architecture and slate has now replaced straw for roofs.

The west is the land of fear. The names of its islands and its promontories sound like so many assurances of drowning. This is a hard and hostile environment bordering on the savage, often mixed with something of the supernatural. It is an environment which, as a reaction and as a necessity, the people have woven a net of mutual solidarity.

But is the Ouessant, the Uximana of the Pytheas, the Greek navigator, who was also called "the very tall," a land of humans? Rather it is a desert of minerals where trees do not grow. It is where, until not very long ago, people slept in homes with furniture made from flotsam wood painted blue and white. It is where homes were heated with a strange combustible mixture made from goemon and dry cow dung. It was where the proper functioning of social life was entrusted to the women with long, dark, flowing hair who, what's more, claimed the right to ask for the hand of the man they had chosen! Now the large eye of the Cyclops Creac'h, lovingly kept by Théo Malgorn, lights with its yellow ray, the longest in the world, the terrible "course" of the Ouessant, a sort of lane into which each day about a hundred iron giants crowd, their bellies filled with black, poisonous blood.

Off the shores of Molène, the current of the Fromveur roars like a monster from the deep, among the ghosts of the drowned people from *Castle Drummond*. Meanwhile, from his tabernacle in the Castle in Daol, on the island celebrated for the enchanted piano of Didier Squiban, the great warlock, Erwan Masson, dispenses sparks of life and heat.

To the south, between Cap du Raz and the Île de Sein, which, at 5 feet (1.5 m) above sea level (at its highest point!) has often been submerged by infuriated waves, the "raz" is face to face with hell. "Whoever sees Ouessant sees his own blood," according to the saying, which hastens to add, in an impetus towards equality, "whoever sees Sein sees his own end," just to be welcoming. Brrrr …! We should not be surprised if our forebears, sharp observers, always in direct contact with the back of the mirror, had located in this reassuring comparison the famous Bay of the Departed, in which the *vag noz* docks, "the boat of the night," loaded to the brim with the heavy souls of the drowned. Nor that Anatole Le Braz, letting his imagination run wild, chose the Vieille lighthouse as the setting for *The Guardian of the Fire*, the most macabre of his novels. In this novel, the guard Goulven Denez imprisons his woman and her presumed lover in a room in the lighthouse with a chamber pot as the only piece of furniture and witnesses their interminable agony with morbid pleasure. Neither is it surprising that, exactly in the middle of the sumptuous Bay of Douarnenez, popular imagination situated the submerged city of Ys, the city that the princess Ahés Dahud, the fiery daughter of King Gradlon and Woman from the Other World, built with the help of the populace. Passing the Pays Bigouden, where at the dawn of the 20th century maidens still did suggestive fertility dances around phallic stones and rounding the point of Penmarc'h, the "horse's head," the south offers completely different landscapes.

208 bottom This pair of farmers is cutting the hay that will serve as food for the animals during the winter. This practice is quite rare now because cows and horses, which numbered respectively 600 and 400 at the beginning of the 20th century, have nearly disappeared from the island, which has progressively been converted to tourism.

208-209 With a surface area of 3830 acres (1550 hectares), the ancient Uxisama is one of the largest — and most distant — islands of Brittany. Life there is difficult for the locals. Of the 3,000 inhabitants on the island prior to the First World War, a little over 800 remain. Numerous homes are shuttered up at the end of summer.

208 top The rams of Ouessant are small, with black heads and paws. They had disappeared from the island and would have become extinct without the perseverance of breeders from the region of Vannes. The islanders, for their part, preferred to raise larger rams from the continent, ones that can graze freely on the island from September to February. Each year the breeders bring their animals to the famous fair that, according to tradition, takes place the first Wednesday of February.

209 top At Ouessant the landscape is flat and barren. No trees, few slopes, only a carpet of heather and broom as far as the eye can see. Until recently — the beginning of the 20th century — the islanders dried cow and horse dung to use as fuel.

The south? The south is all in its port towns, large and small, where many people today still live from the generous depths of the sea. Guilvinec and its lobster catchers who leave early in the morning to search in the "large basin." And Concarneau, famed for its maritime museum situated within the city walls and for its fishing boats that leave for tuna-fishing expeditions off the western coast of Africa. And that myriad of sheltered harbors, lit by the first rays of spring sunlight, blossom in a riot of lively colors! Names that are poetry: Merrien, Brigneau, Rosbras, where learning to sail and be initiated in the rudiments of navigation is wonderful. Doëlan, with its pink house that acts as a beacon when you arrive from the Island of Groix, and its Captain Cook cannery, one of the last examples of an industry that gave work to thousands of people, especially women, from Douarnenez to Belle-Île en Mer. Going up the Aven starting from Rosbras, you arrive in the small village of Pont Aven. This is where Paul Gauguin set down his backpack, brushes and easels between 1886 and 1888, inviting his friends and students to stay, from Paul Sérusier to Emile Bernard. All of them were attracted by the rough, authentic coast of a Brittany which, in their eyes, was in no way inferior to the mystification caused by Polynesia. It was this corner of Cornwall that inspired masterworks such as *La belle Angèle*, who not finding herself so beautiful at least in this depiction, categorically rejected the painting. This period also produced *Le Christ jaune* (The Yellow Christ), *Les ramasseuses de varech* (The Seaweed Gatherers), and *Les petites Bretonnes au bord de la mer* (Little Breton girls on the Seashore). Still echoing at Pont Aven are the interminable discussions of Xavier Grall, the most productive Breton poet writing in the French language of the 20th century who, at Nicole Corelleau's bar, with his friends Georges Perros and Glenmor, reorganized the world, Brittany, in particular, which he dreamed would be free and clear of the burden of dishonor.

212 top Rue de Kereon, with its rush-mat buildings that escaped the disastrous fire of 1762, is one of the most crowded streets of the old Quimper. It represents the obligatory and picturesque passage of the Défilé des Guises, which, during the last week of July, concludes the famous Festival of Cornouaille.

212 bottom The Odet, Quimper's river, which rises in the Black Mountains, is an enchanting stream of water, crossed over by numerous little bridges decorated with splendid geraniums.

212-213 Place Laennec is one of the most beautiful squares of Quimper. During the traditional festivals of Cornouaille, when bagpipers and talabarders blow with full lungs on these characteristic instruments, the city reaches the peak of its fascination.

On the opposite shore of the Laïta, to the west of which rises the charming town of Quimperlé, there is Lorient, the ancient Orient, created by Louis XIV to receive the ships of the East India Company, bringing into question its military "vocation" as it was gradually affirming its Celtic identity. Was it not in this great fishing port, in particular, in arsenal buildings converted to civilian use, or de-militarized, that Breizh TV, the "television of the sea, of Brittany, of the Celtic land," received its baptism in September 2000? Can anyone imagine a better symbol, a more stirring program, a change over more sensational and significant? It should be said that the city, which has hosted an Interceltic Festival competently directed by Captain Pichard since 1971, is the Mecca of a Celtic identity which has now liberated itself of complexes, both of superiority and inferiority.

213 top left It is pleasant to walk in Quimper's historical center, freed from the bonds of traffic, wrapped in the perfume of kouign (a typical sweet of flour, eggs and sugar), crêpes and small focaccia.

213 top right At rue Kereon 9, this maiden of multicolored wood wears the glazic costume of Quimper. Until the middle of the 20th century, many dressed in the traditional clothing of the city.

214 center At Belle-Île, the bridge to the closed door of the city built in 1549 and later enlarged and modified by Vauban. It fell into the hands of the English who occupied it between 1761 and 1763. Now private property, it houses an interesting museum devoted to the history of the island and some of its celebrated visitors.

214 bottom Flowering meadows, tamarisk bushes, white walls, red raspberries and blue skies characterize southern Brittany.

214-215 Under the summer sky, the harbour of Sauzon, which numbers 703 inhabitants, on the northern coast of Belle-Île, takes on a vaguely Mediterranean aspect.

215 top Groix, a short distance from the city of Lorient, presents itself as a huge vessel of stone with the prow turned toward the west. The island gave birth to the sweet poet of the Breton language, Yann-Ber Calloc'hn whose most famous verses Me zo ganet e kreizh ar more were set to music by Jeff Le Penven and masterfully interpreted by Alan Stivell.

214 top The southern coast of Belle-Île, swept by storms, is a world of high cliffs and steep promontories. The stacks of Port-Coton had the honor of being painted by Monet, who stayed on the island in 1886.

Facing the great Atlantic port is the Île de Groix which, just like Belle-Île, its neighbor farther to the south, nostalgically recalls the glorious days of prodigious tuna fishing and the canning industry. In the days of the merchant marines, it employed a fairly numerous workforce since its position in the open sea gave it an advantage over Lorient. Here, curiously, on the village tower, it is not a rooster that signals the direction of the wind but, in memory of an opulent past, an albacore tuna!

It is certainly an island of fishermen but also of farmers. It is an island sacrificed to mass tourism (although to a lesser degree than its neighbor) because of its magnificent panoramas, its vertiginous cliffs on the southern coast and its convex Grand Sables beach, starred with fragments of granite. But it is also an island of poets and bards. Yann Ber Calloc'h, the author of *Ar en deulin* (Kneeling), one of the most sensitive poets in the Breton language, was born here. Killed in the trenches in 1917, he left us the marvelous *Me zo ganet e kreizh ar mor* (I was born in the middle of the sea), set to music by the composer Jeff Le Penven and masterfully interpreted by Alan Stivell. Then there is Gilles Servat, who began playing the guitar here at the beginning of the 1970s. Gilles Servat? The bard, originally from Nantes, conveniently established himself a short distance from here near Etel, a place in which you don't know where the water ends and the earth begins. And that must have been precisely what Polo, Gilles' dog, thought the last time we went there to take photos at the very end of the Locoal harbor, lost between the "path of the Chouans" and the "distaff of Saint Brigate," when, slipping on a clump of seaweed, he found himself in the water!

Here you enter into the world of rebels, rebels with big hearts, the world of those who, when the time is right, can rise up against any form of tyranny and oppression.

216 top Straw roofs are a traditional element of Breton architecture. Beginning at the end of the 19th century, following decrees and incentives, slate replaced straw and rush in the coverings. But in the region of Vannetais and in lower Cornouaille, this type of building survives even today, as in the village of Poul Fetan en Quistinic shown here.

216-217 Carnac is the richest megalithic site in Europe. The configuration of Menec, Kerlescan and Kermario can count a good 3,000 menhir, a Breton term that specifically means "long stone." Local legend would have it that you can recognise some Roman soldiers petrified by Saint Cornély, a Christian transposition of the god Cernunos.

217 top left The placement of these megaliths and the arrival of the Celts are as far away in time as the defeat of the Vénètes and the computer civilization! So the appealing Obelix with his menhir on his shoulders is a pleasing anachronism!

217 top right The large menhir of Locmariaquer, broken into five parts, was one of the tallest in Brittany.

216 bottom The Suscinio castle on the Rhuys peninsula, a few steps away from the Atlantic Ocean, is one of the most beautiful forts in Brittany. Built in the 13th century, this residence, preferred by the dukes of Brittany, was altered in the 14th and 15th centuries. It is now the property of the Conseil Général du Morbihan, which has beautifully restored it.

Pressing ahead to the east, you arrive in the territory of the proud Vénètes. At the end of the summer in 56 B.C., in a bloody naval battle off the shores of the Rhuys peninsula, they were defeated by Caesar's ships under the command of Brutus. Their capital was in Locmariaquer, where you find the Merchants' Table, which even now gives rise to controversies and imagination, and the broken menhir, which, before being damaged, was undoubtedly the most important in France or perhaps, after all, the Gulf of Morbihan, which, it is said, includes as many islands as there are days in a year.

In any case, the region is the richest in Brittany with, to the west of Carnac, its covered walkways, its tumuli and its extraordinary alignments if Kermario, Menec and Kerlascan, vestiges, according to the most recent archaeological studies, of ancient astronomic "temples" and, to the east, on the Rhuys peninsula, the castle of Suscinio, superbly restored by the Morbihan General Council.

Vannes was the city of Nominoé, the first King of Brittany, in the 9th century. Later, in the Middle Ages, it became the residence of the Dukes of Brittany and then, after annexation to France and the revolt of the Red Berets, the seat of the Breton Parliament. Within its walls, some parts of which go back to the Gallic-Roman era, this lovely city still preserves an astonishing series of 16th-century rush-mat buildings in Rue Noë and Rue Saint-Samson.

219 left The Hermine Castle, not far from the Saint Vincent gate, is adjacent to the sumptuous French-style gardens of the ancient capital of the Bro Warok.

219 top right The inhabitants of Vannes, nestled at the end of the Gulf of Morbihan, inherited from the Vénètes' maritime power a special attraction for the sea. In the tourist port, freed in the 1970s from the mud that obstructed it, boats of synthetic materials replaced heavy oak vessels, but the passion for sea-going adventures remains the same.

219 bottom right The center of Vannes, near Henry IV square, rue des Halles and rue Saint-Salomon, teems with rush-mat houses from the 16th century.

221 top Blain Castle, construction of which began in 1104, was the property of Olivier de Clisson before passing to the Rohan family, The façade, called the "residence of the king" (15th century) has preserved the fascination of the Breton Renaissance architecture.

221 center This photograph combines evidence of two past eras: the windmill, which recalls to mind Gilles Servat's beautiful song "turn, turn wings of the Guérande windmill" and a megalithic tomb from approximately 4,000 B.C.

221 bottom La Brière is marshy area of about 20,000 acres (8,000 hectares) which is part of a regional park created in 1970. In 1461 the inhabitants of the region were recognised by François II, duke of Brittany, a right of undivided property respected up till our times.

A panorama of Armorica, this coastal stretch some 6 miles (10 km) long that forms the contours of Brittany, would be incomplete without the Pays Nantais which, after the Revolution, made up the Department Loire-Atlantique. In a 1941 decree it arbitrarily separated from the administrative region of Brittany, in total disregard of the wishes of the overwhelming majority of the population.

And thus it was that, at Batz-sur-Mer, in that brackish lagoon that had represented the wealth of the area from the Middle Ages on, Breton was spoken until World, War I. And wasn't the splendid city of Guérande, the Breton Gwenrann, fortified by Duke Jean IV to defend himself from the terrible war of succession that saw the Breton party of Monfort opposed to that of the francophile Penthiève?

220-221 Around the village of Batz, where Breton has been spoken since World War I, the salt marshes are a silent, mineral world. The mirrors of salt water represented the wealth of the Guérandese peninsula in the period when Brittany was exempt from taxes on salt. This "privilege" was inexorably suppressed after the famous night of August 4, 1789.

222-223 *The Graslin di Nantes quarter came into being between 1778 and 1788. Place Royal, with its beautiful fountain, is the symbol of this section of the city, martyred by the bombardments of September 16 and 23, 1943.*

223 *The Loire (Liger in the Breton language) is one of the most beautiful rivers in France. Before being covered, the numerous branches in which it spread out made the historic capital of Brittany a true Venice of western Europe.*

Though the seaside resort of La Baule, the vacation spot for the golden youth of France and Navarre, should be mentioned for having the most beautiful, longest beach in Europe, attentive travelers will indulge with pleasure in Nantes which, in 937, was chosen as the capital by Duke Alain Barbe-Torte, who had defeated the Normans.

In the city, there is still the ducal castle built at the end of the sixteenth century by François II and his daughter Anne, the last sovereign of the country. Following an unjust war, she was constrained to marry the King of France, Charles VIII. The tomb of François II and his wife, Margherite de Foix, sculpted in 1502 by Michel Colombe, is now found in the Cathedral of Saint Pierre while the shrine containing Anne's heart, profaned during the Revolution, can be seen at the Musée Dobrée.

224 top Declared a historic monument, this 1900 brasserie with ceramic decorations on Place Graslin is an peerless temple to the gastronomy of Nantes.

224-225 Nantes is a port city about 50 miles (80 km) from the sea. It was this that made the city's fortune, in particular with the so-called "triangular trade," an elegant euphemism for the sale of slaves. Now the boats calmly moored at the docks wait to sail off on less immoral cruises.

225 top left The Pommeraye tunnel is a true myth for Nantes. Completed in 1843, it joins rue de la Fosse and the stock market located in rue Santeuil. The structure is divided into three levels, which are joined by a staircase made of iron and wood.

225 bottom left Within the Castle of the Dukes of Brittany are preserved the remains of the old Musée des Salorges, devoted to the history of the industrial and commercial activity of the city.

225 top and bottom right Created in 1880, the Musée des Beaux Arts is housed in a 19th-century building. The museum can boast of a notable collection of works by great masters, among them The Denial of Saint Peter by Georges de La Tour; the prized Madame de Senonnes, by Jean-Auguste Ingre; Caïd, Moroccan Captain by Eugène Delacroix; and Gathering Apples by Emile Bernard.

226 top left The "des Forges" pond, in the forest of Brocéliande, recalls the days when the area was mined for its abundance of iron, which gives the earth and the watercourses their characteristic color.

226 top right Whether pond, river or stream, water in all its forms is omnipresent in the forest of Merlin and Arthur and creates a perfect setting in which to let the imagination run free.

226-227 Dawn on a winter's day in the forest of Brocéliande. To the Celts the forest is the sacred universe par excellence, and is inhabited by the creatures of the Other World.

227 bottom The enchanting path of Sainte Barbe au Faouët, in the woods of Cornouaille, evokes the ghost of Marion "Finefont," or 'Marion of Faouët', the famous kilted leader of a band of 'fearless' brigands, who plundered the entire region in around the mid-18th century.

*A*r mor, the sea. *Ar goat*, the "land of woods" — a name which, like the narrow strip of coastline it refers to, echoes with the sounds of an unknown and mysterious world; a world of spirits, no doubt, of the *duz* Gauls and their countless descendents who in various degrees were loved, feared and respected. But it is also a world of outlaws, either terrible or extremely generous. Guy Eder de la Fontenelle, for example, who had nothing in common with Robin Hood and who terrorized the region in the days of the War of the Alliance, or Marion du Faouët ("of the beech tree"), who was hung in Saint Corentin Square, Kemper in 1755 after having cleaned out the Poher district at the head of a band of cutthroats. This is the world of the volunteers of Jean Cottereau, or Jean "Chouan," as he was known for his perfect imitation of the owl, and whose name became associated with the commoners' resistance against a Republic gone mad.

Ar goat! The land of woods that instil terror in those that do not know them and get lost in their depths, as in the case of the legionaries of Postumius in the dark forest of Litania. Yet it is also a hospitable land, a refuge that nurtures materially and spiritually those who for thousands of years have inhabited its forests, becoming part of them, merging with them, like the *korrigan*, the young fawn of the Afterlife, and all the small creatures of the night. The forest, in its association with *nemeton*, the sacred glade, is the heart of a wonderful world capable also of becoming an ally during conflicts, and not only for the sake of putting on an act a defense strategy. According to François Le Roux and Christian J. Guyonvarc'h, "the one true Celtic sanctuary is the dense, living forest which, at the dawn of history, covered immense stretches of Northern and Western Europe. Our Brocéliande is the last strip of that ancient treasure."

Brocéliande! Is this the forest that literally bewitched all the western courts when Geoffroy de Monmouth, Robert Wace, Robert de Boron and Chrétien de Troyes dared to narrate the adventures of the Knights of the Round Table, the madness of Merlin, the passions of Lancelot and Guinevere, the "white specter"? A multiform and multi-dimensional universe it is, which corresponds more to the geography of the soul than that of the land surveyors. Claudine Glot, President of the Centre de l'Imaginaire Arthurien (Centre of Arthurian Imagery) was not wrong when she said, "Brocéliande does not exist in administrative map-making. It is a forest that each one of us carries inside and each lives in the hope of finding."

228 top Built in reddish shale at the end of the 14th century by Jean de Trécesson, the castle that still bears his name today reflects somerly in the waters of the pond in front of it. This is undoubtedly one of the most fascinating parts of the forest of Brocéliande.

228 center The Tomb of Merlin, remains of an ancient covered passageway that was destroyed in the 19th century by a rather irreverent owner, is today the object of a zealous cult. Here hundreds of anonymous hands place votive offerings for the medieval personification of the great Cernunos.

228 bottom Comper Castle, in Brocéliande, houses the Centre for Arthurian Imagery. The most recent part of the building, dating back to 1860, is reserved for exhibitions and cultural events. The 15th-century ruins of the fortress overlook the moat.

Dame Claudine, who has come to identify herself so completely with the enchanted realm that some say she is a fairy, claims that "the Chart describing the habits and customs of Brocéliande Forest, which dates back to 1467, appropriately locates the realm of Merlin near Comper Castle" — exactly where Claudine set up the C.I.A. branch in 1990.

In the waters of the lake of Comper the love-struck Merlin built for his "pupil" Viviane a magnificent crystal palace, which merged with the lake itself, and where she taught Lancelot, making him the most courageous, skillful and beguiling knight of the Round Table.

In the Valley of No Return the terrible Morgana, part fairy, part witch, with the ambivalence typical of the creatures of the Afterlife, imprisoned her unfaithful lovers behind an invisible wall of air, until the handsome Lancelot, immunized by his ardent and pure love for Queen Guinevere, broke the spell forever.

A short distance away, to the northwest of Comper Castle, is the tomb of Merlin with the remains, more poignant than stunning, of a *hent korriganed*, literally "path of korrigan" or, less poetically, a covered passageway that was destroyed in the late 19th century.

Here votive notes are placed by thousands of anonymous hands, in a strange continuance (or revival?) of the worship of ancient figures.

228-229 *According to legend and keen "Arthurians," in a palace hidden at the bottom of the Lake of Comper the fairy Viviane trained the handsome Lancelot, son of King Ban de Bénoïc.*

229 top *The stately splendor characterizing the buildings belonging to the castle of Trécesson, such as this circular dovecot, clearly illustrates the great wealth of the ancient local nobility.*

Here is where Porhoët begins, whose original name *pou-tre-coët* is frequently translated as "Transylvania," although it simply means "wood-covered land."

Not far from Guer the "standing stones" of Monteneuf, which Canon Mahé wrote about in 1825 in his valuable essay on the relics of Morbihan, were patiently put back in place by compassionate hands at the end of the last century, after having been pulled down by Christians with equal dedication at the beginning of the second millennium. Today, these stones form the impressive background for the Arthurian Week celebrations. Here, in the Summer of 1997, the extraordinary Roland Becker and his Breton National Orchestra performed a series of gavottes that were rousing enough to wake the dead.

A few miles south-east and not far from route D 873, on the Moors of Lanveaux, which stretch out their cloak of heath and broom from Rochefort en Terre to Locminé, is the site of Saint-Juste, proof (if any were needed) that Argoat is in no way inferior to Armor from the point of view of its cultural heritage. The mounds of

Château du Bé, overlooked by a *cromlec'h*, the *cairn* of Croix Saint-Pierre, the splendid burial place of Tréal, the Demoiselles de Cojoux and the alignments of Moulin, represent some of the most important megalithic concentrations of Brittany. A short distance away towards the south, where the rivers Oust and Vilaine meet, stands Redon, a city steeped in ancient history. Here, in the year 832, Nominoë, the first king of Brittany, built a monastery for the obvious purpose of claiming this borderland as part of his kingdom. The monastery buildings, today occupied by St. Saveur College, include an abbey church which is considered one of the masterpieces of Romanesque architecture in Brittany. A free port in the 18th century, one of the characteristic features of the city is its charming riverside towpaths in granite. Today it is the heart of the region of Redon, and proud of its cultural and musical heritage. Every year, in late October, the lively Festival de la Bogue d'Or is held, during which the most beautiful voices of "Gallésie" can be heard.

Moving westward, we quickly come to Rochefort-en-Terre, a real pearl of a village nestled in a valley rich in woodlands and orchards. Although the only remains of the ancient settlement are the small castle, certain sections of the ramparts and the outbuildings of Rochefort Castle, the village boasts a number of magnificent 16th- and 17th-century houses with superb granite or wattled façades and many with turrets, which can be seen along Rue du Porche and in the squares of des Halles and du Puits.

231 top right The abbey of Saint-Saveur di Redon, founded in the 9th century by Konwoéon, a relative of King Nominoë, for many years had a great influence over northern Brittany.

On the route from Rochefort to Vannes lies Questembert, once the setting for one of the most famous battles in the history of Brittany, which took place in the year 890 in a place named Coët-bi-han, when King Alain le Grande, known as "Barbe-Torte," defeated the powerful Norman troops. On the site stands a small, obelisk-shaped monument bearing an inscription, both in French and Breton, commemorating the heroic king.

Before leaving the town, a visit to the covered market is a must. The market, which dates back to 1552, is composed of an extraordinarily harmonious structure with three arcades and is one of the last existing examples of its kind in Brittany.

At 9 miles (15 km) to the northeast, along the road from Vannes to Rennes, stands the castle of Largoët (or "the Towers of Elven," as it is still known today), which preserves within its huge stone walls the memory of one of the more unpleasant chapters in the history of Brittany. Owned by the Lord of Rieux, from 1472 to 1476 this castle was the prison of Henry Tudor, later King Henry VII of England, before Charles VIII's French troops burned it down in 1488. Today in ruins, the castle still manages to inspire awe in the visitor — the 11th-Century keep, for example, an impressive, six-story building, is almost 190 feet (57 m) high, making it one of the tallest in Europe.

In the town of Baud, which lies at the westernmost point of the woodland area stretching out across the Moors of Lanvaux, north of the Camors Forest, is one of the most mysterious statues of Brittany, known to the local people as the Venus of Qunipily. Visitors might well wonder how this little moss-covered granite figure, with its thighs like two stumpy tree-trunks and short, toad-like neck, could have come to be called Venus. Yet this stone "beauty" once stood proudly on the hill of Castennec, a few miles north, on the site where archaeologists believe the ancient Gallo-Roman *dunon* of Sulim stood, until it was torn down by zealous Christians in 1661 and hurled into the deepest part of the River Blavet. The statue remained underwater for three years until the local people, firmly attached to their idols and remote pagan rites and staunchly shrouded in superstition, recovered it and restored it to a place of worship. Subsequently, the "iron lady" was again thrown into the river by Reformists and again salvaged from the waters.

And there it would have remained if the local landlord, the Count of Lannion, had not decided — to his credit — to give it a home on his own property! Deprived of their idol, the villagers of Castennec were angered by this decision, but the 'Venus' finally found a place of rest. Roman deity, Egyptian Isis, or matron of the Cyclades, the goddess continues to keep secret her identity. The entire region, in actual fact, is steeped in mystery. A little north of Baud, for example, in the borough of Guénin, is Mane Gwenn ("white mountain" or "sacred mountain"), on which stands the chapel of St. Michel, probably built on the site of a temple dedicated to the god Bélénos. Dug into this extraordinary mass is a basin that continues to raise controversies and questions. Might it actually be a druidic sacrificial altar, as Gwenc'hlan Le Scouézec and Jean Markale believe?

234 *The castle of Pontivy was built in the 15th century by Jean II of Rohan. Of the four original towers two remain, complete with trapdoors and corner turrets. Partly accessible to visitors, the castle houses interesting summer exhibitions dedicated to the history of Brittany.*

234-235 *Burnt down and pillaged during the Revolution, the Cistercian abbey of Bon-Repos, near the lake of Guerlédan and the forest of Quénéquan, was salvaged from the brambles thanks to the perseverance of a commendable group of individuals who dedicated their time and efforts to its recovery.*

235 top left *At Poul-Fetan, in the borough of Quistinic, this magnificent 16th-century village of huts was perfectly restored in the 1970s. The village faithfully reproduces the atmosphere of an ancient village of the Vannes region.*

235 top right *During the summer months in the town of Poul-Fetan a number of cultural associations organize a revival of various themes relating to the everyday life of the ancient inhabitants. Here, for example, we can see several young washerwomen in ancient dress wringing out the laundry by hand.*

On the other side of the N24, which connects Rennes with the large port of Lorient, is the little settlement of Poul Fetan. Carefully and tastefully restored by the Council of Quistinic, this is one of the ancient little villages of huts that make Brittany so charming, especially around Bro Gwened (the region of Vannes). In the village, which dates back to the 16th century, are an ancient communal oven, a potter's workshop and an inn, which today serves a range of traditional Breton dishes. A local association

raises several breeds of *pie-noire* cows, small-hooved but extremely tough animals that produce high-quality milk; during the 1970s the breed risked extinction, victim of the race for productivity. On the subject of the animal and plant life typical of Brittany, the association in charge of the village of Lann Gough in Melrand, a settlement similar to Poul Fetan, is currently working on the recovery of an extraordinary flora and fauna heritage, including the ditch goats, the so-called Ouessant rams and various other animal and plant species that were characteristic of Brittany in about A.D. 1000 — all within an exceptionally well-restored village of huts from the same period. A few miles north lies Bieuzy; here, built on the rock face in a loop

of the River Blavet, opposite the site of Castennec where once stood the city of Sulim, is a magnificent chapel dedicated to Saint Gildas de Rhuys. Not far from the D2, on the winding road leading to Pontivy, is the 15th-century chapel of Quelven, which is famous mainly for the fact that it houses an extraordinary polychrome statue of St. George and the dragon, as well as for one of the rare opening Virgins of Brittany. During the August 15th processions (reminiscent of local pagan customs that the Church eventually adopted after failing to abolish them) an "angel" descends from the bell-tower of the parish church on a rope and proceeds to light a *tantad!* Towards the north-west, in the area of the Côte d'Armor, stands the Cistercian abbey of Bon-Repos (12th century), which was devastated and pillaged like many other religious monuments during the French Revolution. The picturesque ruins of the abbey are reflected in the emerald waters of Lake Guerlédan, a jewel nestling among the 6175 acres (2500 hectares) of beech and fir trees that make up the forest of Quénéquan. Ancient fief of the Rohan family, Pontivy has a magnificent fortified castle that today still boasts two large towers, complete with trapdoors and crowned with smaller watchtowers, which overlook the ancient town with its many 16th- and 17th-century buildings. Was it to cover up the fact that the Rohan family spent more time with the French royalty than with the dukes of Brittany, or that in the period of the Empire the bourgeois had renamed the town Napoléonville, that the independent movement set up a short-lived independent Breton government in July of 1940?

236 To the north of the moorlands of Lanvaux, in the heart of Porhoët, Josselin (the "village through the wood") is a charming, peaceful little town bounded by the River Oust.

237 top The Basilica of Notre-Dame du Roncier, in Josselin, houses the 15th-century mausoleum of Olivier de Clisson, who succeeded Bertrand du Guesclin as constable of France, and of his wife Marguerite de Rohan.

237 bottom The castle of Josselin, destroyed in 1488 by order of Duke François II as a punishment for the betrayal of Jean de Rohan, was rebuilt in the late 15th century. The stone interlacing of the central part of the castle contrasts strongly with the austere fortified structure of the interior façade.

Moving eastward, we come to Josselin, a delightful medieval town washed by the calm waters of the River Oust. This Breton town has the highest percentage of ancient wattled houses, of which that standing at no. 3, rue Georges Le Berd dates back to 1538. The castle, which has an internal façade covered with lace-like Gothic-flamboyant decorations, was first damaged by Duke François II, the father of Anne of Brittany, as a punishment to the owner, Jean de Rohan, guilty of offering his services to the King of France. Subsequently, at the beginning of the 17th century, Cardinal Richelieu had five of its nine towers destroyed. Nevertheless, the remains of the castle are truly magnificent, lending a touch of loftiness to the surrounding landscape. On the edge of the forest of Paimpont lies Ploërmel, which boasts some fine examples of 16th-century houses, especially in rue Beaumanoir, whose name recalls the heroic Combat des Trente, a battle fought at the height of the War of Succession of Brittany between thirty cavaliers of the pro-English faction and thirty paladins of the pro-French party. The church (on the porch of which the figure of a boar engaged in gustily playing the bagpipes clearly illustrates the ancient attitude of the clergy toward musicians) contains the tombs of dukes Jean II (1286-1305) and Jean III (1312-1341).

238 top left Although it belonged to the bishopric of Cornouaille, Langonnet, not far from the River Ellé, became part of Morbihan in the Revolution. The Cistercian abbey, founded in 1136 by Duke Conan III, includes the remains of a Roman nave and a 13th-century chapterhouse.

238 top right In Faouët, the polychrome wooden roodscreen in the chapel of Saint-Fiacre is a masterpiece in Gothic-flamboyant style, depicting animals, Biblical characters and scenes from everyday life. Next to the nave a series of statues portray scenes of the Temptation.

238-239 The chapel of Sainte-Barbe, in Le Faouët, built in 1498 in Gothic-flamboyant style on the sheer rock overhanging the River Ellé, is a celebration of the union of stone and wood.

239 top A detail of the roodscreen of Saint-Fiacre illustrating its vivid polychromy and richness of detail.

239 bottom The chapel of Saint-Fiacre in Le Faouët boasts one of the finest examples of the fortified bell towers that appeared in Brittany in the late 15th century.

Moving southeast, past Guémené sur-Scorff and Lignol, where the brave young marquis of Pontcallek was arrested, we come to Le Faouët which, although situated in the present-day district of Morbihan, is still part of the historical diocese of Cornouaille.

This parish, as well as having a magnificent 16th-century covered market, boasts two of the most beautiful chapels of Argoat. The 15th-century Chapel of Saint-Fiacre has one of the finest fortified bell-towers in Brittany; its *jubé* is virtually an embroidery in wood depicting the human sins, of which lust is actually represented as a *biniaouer*!

The other chapel is that of Saint Barbe, also in Gothic-flamboyant style, built on a rocky spur overlooking the green valley of Ellé, a true feast for the eyes and the soul.

Along the D769 we come to Langonnet, where Alan Stivell lived for some years with his family before moving to the region of Rennes.

The parish is worth a visit, especially for its abbey, which was founded in 1136 by Duke Conan III. Of the splendid Cistercian complex remains the magnificent Romanesque central nave, whose mysterious decorations "seem to appear out of the darkness of time — masks with enormous eyes gazing on the Other World, monsters that dance in a battle of wild beauty." (Marc Déceneux, *La Bretagne romane*.)

240 In the rugged landscape of the Black Mountains, at the beginning of the 20th Century, the last of the Breton wolves were hunted down and killed by the merciless Countess Vefa de Saint Pierre.

240-241 The Black Mountains are a range of mountains eroded by time, whose peaks reach the height of just 300 meters. In this photograph, taken from the borough of Laz, the pointed stumps of the reier can be seen.

At a short distance northward, from the heights of Glomel that still reverberate with the lyric and epic verses of the local bard Glenmor, to Karreg an Tan, which dominates the town of Gouézec, the Black Mountains align their "peaks." It takes the imagination of the local people to define as mountains this series of *menezioù*, hills with long, rounded tops alternated with *reier*, peaks of hard, jagged shale. It is around here, in the area of Toullaëron, the "culminating point," that in the early 20th-century Countess Vefa de Saint Pierre, a kind of Celtic Amazon who lived in the manor of Manez Cam, killed the last of the Breton wolves. At Gourin visitors should not be surprised to find in the Place de la Victoire a copy (more modest in size) of the famous Statue of Liberty of the port of New York. The "capital of the Black Mountains," in fact, is also the capital of emigration to America, which began in 1881 when Nicolas le Grand, not the Tsar of all the Russias but a humble tailor of Roudouallec, decided to seek his fortune on the far shores of the ocean. Today kinships are well-established, and every family of the Mountain has its own "American uncle." The association Bretagne-Trans-América, expertly run by the energetic Cristiane Jamet and Daniel Le Goff, who is also the organizer of the championship of musician duos *(biniou-bombarde)* that is held in the first weekend of September, is constantly in operation to maintain relations between the 4700 inhabitants of Gourin and the 7000 or so members of the Brittany-New York diaspora, and the others living in other American states or in Québec! Today the Black Mountains no longer echo with the noise of iron bars in the slate quarries which, represented the pride and wealth of the region. While the Société d'Exploitation des Ardoisières de Maël-Carhaix, with some ten employees, is considered an industry, and in Motreff, Honoré Maurice, last of the "Mohicans of the blue" (slate), exhausts himself tearing layers of *mordorè* (purplish-brown) slate from the hillside, at the same time the region of Poher does not rest on its laurels. The county of Conomor the Damned, a Breton version of the Irish Conchobar, and of King Morvan, who stood up to the Franks of Louis the Pious, is determined to stem the population 'haemorrhage' that has slowly but relentlessly been draining the *Kreizh Breizh* (the center of Brittany). The borough of Spezet has for years hosted the *Gouel Broadel ar Brezhoneg*, the National Festival of the Breton language, and its the bilingual signs on all the public buildings are a clear defiance of destiny. Here Breizh Co-op, with a staff of around forty, is dedicated to creating, publishing and circulating the *ne plus ultra* of the Breton culture. Carhaix, the ancient Celtic and later Gallo-Roman settlement of Vorgion, who rebelled against the imposition of stamped paper and proclaimed a (sadly short-lived) local republic. It was here, in fact, that the first Lycee de l'Ecole Bretonne immersive Diwan was set up and that autonomist mayor Christian Troadec intends to create an entire 'technopolis' of Breton culture, of which the Espace Culturel Glemnor, opened in 2001 and hosting so far the *Gouel levrioùe Breizh* (the Brittany Book Festival), may be considered the first brick.

242 top On the peak of Menez Mikael, or Menez Kronan, as it was named in past ages after a Celtic god similar to Cromm Cruach, a bloodthirsy Irish deity, the chapel bearing the same name stands watch over the bleak range of the Monts d'Arrée and the 'infernal' marshland of Yeun-Ellez.

242 bottom The marshland of Yeun Ellez, the surface of which can be seen at the bottom of the picture, was where the ancient Bretons claimed the entrance to Hell lay. Here, in fact, the souls of traitors were hurled, personified by terrible black dogs in the bottomless pit.

242-243 Created in 1969, the Parc d'Armorique is one of the oldest regional parks in France. Stretching out from Ouessant and the archipelago of Molène on the west side as far as the borough of Guerlesquin, the park's 112,000 hectares of land and 60,000 hectares of sea include 39 boroughs.

To the northwest is the *kein Breizh,* "the backbone of Brittany." The mountain range begins with Menez Hom, a mountain that was once sacred and later holy, at the foot of which, in 1913, a farmer discovered a charming mask of the Dêua Brigantia, patron of the arts and goddess of fertility. The range then continues with the shale peaks of the Arrée Mountains and ends in the east with the moorlands of Mené, whose name means precisely "mountain." The rugged Mountains of Arrée, the tallest peak of which measures just 1,320 feet (400 m), are truly unique — a world of rock, pounded in winter by the violent *gwalarn* and where in the early morning long scarves of mist curl around Roc'h Trévézel, Menez Mikaël or Tuchen Gador. The region, it is true, is steeped in the presence of the Other World. Around the Lake of Brennilis roams the *Ankou,* a strange creature draped in a black sheet and carrying a scythe with the handle back to front for more easily tearing the souls from the living. The Washerwomen of the Night, at a stone's-throw from the entrance to the icy Hell of the Celts, as in the story by Émile Souvestre, watch out for drunks who linger on the road to force them to wring out their own funeral shroud. All around this area are the mysterious ponds of Yeun-Ellez — a name that instils fear in even the most daring. It was rumored, in fact, that in these bottomless depths wandered lost souls, caught between heaven and earth, in an endless search for eternal rest, and tormenting the living in an attempt to find relief. Evidently, through living so long with these creatures, the living must have finally tamed the dead and established good relations, since, for the past few years, the region has begun to come back to life.

244 top The nurturing and protecting forest is the refuge of the deer, the totemic animal of the great Cernunos and the magician Merlin, as well as messenger from the Other World and the guide of souls.

244 bottom Wild boar, totemic animal of the Druids, are gradually coming back to inhabit the brushwood, thanks in part to the protection guaranteed by the institution of the founding Parc d'Armorique.

244-245 In Huelgoat, the 'tall wood', the Rivière d'Argent, whose waters have also returned after the closing down of the mines, surges around a turmoil of rocks. Here is where, according to legend, Ahès-Dahud had the lifeless bodies of her many lovers hurled.

Armorica Park, opened in July 1969, has its reception point in Menez Meur, with structures designed for the observation of wild animals — boars, wolves, deer, foxes, etc. — as well as domestic animals — Breton 'pie-noire' cows, Ouessant rams and the semi-wild horses of Brittany.

The Maison Cornec of Saint Rivoal, with its remarkable façade, known as "apothéis," houses an eco-museum dedicated to the history of rural architecture and farming implements.

In Commana, on the mountaintop, the covered passageway of Mougau (2000 B.C.) demonstrates that man has inhabited these mountains since remote times. This exceptionally well-preserved and impressive monument is made up of five slabs supported by 28 pillars. Inside several rock paintings are still visible, portraying spears, knives and three pairs of breasts of the Mother Goddess. The forest of Huelgoat, or "high forest," directly below the line of the mountaintop, lends an atmosphere of magic to the entire area. The magnificent Rivière d'Argent winds its way sensuously through a chaos of mossy rocks, in the shade of time-honored oaks and beeches still haunted by the presence of King Arthur. Certain ancient ruins in the area, claimed by local folk tradition to be an "encampment" of the providential king, are, in actual fact, the remains of an *oppidum,* a fortified site of the Osismes, dating back to the first century B.C., an age in which the populations of Armorica were at war with Caesar. According to legend (or, more simply, literature), moreover, here in this majestic forest was the abyss into which the damned soul of Ahés Dahud, the Queen of Ys, threw the lifeless bodies of her many lovers. On the northern slope of the Menez Arrée the charming ruins of the abbey of Relecq reflect in the waters of a shady lake. The church of the abbey, a 12th-century Romanesque building of typically Cistercian layout, was erected on the site of a monastery founded in the 6th century by Saint Tanguy and Saint Pol Aurélien.

245 top *Argoat represents the holy alliance between ancient sacred buildings and the timeless woodlands, like the* nemeton, *wood of the ancient Celts, where priests, poets and musicians gathered together to pay homage to the deities.*

246 top The church of Saint Thégonnec houses a valuable Calvary and an ossuary, both of which date back to the 17th century. The church suffered severe damage in a fire in 1998, after which, fortunately, it was quickly restored.

246 bottom The parish church complex of Guimiliau contains what is perhaps the finest Calvary in Brittany. Created between 1581 and 1588, it portrays around two hundred characters, including the strange Katell Golet (Catherine the damned) with breasts swollen with desire and sin. In Brittany the complex is traditionally entered through the south porch, which can be seen in the picture.

246-247 The Calvary of Saint-Thégonnec, dating back to the early 17th century, is one of the most interesting in the famous circuit of parish church complexes. The group of sculptures portraying the "Abused Christ" has been created on the basis of a perfect symmetrical axis. The scene recalls the Breton Mysteries, representations of episodes in the life of Christ.

If there is an art in which the folk genius of Brittany — very often anonymous — has proved to excel, it is sacred art. This includes the parish church complexes, the dolmens, the menhirs and the lec'hioù, which represent the most ancient expressions of the intense spirituality of the Bretons. These complexes, which center around the parish churches, include the porch, where, until recently, the deceased of the clan were buried, the ossuary, situated on the west side facing the direction of the Celts' "Tir na n'Og," and a Calvary depicting scenes of the life of Christ.

Descending the slopes of the Mountains of Arrée, down on the plain of Léon is the triptych Guimiliau-Lampaul-Guimilau-Saint-Thégonnec, a truly marvelous work in granite, covered by a delicate embroidery of grey and golden lichens.

The Guimilau Calvary, constructed between 1580 and 1588, contains about 200 figures, including a serpent strangely resembling Morgana, the ancient goddess of the waters and Woman of the Afterlife, and a figure of the poor Katell Golet ("Catherine the Fallen"), an incarnation of lasciviousness condemned to suffer the torments of Hell.

The Calvary of Saint-Thégonnec, which dates back to 1610, depicts a particularly moving version of the humiliated Christ.

The most ancient complex is, however, that of Lampaul-Guimilau, which dates back to the early 16th century.

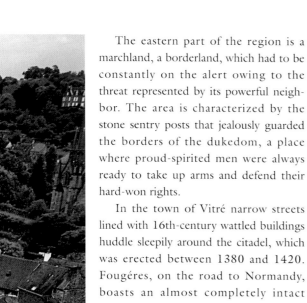

The eastern part of the region is a marchland, a borderland, which had to be constantly on the alert owing to the threat represented by its powerful neighbor. The area is characterized by the stone sentry posts that jealously guarded the borders of the dukedom, a place where proud-spirited men were always ready to take up arms and defend their hard-won rights.

In the town of Vitré narrow streets lined with 16th-century wattled buildings huddle sleepily around the citadel, which was erected between 1380 and 1420. Fougéres, on the road to Normandy, boasts an almost completely intact fortress which, in 1793, was the refuge of the Chouans of Marquis de la Rouérie.

The watchtowers of the castle of Combourg, purchased by a (priest) collector in 1793 at Saint Malo, still house the dreams — and fears — of François René de Châteaubriand, author of the *Mémoires d'outre tombe* and forefather of the great Romantic movement.

Of the fortified town of Saint Aubin du Cormier, once the scene of the fatal battle of 1488 and subsequently destroyed by the French in retaliation, there remains only a mass of ruins, evocatively reflected in the backwater.

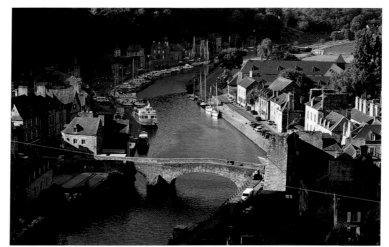

At a distance of about 12 miles (20 km) to the west, overhanging the deep and winding River Rance (along which it is possible to take a boat ride as far as Saint Malo), lies Dinan, like "a swallow's nest," to use the words of Victor Hugo, one of the most beautiful and most complete of Brittany's fortified cities. It is worth dedicating at least a day to the town of Dinan, to admire the 13th-century ramparts, the evocative 14th-century castle, of which the tower of Coëtquen still stands, the impressive keep of Duchess Anne, the Basilica of Saint Saveur, erected in 1120 and the historical center, where there are ancient workshops with wooden beams and the characteristic benches outside. The best periods to visit the town are during the first fifteen days of July, when the prestigious Rencontres Internationales de la Harpe Celtique (International Celtic Harp Conventions) are held, or in September for the Medieval Festival.

At a short distance from the N137, which at the weekends brings the inhabitants of Rennes to the corsair city (today a seaside resort) of Saint-Malo, stands Bécherel, an ancient fortified town with characteristic granite buildings. For the past twenty years or so this town, like its Welsh cousin Hay-on-Wye, has been totally dedicated to the service of book-lovers and book-collectors, so much so as to earn the prestigious title of the first "book city" of the Hexagon (France).

Lastly, it would be quite inconsiderate towards the sharp-witted and hardworking inhabitants of the forests to leave Brittany and end this introductory journey without paying our respects to the most impressive, most prestigious and most enormous of the megalithic monuments of Argoat. The Roche aux Fées ("Fairies' Rock"), in the borough of Essé, is a magnificent dolmen which consists of a 63 feet (19 m) corridor made up of 42 rock masses covered with slabs, each weighing the modest total of 40 tons. This construction is so huge, in fact, that folk tradition attributes it to the fairies which, before they were driven out by "modern" civilization, inhabited in great numbers the forests of the region.

Rennes, with the same importance for Argoat as Nantes has for Armor, is a city that is rich in history while at the same time keeping its sights firmly set on the future. With 212,000 inhabitants (375,000 the entire metropolitan area), the ancient Gallic and later Gallo-Roman settlement of Condate, city of the Redones, as well as the site of the last album of Asterix, Rennes is the smallest French city to have its own subway system. However, it became the seat of the regional government of Brittany only in 1554 with the setting up, after the annexation, of the Parliament of Brittany, the most important institution of the country, which defended the rights of the 'province' until it was abolished by the Revolution. Louis XIV, in order to punish the zealous jurists suspected of having stirred up, or at least encouraged, the insurrection of 1675 (known as the 'Stamped Paper Revolt') which began in Rennes and spread throughout Brittany, decided to 'exile' them to Vannes. It appears, however, that this institution retained its spirit of rebellion until at least the following century; the general proxy La Chalotais, in fact, was himself imprisoned by order of Louis XV. The parliament building, the work of Salomon de la Brosse, which became the

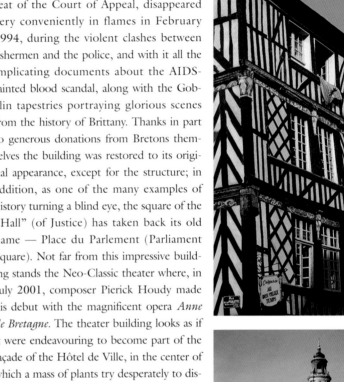

seat of the Court of Appeal, disappeared very conveniently in flames in February 1994, during the violent clashes between fishermen and the police, and with it all the implicating documents about the AIDS-tainted blood scandal, along with the Gobelin tapestries portraying glorious scenes from the history of Brittany. Thanks in part to generous donations from Bretons themselves the building was restored to its original appearance, except for the structure; in addition, as one of the many examples of history turning a blind eye, the square of the "Hall" (of Justice) has taken back its old name — Place du Parlement (Parliament Square). Not far from this impressive building stands the Neo-Classic theater where, in July 2001, composer Pierick Houdy made his debut with the magnificent opera *Anne de Bretagne*. The theater building looks as if it were endeavouring to become part of the façade of the Hôtel de Ville, in the center of which a mass of plants try desperately to disguise a surrealistic emptiness. In this niche, in fact, once stood the so-called "Statue of shame" portraying Brittany kneeling at the feet of the King of France, which was blown up in August 1932 by the underground national independence movement Gwenn ha Du, in occasion of the 400th anniversary of the annexation. Just outside the classical center, in the "medieval" districts of the city around place Sainte Anne and place des Lices, where tournaments were once held, are the finest examples of wattled houses in the whole of Brittany. Those, that is, that survived the terrible fire of 1720, in which more than one hundred people lost their lives and 8000 were left homeless.

THE AWAKENING
OF IDENTITY

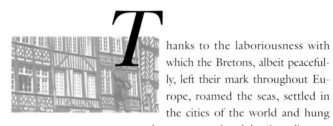

254 In Brittany the traditional costume is undoubtedly considered a strong identifying element. To wear the time-honored headgear or waistcoat during important traditional events is an expression of the pride shared by a population that continues to refuse collective amnesia.

255 With the natural elegance of youth these young girls of the Fouesnant region show off a costume that enhances their gracefulness. The combination of the giz-Fouën bonnet and the collar make this costume of the Rias region one of the most attractive in Brittany.

Thanks to the laboriousness with which the Bretons, albeit peacefully, left their mark throughout Europe, roamed the seas, settled in the cities of the world and hung around ports across the globe (in a diaspora which, although smaller in numbers than those of the Irish or Scots, was nevertheless considerable) they quickly became distinguished as a population, and known as a people whose identity was bound inseparably to its soul. The identity of the Bretons was obviously related to their language, the last Celtic language of the continent which, although it is still spoken today by around 300,000 people, risks dying out before the next century if the French government fails to ratify and apply as soon as possible the European Map of Regional Languages and Language Minorities.

Naturally, the rich and multiform identity of the Bretons is expressed also in their traditional costumes, the extraordinary variety of which dates back to the 18th century, although their heyday was in the mid-19th century, when they were immortalised in the paintings of Perrin, Grignel and Lalaisse. Each individual community was distinguished by the women's hairstyles, the height of the men's hats, the size of the belt buckles and the width of the *bragoù-braz,* the strange, baggy trousers that were worn with leggings. The extravagance of these costumes was matched only by the veritable orgy of colors in which they appeared — the violent reds and deep mauves of Plougastel's costumes contrasting with the stunning burnt gold of those of Bigouden. A race of lords, we might be tempted to remark while

viewing the impressive showcases at the Musée Départemental Breton of Quimper, if we did not know that those magnificent "costumes" were in actual fact worn for the festivities of the rural aristocracy while, in the same period, the farm laborers went about in rags. Today, the traditional costumes are worn only by the eldest women and only in certain places, such as the peninsula of Plougastel or Bigouden, or for events that are now defined as "folklore festivals."

However, thanks to certain idealistic and generous individuals, such as R.Y. Creston, a distinguished member of the *Seiz Breur* art school, several of these garments have been immortalized as symbols. The famous *kabig,* for example, before being appropriated by the students, was actually the working attire of the fishermen of Lyons. Over the past decade a number of young and talented fashion designers (such as Val Piriou of Quimper or Christian Le Drezen of Bigouden, who prematurely passed over to the Paradise of the Celts after promising international debuts), have adopted the traditional Breton motifs and models and adapted them to the brilliant imagery of high fashion. Besides its language and its costumes, however, Brittany is also famous for its dances, which today are enjoying a popularity that is perhaps even greater than ever before. Immediately after the war, when all Breton political activities were strictly forbidden, the energy of the young people found expression in cultural pursuits. The Celtic clubs (the first of which was created in Paris in 1911) underwent a true explosion. On his part, Loeiz Roparz, a young teacher in the "mountain" area of Pollaouenn, had the idea of "modernizing" the old, rural

*256 top left A local girl
from Pont-l'Abbé wears
with pride her typical
pays bigouden
(Brittany) bonnet; this
headgear is such an
emblematic element
that it has become the
symbol of the
extraordinary variety
of Breton traditional
dress.*

night-time festivals known as *fest-noz*. He was the first to organize evening dances in halls, with the dancers separated from the singers, who were set on a makeshift stage and eventually even equipped with microphones. Since then, the "Breton dances," as they came to be called, have enjoyed overwhelming success, kindling an enthusiasm that affected city and country folk alike and producing true "stars" such as the Goadec sisters or the Morvan brothers.

Today, these "night-time parties" attract every Saturday a public composed of all age groups and all social categories, who dance together the *gavotte* or form Circassian circles to the sound of the *kann ha diskann* — the famous *tuilé* singing of the *Kreizh Breiz* — accompanied by the inseparable bombarde-bagpipe duo. Besides the traditional *festoù-noz* there are many other occasions for dancing, including innumerable festivals, in which the Celtic clubs show off their skill and initiate tourists into such traditional dances as the *kost-ar-c'hoat* or *the an-dro*. While the Cornouaille Festival at Quimper is without doubt (as its president Jean-Michel Le Viol claims) the "flagship of the Breton culture," in summer months there are an astounding number of events throughout Brittany, each with its own particular identity: Hortensias in Perros-Guirec, Saint-Loup de Guingamp, dedicated to folk dances, Fleurs d'Ajonc at Pont-Aven, in the region of Gauguin and at Concarneau, Les Filets Bleus, a great folk event that began in the early 20th century as a way to help the fishermen who had been impoverished by the disappearance of the sardine shoals. Of all these, however, it is the Festival Interceltique of Lorient, which

has managed to avoid the double trap of folklore and closing-down, that best represents the Breton culture today.

If the folk dances of Brittany can be said to be one of its finest expressions, this is even truer of its music and songs. The Bretons have been singing, in fact, ever since the traditional motives, recited by the bards to the sound of the *telenn* (Celtic harps) or the *crwth*, enchanted courts throughout Europe with the story of the unhappy love between Tristan and Isenlt or the adventures of the valiant knights of the Round Table. The Breton harp actually disappeared from the continent in around the 14th century and was replaced by a coarser, less refined copy, which went on to incarnate the seductive power of the music of Brittany. Right from the 18th century the combination of the *biniou*, small bagpipes with a high tessitura and very short pipes, and the bom-

256 top right For the Filets Bleus festival of Concarneau this girl is wearing the costume of the "salters" of the Guérande region, which owes its prosperity precisely to the salt trade.

256-257 Elegant collars resembling gulls' wings, bonnets of white lace on sky-blue satin coëff-blew, *bodices finely embroidered in iridescent colors — these are the "broom flowers" of Pont-Aven that were so admired by Paul Gaugin and his "nabis" friends.*

257 top A woman wearing the traditional dress of Bannaleg. The bodice is plain black and the collar is much more modest than that of the costume of nearby Pont-Aven.

257 bottom At the embroiderers' festival in Pont-l'Abbé, these young men pose in their Quimper costumes. The men's baggy, puffed trousers, known as bragoù-braz, *date back to the 19th Century and were worn in Cornouaille and the region of Vannes until 1900.*

barde, a medieval oboe usually made from box-wood, has been synonymous with Breton folk music. After a considerable decline just before the war, this music, which was mainly an expression of the farming culture, later underwent an extraordinary revival, gaining popularity from city to city thanks to the *Bogadeg ar Sonerien* (Assembly of Pipers). The stroke of genius of these musicians was to create, on the Scottish model, a Breton pipe band, which was initially called a *clique* (gang, band), then later band, followed by *bagad-sonerion*, until in 1950 it became simply *bagad*. The music of Brittany would not have such a widespread popularity today if it had not been for the efforts and perseverance of Jord Cochevelou, a native of Gourin, who, in his Paris exile, decided to bring back to life the ancient *telenn*, the harp of the Celts. His son Alan, who was later to become famous with the surname of Stivell (the "spouting spring"), played this harp for the first time at the Maison de la Bretagne in Paris, in November of 1953, winning overnight success. However, the turning point in Alan's career was the concert at the Olympia in January 1972. This marked the beginning of a revolution, manifest by the elated Breton youth of the capital, who went around singing at the top of their voices old battle songs like *An Alarc'h* and the famous *Suite Sud Armoricaine*. The way was paved for the rebirth of Brittany and the rediscovery of its identity. Following in the footsteps of Stivell came those whom Xavier Grall, from his refuge of Bossulan, affectionately defined as "the enlightened" — the guardians and the seers, those who imagine a future that meets the needs of the country: Dan ar Braz, who brought together the Celtic heritage, Myrdhin, Kristenn Nogués, Triskell, Tri Yann, Gweltaz ar Fur, Kirjuhel, Kerguiduff and Servat, whose "Blanche hermine" was to become a second national anthem. It is impossible to give a faithful description of the Breton people without including their feeling for the sacred, the ardent and all-consuming spirituality that throughout the ages has remained the most characteristic feature of the Celts.

Theirs is a spirituality that, since time immemorial, has always found its best expression through the popular, clan-oriented veneration of a myriad of saints (nine hundred, according to Gwenc'hlan le Scouézec), of which only one, the national saint Saint-Yves, is recognized and listed among those of the Catholic Church.

260 top The Troménie is actually the revival of a procession dating back to the days of the Druids (or perhaps even earlier) and corresponding to a precise solar calendar. All along the sacred route small "altars" are placed, decorated with flowers and vegetables, in honor of saints who are totally unknown to the Catholic Church.

260 bottom Standards are a glorious and essential part of the pardons. Mainly written in the language of Brittany, they represent a sign of prosperity and a symbol of identity.

261 Saint-Ronan, along the Troménie route on the sacred mountain, where in August the ancient

Celtic celebrations of Lugnasad-Lugunassatis are held. Descending along the path lined with ferns and broom, the women and girls seeking to have children sit on the gazez vean, the ancient fertility stone.

The others, such as Arzhel, Miliau, Mélar, Nona, Gireg, Maodez, Efflam, Enora and Tudwal, are today basically unknown, their origins lost in the collective memory and the dawn of time.

It is not difficult, however, to discern behind the mask of Santez Anna, Patron Saint of the Bretons, the smile of Deva Anna, the Great Mother of the Celts and the gods, just as the great Cernunos can be seen in the polychrome paintings depicting old Cornely, the horned protector of animals venerated in Carnac.

To cater to all these "idols" of this little world of stone and wood there had to be festivals, ceremonial worship, tribal adoration. Thus the processions known as "pardons" were created, which, after being abolished during the "enlightenment" of the French Revolution, became extremely popular again in the 19th century with the Romantic movement, the rehabilitation of the supernatural and the triumphant mania for the Celtic culture. Extremely picturesque, these processions represented a veritable celebration of the mystic and many of them, such as the famous troménie of Locronan, reintroduced ancient sacred Celtic and solar routes.

After the Tan Tad (the Purifying Fire), also of ancestral heritage, and the great procession, the "pardon" gave way to the profane festival. Anatole Le Braz describes the "pardon" of Sainte Anne La Palud as follows: "A kind of nomadic city took shape before our eyes. As in the days when the herding populations migrated, as far as the eye could see there were tents of all colors and all shapes, clustered in groups and rip-pling in the wind, resembling a Barbarian camp or, better still, the breaking of the waves on the sea."

After the religious ceremonies there are banquets, Breton wrestling, and dances accompanied by the music of biniou and talabard players, who blow so hard on their instruments as to burst their cheeks. From a sacred celebration the "pardon" is capable of transforming into a Dionysian orgy, or a great hullaballo.

These parish, diocesan or national rallies are, naturally, also occasions for dressing up and showing off the most colorful costumes. In around the mid-19th century Emile Souvestre gave the following commentary: "(it) gathered an immense crowd together in Lannion. All the parishes of the Côtes-du-Nord had sent their representatives. There were the roses of Trégor, whose slender hats recalled the shape of the American piraguas; the hot-blooded maidens of Lamballe with imploring eyes and inviting lips, with their flowing, black locks that fell from their Italian bonnets; there were the girls of Lannion, who blossomed beneath the locks of hairstyles resembling the wings of a moth.

Following these were the men of Menez Bré, with their garments of white cloth, their long hair and enormous fire-hardened clogs."

After a short period of estrangement these events, so deeply-rooted in folk tradition, are once more gaining popularity with the reassertion of the Breton culture, as it rediscovers its original vocation and the almost pagan identity of which the renowned philosopher Ernest Renan was so fond.

Castles of the Loire

SECTION THREE

262-263 Chaumont
Castle was rebuilt
between the 15th
and 16th centuries
on a hill that
overlooks the village
of the same name.

Its "gentle"
appearance typical
of the Renaissance
fashion, with its
unmistakable conical
roof, softens the heavy
fortress-style structure.

F rom Giens to Angers, by the calm waters of what has been called the loveliest river in France and along its major tributaries, hundreds of fortresses and castles appear as if by magic from the woods. But why should there be so many princely residences in this area?

One tragic night 600 years ago, the Burgundians put Paris to fire and sword. Tanguy du Châtel, a faithful servant of King Charles VI, hastened to the palace and, with a group of horsemen, escorted the 15-year-old dauphin of France to safety at Chinon Castle. Thus, on the night of May 28, 1418, began the history of the castles of the Loire. For a century the court of the kings of France, with their

retinue of noblemen and dignitaries, moved to the banks of the river. The dauphin (who ascended to the throne as Charles VII) and his successors found the Loire Valley to be the ideal refuge from the threats of a turbulent, unsafe capital. Great castles were built, ancient city walls restored and patrician residences erected, housing a wealth of splendors, intrigues, vendettas, courtly pageants and decadent love affairs.

264 top The walls of Chaumont Castle, shrouded in the morning mist, conceal a multitude of secrets and mysteries.

264-265 Chambord Castle, so grandiose as to seem almost unreal, looms up in the distance like a mirage.

265 Shooting parties take place every year in the huge grounds of Cheverny Castle, and the pack of dogs are exercised along the paths of the park under the guidance of a trainer every day.

*266 and 266-267
Chambord Castle
ends the saga of the
Loire Valley. Bristling
with pinnacles and
turrets, containing
endless halls and*

*chambers, the castle,
built on the banks of
the magical river,
was a king's last
dream, intended by
Francis I to evoke an
entire age.*

But in a letter written on his return from Madrid on March 15, 1528, Francis I manifested the desire to return "to sojourn in the good city of Paris." The Loire had lost the privilege of being the Valley of Kings. When the court left, the noblemen who had built princely residences, no less magnificent than the royal castles, left too. Thus the lights went out on that enchanted world that, centuries later, still evokes a dreamlike fascination. Princes and kings, courtiers and minstrels, queens and dukes still seem to tread that great stage. An invisible hand holds the strings of their memories. From the time of Louis XI to the present day, it has been said, the centuries have never obscured the fame of this garden, where François Rabelais plucked the roses of life. A million tourists visit it every year not only because of the castles, but also for the countryside, the cuisine, and the secrets held by a region that always has something to say. The villages, with their quiet squares basking in the sun, encircle the larger towns, where the living heart of the Loire beats. Through its markets, riverside restaurants and souvenir shops, to the backdrops of its better known castles, the history of the Loire is recounted in "sound and light." Every stone tells a story, every garden bears witness to the idle pleasures of a king, and every drawing room rings with the echoes of a bygone world. But the Loire Valley is only the main artery of a much larger green heart, also studded with castles steeped in history; the whole region is just waiting to be discovered, by traveling from castle to castle like a courtly minstrel. There are the more famous ones, perched on its banks or nestled in the woods: Chambord, Chenonceau, Blois, Amboise, Azay-le-Rideau, Langeais, Chinon, and so on. To the south, in the ancient land of Berry, there are the more defensive castles designed as military outposts, like the fortress of Culan, Meillant Castle, shrouded in the green mantle of the forest of the same name, and the castle of Ainay-le-Vieil. And there are the lesser known castles to the north, behind the Loire, such as Châteaudun, perched on a steep crag, Montigny-le-Gannelon, with its magnificent furnishings, Maintenon, still as it was when Louis XIV's secret wife lived there and, just outside Paris, Anet Castle, the little kingdom of Diane de Poitiers, mistress of King Henry II, which brings to an end the romantic and dissolute history of the Loire Valley castles.

267 top Starting from the northwestern side, the Chapel Tower is followed by the west wing of the galleries (top right), the Dieudonné Tower, the Francis I Tower, the east wing of the galleries and the Robert de Parme Tower.

270-271 The castle of Sully-sur-Loire, which has the tallest slate roof in the Loire Valley, stands like an island of pale stone suspended over the water.

The castle of Sully-sur-Loire

Chambord Castle

Valençay Castle

Ussé Castle

Azay-le-Rideau Castle

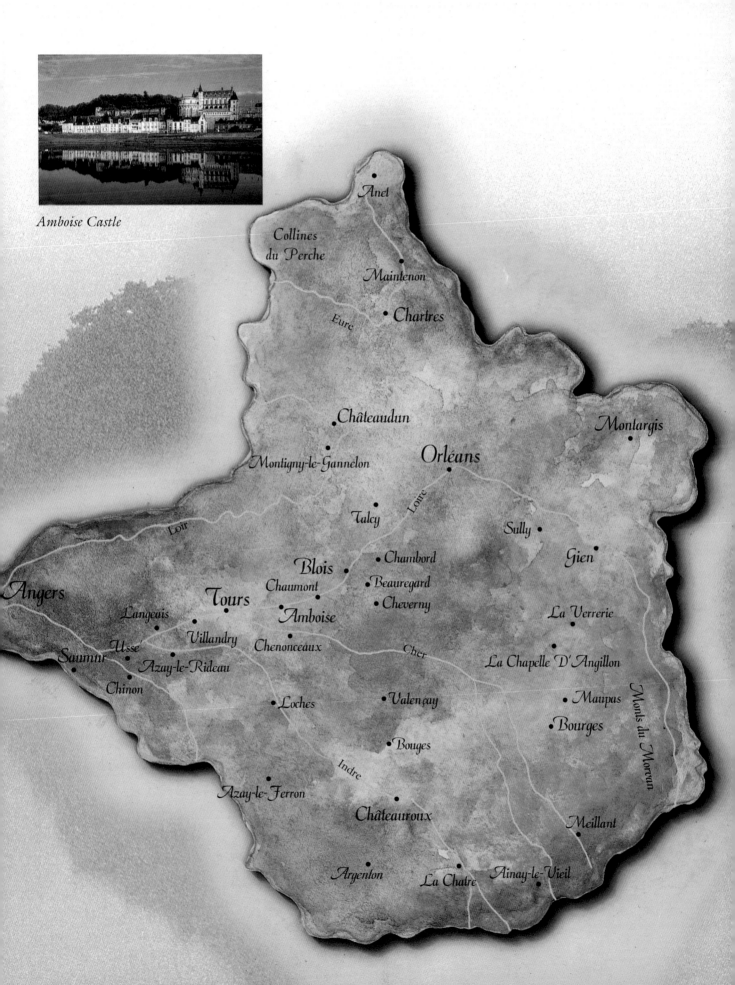

Amboise Castle

Anel

Collines
du Perche

Maintenon

Eure

Chartres

Châteaudun

Montargis

Montigny-le-Gannelon

Orléans

Talcy

Loire

Sully

Gien

Chambord

Blois

Beauregard

Loir

Chaumont

Cheverny

Tours

Angers

Amboise

La Verrerie

Langeais

Chenonceaux

Villandry

Cher

La Chapelle D'Angillon

Ussé

Saumur

Azay-le-Rideau

Valençay

Maupas

Chinon

Loches

Bourges

Monts du Morvan

Bouges

Indre

Azay-le-Ferron

Châteauroux

Meillant

Argenton

La Chatre

Ainay-le-Vieil

THE GENTLE
SOUTHERN
COUNTRYSIDE

272 top left The fortress of Culan, standing high on a crag, overlooks the Arnon River.

272 center left The perfect French-style garden of Bouges Castle, a linear square of pale Touraine stone with a classical beauty; the castle has no pinnacles or Renaissance influences.

At the southernmost border of the central Val de Loire region, before the architectural grandeur of the famous valley begins, the department of Cher has constructed the historical Jacques Coeur route, which leads to villages and castles. These castles were the theater of war centuries ago, when the area, which forms part of the ancient region once called Berry, divided the possessions of the king of France from those of the king of England. Visitors can still admire these outposts of bygone deeds, long roads and unusual itineraries entwining with the great river, until reaching Bouges Castle—with its precious furnishings—and Valençay Castle—residence of statesman Talleyrand—bring them back to the charm of castles that have never known war. In Culan, the 12th-century stronghold standing high on a spur of rock has the austere features of one who has known the hardships of sieges. It is an awe-inspiring fortress, with mighty round towers overlooking the Arnon. The great 15th-century fireplaces, two precious paintings attributed to Caravaggio, the original windows and precious historical relics testify to its past splendors. Its grandeur was due to the feats of Louis de Culan, admiral of France, who fought all over the world and was Joan of Arc's comrade in arms at Patay and Orléans. Famous personalities and leading statesmen have stayed at the grandiose castle, last but not least being General de Gaulle in November 1951. Indre, which borders on Cher, is another department whose treasures are worth a visit. The most romantic is the magnificent country home of George Sand at Nohant, an aristocratic mansion with many rooms and a peaceful garden on the outskirts of La Châtre village, which inspired the scenario often described in her novels. George Sand, born in Paris in the early 19th century, came to live at her grandmother's house as a child. From Chateauroux it's just a short trip to La Brenne, a little-known region that few tourists visit, except for the elite band of nature lovers who travel with sleeping bags and sleep under the stars. There are no trees, just scrub, moors, meadows, great silences and 400 ponds in this nook where unspoiled nature has an austere, melancholic charm. Every so often, scattered over the wide open spaces, there's a cottage, a castle, like the splendid castle of Azay-le-Ferron, or a secluded village. To the north of La Brenne are Bouges Castle and Valençay Castle, still in the gentle Berry countryside. Fields and forests lead to the discreet elegance of Bouges Castle, a severe square of pale Touraine stone with a classic beauty, devoid of pinnacles, in perfect Louis XV style. It recalls the Trianon at Versailles, partly because of the antique furnishings, collected in a lifetime's research by the last owners, M. and Mme. Viguier, who bought it in 1917.

272 bottom left The mansion of George Sand, in the Berry countryside, where the author lived as a child and later took refuge for long periods of her life.

272 right George Sand's intense look in a portrait at her Nohant mansion.

273 Meillant Castle, shrouded in the green cloak of the forest of the same name, was more defensive than romantic. A flamboyant Gothic polygonal tower can be seen on the inner side of the castle.

GRACE AND STRENGTH: AINAY-LE-VIEIL CASTLE

Ainay-le-Vieil is the southernmost castle in the Loire Valley. The thick octagonal walls of this intact medieval fortress surround the Renaissance grace of the central building, added centuries later, next to the 16th-century Renaissance tower. It is still inhabited by the descendants of Charles de Chevenon de Bigny, the noble knight who bought the property from the Lord of Culan in 1467. It houses historical relics associated with Colbert, Marie Antoinette and, still longer ago, Louis XII and Anne of Brittany. The parapets pass from tower to tower, surrounding the castle with a continuous circle of walls that has won the impressive building the nickname of "Petit Carcassonne." In the great hall is a huge fireplace, meticulously carved with symbols and the royal initials L and A against a blue background of gilded fleurs-de-lys. When spring comes, a thousand varieties of old roses bloom in the castle garden, while in summer the historic castle presents thematic exhibitions and some very popular events.

*274 and 275
Ainay-le-Vieil, the southernmost castle in the Loire Valley, on the borders of Berry, is an extraordinary medieval fortress dating from the 14th century. Massive*

towers intersect the polygonal design of the outer walls, which enclose the attractive inner courtyard of the castle, with its Renaissance tower and beautifully furnished interior.

The castle has belonged for five centuries to the descendants of Charles de Chevenon de Bigny, the noble knight who bought the property from the Lord of Culan in 1467.

THE RESIDENCE OF BEAUTIFUL DUCHESS: VALENÇAY CASTLE

A few miles away, Valençay Castle bears witness to the splendors of the First Empire. "Lord of Talleyrand, it is my wish that you purchase a beautiful residence where you can receive the diplomatic corps and foreigners accredited to Paris," said Napoleon to his prime minister in 1803. Talleyrand did not need to be asked twice. At Valençay he found a ruined 16th-century castle, built by Jacques d'Estampes, with an east wing added in the 17th century. He transformed it into that perfection of style and furnishing that can still be admired today by moving from room to room along the grandiose first-floor gallery and looking out over the park, where deer graze. Napoleon paid most of the price so that he could use Valençay Castle himself. In fact, he used it for six years to accommodate the Spanish king Ferdinand VII, who lost his throne through the emperor's fault. On regaining possession of the castle in 1814, Talleyrand refurbished the interior, and after the Congress of Vienna went to live there permanently with his niece by marriage, Dorothée, duchess of Dino. The grandiose palace, which has remained intact since the early 19th century, witnessed 20 years of balls, receptions, literary salons and meetings of the leading contemporary figures in politics and art.

*276 bottom The halls
of Valençay Castle
contain antique
furniture and
original paintings,
like the splendid oval
frame containing the
portrait of Princess
Bénévent of Vigée-
Lebrun.*

277 top *The magnificent collection of paintings at Valençay includes a portrait of the famous minister Talleyrand (left), and one of Victoire Alexandrine Eléonore de Damas, countess of Talleyrand-Périgord, who lived in the late 18th century (center) and was the mother of Charles Maurice Talleyrand, portrayed by Prud'hon (right).*

278 and 279
Talleyrand de
Périgord had to give
up his lovely residence
at Valençay between
1808 and 1814 to
Ferdinand VII, King
of Spain, who was
exiled there after being
deposed by Napoleon.
Visitors can see his

chamber (large photo),
in First Empire style,
then proceed along the
large gallery on the
first floor to other
magnificently
furnished rooms like
the Blue Room
(bottom left) and the
cabinet de toilette
(top right).

280 and 281
Napoleon's prime
minister, Talleyrand
de Périgord, regained
possession of his castle
in 1814 and partly
renovated the interior
decoration. Some of
the most interesting
rooms are the ground-
floor hall containing
the table around
which the signatories
of the Congress of
Vienna sat (left-hand
page), the Great Hall
(top left), the Portrait
Gallery (top right),
and the Prince's
Chamber (bottom).

282 and 283 The
Renaissance tower by
Michelangelo's pupil,
Fra Giocondo, and a
window in flamboyant
Gothic style stand out
on the south façade of
Meillant Castle. The
defensive structure of
the castle, which is
still inhabited, can be
clearly seen from the
entrance moat. The
building contains a
wealth of furnishings,
halls and chambers
with painted coffered
ceilings.

FRA GIOCONDO'S LOVELY TOWER: MEILLANT CASTLE

Meillant Castle, enveloped in the green mantle of the forest and the scent of lime trees in spring, reveals its pretty Gothic style with a lawn of strutting peacocks, glistening ponds and the "Lion" tower—a Renaissance construction by Michelangelo's pupil Fra Giocondo—that stands at the center of the façade. Remember this tower when viewing the more famous one at Blois Castle; the Italian Renaissance touch left the first trace of its brilliant harmony here. In fact, it was Charles II d'Amboise, lord of Chaumont and governor of Milan, who introduced into Meillant Castle discreet but perceptible signs of the art he had seen flourishing across the Alps. In the inner rooms, 17th-century Dutch furniture; a great banqueting hall with minstrel's gallery and tapestries made to a design by Raphael; and a spectacular dining room with a Renaissance fireplace, a gilded coffered ceiling (partly painted in bright colors) and Cordova leather wall hangings all bring to life the age of the duke of Charost, owner of the castle during the Revolution, who had a philanthropic bent. The epitaph on his tomb in the castle chapel states, "Everywhere and at all times he did nought but good."

284 top The impressive statue of Jacques-Coeur (left) stands in the heart of Bourges opposite the famous merchant adventurer's mansion (right); the Jacques-Coeur route, which takes in the major castles of the southern Loire region, is named after him.

284-285 In the austere rooms of La Chapelle d'Angillon Castle, author Alain-Fournier found his inspiration for the characters of his famous novels, including Le Grand Meaulnes.

THE LAND OF JACQUES-COEUR

The echoes of war give way to an ancient, bucolic landscape, while the Jacques-Coeur route continues north. After the calm sight of Apremont, the prettiest flowery village in France, comes Bourges, and the impressive statue in the town center of Jacques-Coeur, who gave the capital of Cher its most precious castle. Tall, handsome, and a lover of the sea and great ocean routes, he founded a shipping company whose sailing ships traveled far and wide to supply the king's court with spices, silks, silver, carpets and majolica. He financed Charles VII's military campaigns and was his private and most trusted banker until he fell into disgrace, it is said, because of the pretty Agnès Sorel, the king's mistress, and was thrown into prison. He escaped, embarked on a ship of the papal fleet that attacked the Turks, and died in 1456. His statue, which stands on a stone pedestal opposite the entrance, swathed in marble drapery, seems to admire his castle for eternity. In the heart of Henrichemont Forest, studded with pastures and clearings, castles are still the main leitmotiv. Maupas Castle is famous for its collection of 887 china plates from the oldest and most famous French pottery works, many of which hang on the walls alongside the wooden staircase, and for a silk tapestry of Italian manufacture given by the count of Chambord to the marquis of Maupas in the 19th century. Literary memories and the personalities invented by Alain-Fournier give a special appeal to the castle of La Chapelle D'Angillon. "I have returned to my land, the land that can only be seen by moving branches aside. I have never seen it so fresh, so concealed," wrote Alain-Fournier, when he was already beginning to imagine the adventures of *Le Grand Meaulnes* (published in English as *The Lost Domain*).

Cher, the department that, together with Indre, partly includes the ancient Berry, was a source of inspiration and peace for the author. He learned to read and write at the Epineuil-le-Fleuriel village school, enjoyed staying with his uncle in Nançay, a village comprising a few houses built around a single square, and daydreamed as a child in the great castle of La Chapelle D'Angillon. The dramatic destiny of the Princess of Clèves and the adventures of Le Grand Meaulnes, a young man lost in the memory of a mysterious kingdom where the enchanting Yvonne de Galais lived, accompany the visitor through the austere rooms of this castle. Alain-Fournier, the author of some famous novels, was born in 1886 in the village not far from the castle, but it was the great halls of the historic building that set light to his imagination. Two of them house relics of the writer's fantasy world, while others feature impressive fireplaces, beautiful paintings; a Luca della Robbia sculpture stands in the chapel, and a curious gallery is designed for *jeu de paume*, a fashionable game that was the forerunner of tennis.

SMALL WORLDS,
SPECIAL ATMOSPHERES

*T*he land veined by the Cher River still encloses small worlds and an atmosphere of stillness: sleepy villages, roads that disappear into the countryside, abbeys, castles and landscapes untouched by the passage of time. The gentle countryside of Berry leads to the castle of La Verrerie. The Scots were at home here, because Charles VII gave this solitary castle to James Stuart in 1422. They kept it until 1683, when Louis XIV donated it to Countess Louise de Kéroualle, Duchess of Portsmouth, and Charles II's mistress. In 1843 a descendent gave it to an ancestor of the present owners, the De Vogüé family. Nested in the greenery of Ivoy Forest is the classic castle with turrets, Renaissance porticoes, richly decorated halls, secret archives, huge, silent grounds, and a stream to provide silvery highlights. Visitors can admire the Gothic chapel, the reception rooms, the billiard room and the library. Some rooms are set aside for paying guests who wish to spend a night as a king amid velvets and canopies, ancestral portraits, tapestries and antique furniture. The world of fishing also appears on a royal frame. A few miles from Gien stands the lonely gray castle of La Buissière, already a fortress in the 12th century. Since 1962 the castle has housed the Fishing Museum, which contains exhibits of all kinds: fossil fish, silver fish, stuffed fish, sculpted fish, drawings of fish.

286-287 The gentle Berry countryside and the thick Ivoy Forest surround La Verrerie Castle, with its Renaissance portico in the inner courtyard, and rooms furnished with antique furniture and damask fabrics. Some of the rooms are reserved for paying guests who would like to spend a night in the magical atmosphere of a great château.

ANNE DE BEAUJEU'S RESIDENCE: GIEN CASTLE

The history of this small town, which stretches along the banks of the Loire, is closely linked to that of its castle, the first of those overlooking the Loire if the route of the famous river is followed towards the sea. The castle, standing high above the river at a point where the view is limitless, has offered hospitality to Joan of Arc among others. Before attending the coronation of Charles VII, the famous heroine spent a night praying in the wing of the castle now named after her, the only surviving part of the original feudal building.

The castle, overlooking Gien and the Loire, was built of brick and stone for Louis XI's daughter Anne de Beaujeu, Countess of Gien, in 1484. Francis I, Henri II, Charles IX and Henri III all stayed here. It survived unscathed the bombing of the Second World War, which razed the red-roofed town to the ground.

Since 1952 the castle has housed the Hunting Museum, which contains 15 rooms full of weapons of all ages, costumes, rare collections of buttons inspired by the hunt, works of art associated with the subject, tapestries, majolica, watercolors, lithographs, paintings by François Desportes, the famous animal painter to Louis XIV and Louis XV, and the Claude Hettier de Boislambert Collection of 500 hunting trophies. As well as the castle and its museum, Gien also offers another interesting attraction: the ceramic works founded in 1821 by Englishman Thomas Hulm, known as Hall, who wished to introduce the manufacture of fine English china into France. He found the right kind of clay for the purpose near Gien, while wood from the great forest of Orléans stoked the kilns that produced Gien blue, a color that remains inimitable today.

288 top Gien Castle, the first of the castles overlooking the Loire as the course of the famous river is followed, was built on the foundations of a hunting lodge erected for Charlemagne. Its involvement with hunting thus has ancient origins, and still continues today. The castle houses the magnificent Hunting Museum, which includes some lovely tapestries like the one woven following a cartoon by Laurent Guyot (right).

288-289 and 289 The large hall featuring paintings by François Desportes (1661–1743), with its mighty woodwork, contains numerous works by this famous animal painter who worked at the court of Louis XIV and Louis XV.

SULLY,
A ROMANTIC CASTLE

S ully Castle, a good example of defensive architecture on the border between Berry and Sologne, rises from the water like a romantic vision on the left bank of the Loire and its tributary, the Sange. The great hunting parties of yesteryear took place here, in the huge wooded Sologne Forest. The square tower at the entrance, the round tower on the southeastern side and the keep date back to the 15th century. From the knoll visitors can admire the castle, the park and the moats. Amid the greenery stands the marble statue of the duke of Sully, with a laurel wreath and the marshal of France baton. The Guard Room, with its coffered Vosges wood ceilings, leads to the Great Hall where Voltaire, exiled here after libeling the Prince Regent, Philippe d'Orléans, staged some of his plays between 1716 and 1719. Near the Great Hall, separated by a solid iron door, is the oratory, followed by the King's Chamber, with tapestries, a four-poster bed with blue canopy and wood-paneled walls. Finally, 40 steps lead up to the top floor, where visitors can see the framework of the roof: a brilliantly engineered wooden skeleton. This very tall pitched roof, which dates from the late 14th century, has undergone catapult attacks, but has always withstood them and is still there, like a great upside-down ship's hull, waiting to be admired for its latticework of beams and the unusual design of its roof.

290 and 291 The romantic sight of Sully Castle, a good example of defensive architecture, rises from the water on the border between Berry and Sologne. Among its attractions are the Guard Room, with its ceiling painted in pure gold, the King's Chamber—with tapestries portraying scenes from classical mythology and a blue damask canopy to match the walls—and the extraordinary roof frame, with its upturned-hull shape.

A WORLD PRESERVED IN STONE

Tourists who travel through the Loire Valley or merely hear stories about its magnificent residences wonder why so many castles and princely residences were built there. Why by the Loire, and not the Seine, for example, or other no less famous rivers? Because the Loire Valley, with its warm, dry climate, has always been the garden of France; because along the riverbanks there were already fortresses and castles able to accommodate royal guests; and because in the 15th century the king's political survival depended on the resistance offered along the Loire border by the dukes of Berry and Orléans in the south against the English and in the north against the Burgundians. Even after his accession to the throne, Charles VII remained fascinated by the climate and landscape of the gentle Loire Valley. After the Treaty of Troyes (1420), which stripped him of his kingdom, he lived at Chinon, Loches and Amboise with the sole title of Roi de Bourges. Following the legendary liberation by Joan of Arc of Orléans, besieged by the English, in May 1429, Charles VII began to win back his kingdom, but when he was finally able to return to liberated Paris on November 12, 1437, he only stayed a few days. Homesick, he took the court back to Chinon, preferring to pass his life in the gentle Touraine, where he had been bewitched by the beautiful Agnès Sorel. His son, Louis XI, who grew up at Loches Castle, though a restless wanderer by nature, nearly always lived in the castles of Amboise and Plessis-lez-Tours. Charles VIII, who was fond of Amboise, also had no desire to transfer the court to Paris.

After his marriage he spent a year at Langeais Castle; then, on his return from the Italian campaign in 1495, he decided to live at Amboise and convert the castle into a modern residence, for which purpose he summoned skilled craftsmen and artists from Italy. His successor, Louis XII, also chose the Loire, as did Francis I who lived at Blois Castle in the early years of his reign. Three years after his coronation began the construction of his own castle, Chambord. Today, in the summer, many castles stage historical reenactments; sound-and-light shows, pageants and plays to familiarize the public with the history of the best-known castles. The Francis I route follows the ancient road traveled by the king on his way to Italy, while the Vallée des Rois route leads to royal residences and sleepy old-world villages. Even without following a set route, the castles follow one after another. The castle of Chenonceau, the best known and most visited, recounts tales of love and the revenge of betrayed mistresses, while Villandry's charm focuses on its gardens. Cheverny is still inhabited, and the pack of dogs used for fox hunting in the autumn can be seen in its avenues in the afternoons.

Then there's Azay-le-Rideau; Langeais with its tapestries; Ussé, so unreal that it inspired the fairy tale of Sleeping Beauty; Blois, where French history was made and the duke of Guise was assassinated; Chinon, which featured in the destiny of Joan of Arc; Amboise, linked with Italy because of its association with Leonardo da Vinci; and Chambord, which, with its huge size, its 380 chimneys and 406 rooms, exemplifies and concludes the saga of the Loire castles.

292 top left Feudal towers and outer walls give Chaumont Castle, which stands on a hill overlooking the Loire, the appearance of an impregnable fortress. The castle has an air of mystery, the legacy of its association, at the height of its splendor, with a court astronomer who was more of a magician and fortune-teller than a scientist.

292 top right Villandry Castle is a magnificent residence, but its fame is not so much due to the interior as to its magnificent flower and vegetable gardens, whose colors change with the seasons and the crops. These gardens were inspired by ancient documents written by medieval monks.

292-293 Little Azay-le-Rideau Castle, framed by a romantic natural setting of rare beauty, overlooks the Indre River amid lush vegetation with plane trees, lime trees and tall oaks.

THE INFLUENCE
OF ITALIAN ART

The Loire Valley is an immense setting that, in a way, belongs to the marvelous period of the Italian Renaissance. In the stone friezes, spiral staircases, windows lighting the halls, and castle porticoes – almost everywhere, in fact – Italian influence has left the unmistakable imprint of its grandeur. The façade of Valençay Castle has the same scenic perfection as the 15th century palazzi of Florence, the staircase of Blois Castle repeats the floral motifs of many Tuscan portals, and the names of many famous personalities are linked with the Loire Valley. One such personality was Catherine de Médicis who, when she married Henri II, brought to France the art of good living, the gaiety of the *volta* (a rather daring dance that delighted the court), and the elegance and taste of the great balls and banquets held in Florence under the Médicis.

Another was Leonardo da Vinci, who ended his days at the castle of Clos-Lucé in Amboise, given to him by Francis I. He arrived from Florence, his mules loaded with the canvases of the Mona Lisa, St. Anne and John the Baptist. He warmed himself by the fire in the Great Hall, and in the peace of that retreat organized magnificent parties for his French king, creating flying machines and robots that, when struck on the chest, released pure white lilies and perfumed roses onto the guests.

After his death and the return of Francis I from the Battle of Pavia (1528), the time was ripe for the king to return to the capital. The destiny of the Loire as the headquarters of the court was over. Chambord Castle was finished, and from then on was only used for holidays and hunting parties. However, distant sounds still seem to issue from that kingdom of keeps, pinnacles and parapets: the rustle of silk, the clank of armor, dance steps and the gentle notes of lutes and rebecs.

294-295 Chambord: a sight that seems like a mirage. Standing alone at the end of a huge park, Chambord Castle incarnates the megalomaniac dream of a king who wished to conclude the age of the splendors and legends of the Loire Valley with the most magnificent castle ever built on the riverbanks.

295 right Blois Castle stands in the heart of the town of the same name on the right bank of the Loire, about 37 miles from Orléans. In the 15th century it was the favorite royal residence of Louis XII, who ordered large-scale extension work.

IN THE FOOTSTEPS OF JOAN OF ARC: CHINON CASTLE

*O*rléans commemorates Joan of Arc every May 8, when 1,000 banners fly from Fort des Tourelles to Place St. Croix. The famous Maid of Orléans, played by a young girl, walks at the head of a great procession. This pageant commemorates the day in 1429 when Joan arrived to liberate the city from the English siege. Her "crusade" had set out from Chinon Castle, where Charles VII had taken refuge after escaping from Paris. Joan arrived there on March 9, 1429, escorted by six men, asking to be brought before the king. It was a dramatic time for France.

Henry IV was king of England and king of Paris; Charles VII was only king of Bourges. The states general of the central and southern provinces, which had remained loyal to him, had decided to finance the war against the English, but the dauphin hesitated. Joan waited for two days, praying, until she was eventually received in the Throne Room (sadly now partly demolished; only the monumental fireplace remains, to-gether with what, according to legend, is the footprint of the famous heroine). King Charles VII, who had exchanged clothes with a courtier, was concealed among 300 costumed nobles. But Joan was not to be deceived. She walked straight up to the king, embraced his knees and said, "My name is Joan, and I am sent by the king of Heaven to tell you that you will be crowned true king of the French at Rheims Cathedral." The king doubted her word and sent the girl to Poitiers for medical examinations, to establish whether she was a witch or an envoy of God. Eleven days later, convinced by the results, Charles VII permitted Joan of Arc to march at the head of his army against the English. Until 1450 Chinon Castle on the Vienne, a tributary of the

Loire, was the headquarters of the court, which later moved to Amboise and Blois. The castle was used once more by Louis XII in 1498 to receive Cesare Borgia, sent by the Pope to deliver the papal bull annulling his marriage with Joan of France so that he could wed Anne of Brittany, thus uniting Brittany and France. The chronicles tell of a grandiose entrance of 68 mules bearing trunks, crates and chairs covered with gold brocade, accompanied by pages, minstrels and drummer-boys. Men and animals draped in brocades and crimson velvets preceded Duke Cesare, who rode a horse decked out with precious stones and pearls. The duke's costume was so precious and studded with gems and diamonds that it "shone like a lighthouse." The duke, son of the Pope, was received with full honors, although it was already known that as cardinal he had been his sister's lover and his brother's murderer. Little now remains of Chinon Castle apart from the grandiose foundations and some towers, including the Tour de l'Horloge with the bell, Marie Javelle, which has struck the hours since 1399, and the Tour d'Argenton, built towards the end of the 15th century, in the location where Louis XI is said to have held his prisoners.

The king's mistress, Agnès Sorel, lived in the adjacent Coudray Castle, which the sovereign reached via secret underground passages. Joan of Arc was held prisoner in the tower of the same building, as were the Templars, whose heartrending messages can still be read on the walls, centuries later. The countryside around Tours is characterized by precious vineyards that produce the red Chinon, Bourgeuil and Saint Nicolas and the white MontLouis and Vouvray wines that accompany the gastronomic delights of the Loire Valley.

296-297 Seen from the Vienne River, Chinon Castle reveals the defensive and military features of what was one of the most famous fortresses of the 15th century. Here the dauphin of France took refuge when he left Paris during a night of terror; Joan of Arc came to the castle too, to implore the king to grant her the honor of marching at the head of his troops against the English army besieging Orléans.

298 top and 298-299
*Ussé Castle still
breathes the enchanted
atmosphere of* Sleeping
Beauty, *the fairy tale
by Charles Perrault
that made it famous.
Its towers, with their
gray conical roofs, and
the thick forest all
around have helped
preserve the magic of
this spot over the
centuries.*

299 bottom *The
world-famous Ussé
Castle is now a
favorite destination
of couples looking for
a romantic setting
for their wedding.*

USSÉ: SLEEPING BEAUTY'S CASTLE

*U*ssé Castle, an enchanting mixture of pinnacles and pointed turrets, is known as Sleeping Beauty's castle. It was an ancient fortress when it belonged to Jean de Bueil, who married a daughter of Charles VII and Agnès Sorel. Work later began on converting it into a less severe home, bristling with towers and pinnacles. It was such an enchanted castle that it inspired Charles Perrault to write his famous fairy tale; so magical that it has caught the imagination of the Japanese, who travel halfway across the world to get married in this romantic setting. The castle is quadrangular in shape, bounded at the corners by keeps and pinnacles. However, like nearly all those in the Loire Valley, the appearance of the building and the original architectural plans, which date back to the 15th and early 16th centuries, were changed by the various owners. The interior of Ussé Castle is richly decorated, and its rooms, with their 18th-century tapestries and 17th- and 18th-century furniture, constitute veritable museums. Some tapestries also hang on the walls of the long gallery, with its black-and-white tiled floor. Paintings of famous schools line the main staircase and the Salle Royale. A rare piece of Renaissance furniture inlaid with ivory occupies almost an entire wall of the *cabinet florentin*. The chapel, which has a nave with no aisles, was built between 1523 and 1535. It contains 16th-century wooden choir-stalls and an enameled majolica Virgin attributed to Luca della Robbia.

299 top Two ancient cedars (legend has it that they were planted by Chateaubriand) protect the 16th-century chapel. The interior, which has a nave but no aisles, is decorated with wooden choir-stalls dating from the period when the chapel was built. However, the most valuable item is an enameled terra-cotta Madonna made by Luca della Robbia around the mid-15th century.

300 and 301 The
wealth of the interior
of Ussé Castle
matches the charm
of the exterior. The
furnishings, especially
the tapestries and
furniture, enhance
the magnificence of
the 18th-century
galleries and halls.
The Aubusson
tapestries and those
by Flemish craftsmen
depicting rural scenes
are particularly
exquisite. Ancient
weapons and
paintings of a
good artistic level
alternate with
Italian furniture,
like the rare ivory-
inlaid specimen in
the cabinet florentin.

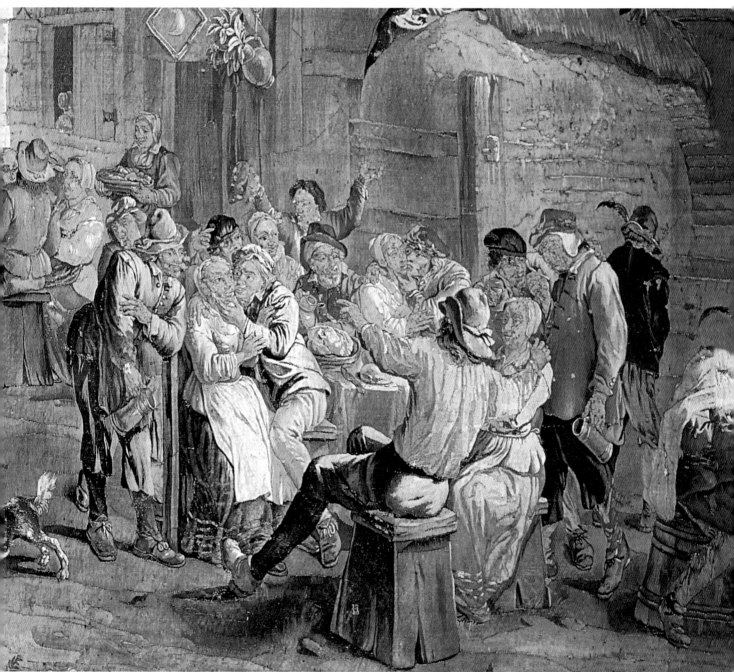

MORE TALES
OF LOVE AND WAR:
LOCHES CASTLE

Between one military campaign and the next, the sovereigns who lived by the Loire devoted a great deal of time to feasting, jousting and love affairs. They had mistresses whose names have gone down in history and who, in exchange for their loyalty, were rewarded with castles and riches. Charles VII and Agnès Sorel were bound by a true passion, and a castle was the reward for every child she bore (four in all). Loches Castle, the largest, had existed since the 6th century with the name of Castellum. In 840 Charles the Bald gave it to a loyal knight, who passed it on to a niece who married Foulques the Black of the House of Anjou. The castle has an exceptional defensive system of walls and towers. It underwent lengthy sieges in the 13th century in the battle fought for possession of Touraine between the Plantagenet King Henry II of England and his sons Richard the Lionheart and John Lackland against Philip Augustus. In the 15th century it became the favorite residence of Charles VII and Agnès Sorel. She died in 1450, and her body lies in an alabaster sarcophagus in the tower that bears her name. A portrait of the king's mistress in another room (a copy of the original, which is in a private collection) shows the delicate grace of her body and a naked breast escaping provocatively from the laces of a corset. From Loches it is just a short walk to Montrésor, one of the prettiest villages in France. The most famous lord of the manor was Imbert de Bastarnay, who bought the existing fortress in 1493 and converted it into the pretty castle that now belongs to the descendants of Count Branicki, the Polish nobleman who bought the property in the 19th century. A friend of Napoleon III, he was a leading financier and a collector of valuable works of art, now on display: paintings by Raphael, Caravaggio and Veronese, silverware belonging to the ancient kings of Poland, hunting trophies, jewelry and furniture from the Italian Renaissance period.

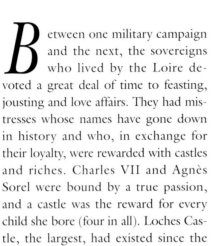

302-303 and 303 top *The warm light of sunset mellows the austere design of Loches Castle. More of a defensive bulwark than a romantic castle, it has survived intact over the centuries, with its famous tower, the royal gate, and the chancellery built by the Counts of Anjou. The Counts, who were among the first owners of the castle, also ruled over the town, with its narrow medieval lanes huddled at the foot of the crag.*

304 top left Huge fireplaces, shining armor and splendid windows give the interior of the castle a unique atmosphere.

304 top right A young Charles VII, a central figure in the history of Loches, is portrayed in this fine glass window in the castle. The monarch, was the man who succeeded in leading France out of the Hundred Years War.

304 bottom right It was in this room that Joan of Arc delivered her famous speech to King Charles VII in June 1429, urging him to go to Rheims to be crowned king of the French.

304-305 The beautiful Agnès Sorel had a long love affair with Charles VII. Her tomb, watched over by an angel, lies in a tower of the castle.

305 bottom Pages of history have been written at Loches Castle, from the long love affair between Charles VII and the lovely Agnès Sorel to the imprisonment of Cardinal La Balue, counselor to Louis XI, who betrayed the king to Charles the Bold. He was imprisoned in the Martelet, the gloomy prison with three tiers of cells (cachots) constructed in the Tour Neuve, where Ludovico il Moro, duke of Milan, was also held prisoner by Louis XII.

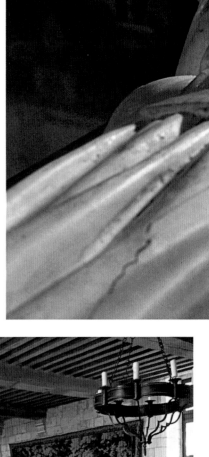

*306 top and 306-307
and Saumur Castle,
a quadrangle
bounded by polygonal
towers with conical
slate roofs, stands on
a rocky promontory
that seems to watch
over the last stretch of
the Loire as it flows
towards the sea.*

THE CASTLES
OF ANJOU

*H*ere the Loire enters Anjou, and before reaching the sea passes by two more famous castles, those of Saumur and Angers. The castle of Saumur, the town that contains the leading French riding school, stands on a rocky promontory. The castle, a quadrilateral with polygonal corner towers, conical roofs of bluish slate and Renaissance-Gothic decorations on a visibly medieval structure, is reached by walking up narrow, steep streets, until the effort is rewarded by a superb view and a visit to the richly decorated rooms. The castle dates from the late 14th century, although its appearance reveals some later additions.

It was the Italian Bartolomeo who built the outer fortifications, which herald the form of the typical Vauban ramparts. A Huguenot stronghold in the 17th century, then a barracks and a penitentiary, it was restructured at the turn of this century and houses three museums: the Decorative Arts

Museum, Toy Soldier Museum and Equestrian Museum, which displays harnesses, trappings and uniforms.

Although it has the resources and dynamism of a big city, Angers, with its close-knit network of squares and pedestrian precincts and its clusters of houses over 500 years old, looks like a large village. At the center is its symbol: the squat pentagonal fortress erected by Blanche of Castille, mother of St. Louis, in the early 13th century as a bulwark against the restless Breton populations. Later, at the end of the 13th century, residential buildings, hanging gardens and a chapel for the ducal family of Anjou were added. What was once the residence of the poet-prince René contains the famous *Apocalypse*, about 118 yards of allegorical scenes made with the tapestry technique by 14th-century artists. It has six sections, each divided into 14 episodes, featuring red-blue shades, dragons with huge heads, quadrupeds ridden by Death, sea creatures with macabre features and crude representations of the human face. This is the best visiting card for the itinerary that starts from the castle and continues as far as the "*promenade du bout du monde*," leading the visitor to the attractive historic buildings in the town center.

307 left and top right Saumur Castle dates from the late 14th century, but like all those in the famous valley it was altered over the centuries and also served various purposes: it was a Huguenot stronghold in the 17th century, then a barracks, and then a penitentiary. It now houses three museums: the Decorative Arts Museum, the Toy Soldier Museum and the Equestrian Museum.

307 bottom right The mighty Angers Castle, a squat pentagonal fortress, was built by Blanche of Castille, mother of Saint Louis, in the early 13th century, to protect the area, which was threatened by the restless Breton populations.

A LADY'S ROMANTIC
DREAM: AZAY-LE-RIDEAU

*308 and 309
The greenery of the
park contrasts with
the silvery veil of the
Indre River as it
flows past Azay-le-
Rideau Castle,
creating a romantic
atmosphere. An
enchanting blend of
pinnacles and sharp
turrets, the castle
houses valuable works
of art such as a 16th-
century portrait by
an unknown artist
of a young woman
reading, a portrait of
Louis XIV standing,
and a 16th-century
portrait of the duke
of Guise, nicknamed
le Balafré (Scarface).*

*I*n the spot where the road from Tours to Chinon crosses the Indre, a left-hand tributary of the Loire, once stood the watchtower of Azay-le-Rideau. This was a medieval fortification surrounded by a deep moat and manned by a garrison of Burgundian soldiers. For 100 years it was no more than a pile of rubble, after Charles VII set fire to the entire village and the fortified tower in 1418, also killing the soldiers of the garrison, to take revenge for the insults he had received. In 1518 the court financier, Gilles Berthelot, treasurer to Francis I, bought the property and commissioned architect Étienne Rousseau to erect a castle in Renaissance style in a pretty spot where the Indre formed a small lake. The work lasted 10 years, until 1529, and was directed by the financier's wife, Philippa Lesbahy. The result was a residence designed for the pure pleasure of living in it, with no defensive purposes. It was built partly on the water, its romantic white image reflected in the lake, with conical towers, slate roofs and pretty ornaments outside and the great right-angled staircase inside. It was Philippa Lesbahy who gave the residence the elegant furnishings it still retains: drawing rooms full of paintings, a collection of blue majolica plates, and walls hung with Gobelin tapestries. That is why the castle is one of the most beautiful in the Loire Valley and was liked so much by Francis I who, taking advantage of a

conspiracy, had no hesitation in confiscating it and exiling the owner, Berthelot. In the King's Chamber, where Francis I almost certainly stayed, is a great fireplace with the initials F and C (standing for queen Claude). It is followed by the Green Room, named after the huge green damask four-poster bed dating from the 17th century, the Red Room, where crimson damask still prevails in the furnishings, and the Banqueting Hall, with its huge fireplace and valuable Brussels tapestries.

310 More beautiful rooms in Azay-le-Rideau castle bear witness to the famous personalities who stayed there: the Salle à Manger, decorated in Henri II style (top right), the chamber of Francis I with the royal emblem of the salamander engraved on the fireplace (left), and the Blue Room (bottom right), which belonged to Maréchal de la Barre, who was killed in the siege of Nice in 1705.

311 A plain four-poster bed, an original marble table, wall hangings and golden yellow curtains with the most popular flower patterns, and a monumental fireplace are the few concessions to luxury in the simple, cozy bedroom of Francis I.

A CASTLE OF WEAPONRY AND LOVE: LANGEAIS

312 The marriage of
Charles VIII to Anne
of Brittany was
celebrated in Langeais
Castle in 1491. The
hall where the
wedding took place,
with its great
tapestries and beamed
ceiling, remains intact
(bottom right). The
royal bedchamber,
with its four-poster bed
(bottom left),
exemplifies the
furnishings typical of
great 15th-century
mansions. In
Langeais Castle, 13
chambers are hung
with 15th- and 16th-
century Flemish
tapestries. The chapel
(top left) has the
typical inverted-hull-
shaped ceiling.

*I*n the numerous castles that follow the Loire Valley from Gien to Saumur, the desire for beauty replaced the need for defensive security in the century of the Renaissance. Langeais Castle, situated to the west of Tours by the riverside, is the only medieval fortress that has remained intact and has never been changed over the centuries by rebuilding work. After passing through the main door visitors enter the inner courtyard, where they see the ruins of a high wall, part of the ancient fortress built in 994 by Foulques the Red, founder of the Anjou Dynasty, a farsighted politician and strategist, but also a treacherous, cynical feudal brigand.

Langeais Castle and the entire province of Touraine passed to the Counts of Anjou in the 11th century, then to the Plantagenets. During the Hundred Years' War it was occupied by the English on various occasions. The present castle was built by Louis XI. Charles VIII and Anne of Brittany were married there in 1491. The chronicles tell of the magnificent procession that escorted the future bride, clad in a gold and velvet robe decorated with 160 sables, into the king's presence, and of the magnificent banquet with flocks of doves, meat pies, patties containing warblers, quails and turtle doves, and boiled capons covered with fine gold. After the wedding the severe feudal castle must have seemed gloomy to the 15-year-old bride, who only a year later preferred to move with the court to Amboise Castle. Since then, Langeais Castle has never reappeared in the history books, but the austere style of its walls, the rooms hung with 16th-century tapestries and the valuable antique furniture beautifully recreate the atmosphere of its legendary past.

313 Proud and solemn
in its feudal armor,
Langeais Castle has
survived the ravages of
time and war
unharmed. The castle,
whose features are
typical of late 15th-
century defensive
architecture, overlooks
the Loire and the roofs
of the village below.

GREAT HISTORICAL EVENTS:
AMBOISE

*314 and 315
Medieval and
Renaissance styles are
blended in the
majestic Amboise
Castle, with its stone
friezes, spiral
staircases and
windows casting light
on halls and porticoes.
Standing high above
the Loire, the castle
still seems to control
its strategic position
as a defensive
bulwark by the ford.
For centuries that was
its function, with the
result that its walls
have witnessed a
great deal of history.*

Amboise Castle is one of the most important castles in the Loire Valley because of the historical events that took place there and the role it played in introducing Italian art into France. Its origins date from the Gallo-Roman period. In 500 Clovis, king of the Franks, met Alaric, king of the Visigoths, there. They challenged one another to a chivalrous duel, and Alaric was killed. Later, the importance of Amboise grew with the construction of the bridge over the Loire, because there were only seven bridges between Gien and Angers, and anyone who controlled them, thus enabling troops to cross the river, would control the entire region.

The promontory of Chatelliers, a spur of rock at the end of which stands Amboise Castle, was always a crossroads because of its ideal position at the confluence of the Loire and the Amasse. The bridge, town and castle were owned by the Counts of Amboise until the mid-15th century, when Charles VII ordered them to be confiscated in favor of his son Louis XI, who took up residence there with his wife, Charlotte of Savoy. Thus Charles VIII, who became king at the age of 13 and was already a courageous commander by the age of 20, was born at Amboise. On his return from the Italian campaign in 1494 he brought with him not only furniture, carpets and fabrics but also Italian artists, painters, tailors and craftsmen who soon changed the face of the castle. Amboise was transformed.

316 and 317 Charles
VIII, who became
king at the age of 13
and was already an
able commander at
20, was born at
Amboise. He left
Amboise to fight in
Italy, and on
returning to the banks
of the Loire in 1494,
decided to renovate
his castle in the

*Renaissance style he
had so admired south
of the Alps. The new
architectural canons
are evident at
Amboise Castle, where
flashes of Gothic style,
still evident, for
example, in the
Round Arch Room
(left), blend with the
new Renaissance
influences (right).*

Landscape gardener Pacello Mercogliano created the first Italianate garden; brilliant architects and sculptors embellished the residence in accordance with Renaissance style; and hundreds of Turkish carpets and tapestries from Flanders and Damascus adorned the magnificent rooms.

A solemn tournament was held to celebrate its renovation. On April 7, 1498, Easter Eve, Charles VIII, accompanied by his wife, Anne of Brittany, went to the Hacquelebac Gallery on the way to the tournament field. Charles forgot to bend his head, and though he was by no means tall, he accidentally hit his forehead against the entrance architrave. He still watched the tournament, but then fell into a coma and died at 9 o'clock the same evening. He was succeeded by his cousin Louis d'Orléans, who became King Louis XII, married Charles' widow, Anne of Brittany, and gave Amboise to Louise of Savoy, mother of Francis I of Angoulême, who was heir to the throne. When he became king in 1515, Francis I demonstrated a particular fondness for the castle where he had spent his childhood. He completed the wing begun by Louis XII and summoned Leonardo da Vinci from Italy.

318 top and 318-319
*Magnificent furnishings
and original paintings
decorate the rooms of
Amboise Castle, like the
room in Louis Philippe
style dominated by
crimson fabrics and
upholstery.*

319 *The hall is
dominated by the
great portraits
hanging on the walls,
including those of the
duke of Orléans (top
left) and Maria
Amelia of Bourbon
(top right).*

320 top The elegant Salle aux Poutres, designed and decorated between the 15th and 16th centuries, contains exquisite tapestries, beamed ceilings and priceless antique furniture.

320 left and 321 top and bottom The classic, severe style of the Renaissance period dominates these rooms of Amboise Castle; a good example is provided by the chamber of Henri II, with the large tapestries on the walls, great fireplaces, and four-poster beds.

320-321 *The classical style of furnishing characteristic of all the Loire chateaux can be seen in the Salle des Gardes, with its Gothic ceilings, and the rooms adjacent to it.*

322 and 323 Amboise Castle not only provided the venue for some major historical events; above all, it provided the base from which Renaissance art was introduced into France because the great Leonardo da Vinci (shown here in a marble bust at top left) moved from Milan to spend the rest of his life there. His tomb is in St. Hubert's Chapel, constructed in flamboyant Gothic style with large windows and a richly decorated portal.

324 and 325 After loading some precious canvases, including the Mona Lisa, onto mules, Leonardo da Vinci left Florence for Amboise at the age of 64. Here Francis I is shown awaiting the great artist, to whom he donated Clos-Lucé Castle, where he spent the rest of his life.

His spirit can be felt in every room, such as the bedroom with the four-poster bed and large stone fireplace where he died, and in the collection on the basement of scale models of brilliant machines that he designed and about which he left detailed notes.

AN ARTIST'S JOURNEY
AND A KING'S FRIENDSHIP
LEONARDO DA VINCI AND FRANCIS I:
FROM AMBOISE TO CLOS-LUCÉ

*L*eonardo, at the age of 64, loaded the canvases of the Mona Lisa, St. Anne and John the Baptist onto mules, left Florence, and set off for Amboise with his faithful disciple, Francesco Melzi, and his servant, Battista di Villanis. Francis I received the Italian genius at Amboise, and gave him Cloux Castle (now Clos-Lucé) and an annuity of 700 gold scudos. All he required in exchange was the pleasure of conversation with him. From 1516, Leonardo spent the last years of his life in the Loire Valley, masterminding splendid parties, masked balls and artists' conferences, and continuing his studies of engineering and anatomy. He lies in St. Hubert's Chapel in Amboise Castle. On the death of Francis I in 1547, the decline of Amboise began. In the 17th century Louis XIII visited the castle to hunt in the nearby forest, but under Louis XIV the mighty walls became grim state prisons. Amboise castle regained its past glory under Louis XV, who gave it to the duke of Choiseul, and later under Napoleon, who confiscated the castle and gave it to a member of the Directory, Roger Ducos. The latter had insufficient funds to maintain the great building and demolished part of it, but despite this mutilation, the castle still presents a faithful picture of what court life must have been like 400 years ago.

There were two mighty towers, about 22 yards tall, with spiral staircases, in which a horse could be ridden right to the top; the king's apartments, the guardroom, and a wonderful view from the large terrace over the Loire and its tributary, the Amasse, complete the picture of one of the most spectacular castles in the valley. A long walk from Amboise is the magic of Clos-Lucé Castle, the residence of Leonardo da Vinci. The king and the "painter-cum-engineer" got along extraordinarily well; both of them enthusiastically cherished fantastic dreams. Leonardo was planning to build prefabricated wooden houses for the populace, to connect all the Loire castles with a series of canals, to make flying machines with wings. His designs and intuitions were ahead of their time in a century of humanists not given to flights of fancy. The time was not yet ripe for the scientific innovations that continually issued from the mind of the great genius, and everything remained on paper. At Clos-Lucé, in the very rooms that witnessed this outpouring of ideas and the long talks between the Italian artist and his royal patron, the astonished visitor can view the collection of manuscripts and the models of machines reconstructed in accordance with Leonardo's detailed instructions.

326 top and 326-327 Magic and mystery inhabit Chaumont Castle, with its pale stone and sloping slate roofs, situated just a few miles from Amboise and Blois, which were so powerful in the Middle Ages.

A QUEEN'S DARK SECRETS: CHAUMONT

The memory of Catherine de Médicis pervades the halls of Chaumont Castle. In 1560, as widow of Henri II, she bought the castle to take her revenge for her husband's adultery and force his mistress, Diane de Poitiers, to exchange it for Chenonceau Castle, which Henri had given her in 1547, when he ascended to the throne. The beautiful Diane could hardly refuse, but did not stay long at Chaumont, preferring exile at Anet Castle, where she died seven years later, far from the gossip of the Loire Valley.

The memory of the great Catherine is still very much alive at Chaumont. Her adviser on the occult arts, the sorcerer Ruggieri, is said to have stayed there, and the existence of a room connected to a tower by a steep staircase has led to rumors of a secret hideaway where the queen and her adviser retired to conduct magic rites and interrogate the stars about the future. Catherine is said to have discovered the tragic destiny awaiting her three children and the imminent advent of the Bourbons at Chaumont. The castle stands on a hill overlooking the left bank of the river. Until the 15th century it was the feudal fortress of the Counts of Blois; it was later rebuilt with round guard towers and softened by the addition of conical roofs and Renaissance influences. It passed through the hands of various owners, including the chatelain who demolished the north wing in the 18th century to obtain a better view of the Loire, and one Le Ray who, also in the 18th century, arranged for the famous Italian pottery maker Battista Nini to stay there. The latter set up his workshop in the stables, and his great kiln in an old dovecote. He made an important contribution to the history of art by reproducing numerous copies of ceramic medallions of the most famous personalities of the period, some of which are on display in the rooms of the castle leading to the chambers of Diane, Catherine and the astrologer Ruggieri.

328-329 Chaumont Castle, the feudal fortress of the Counts of Blois until the 15th century, was later rebuilt with round watchtowers and ornamented with conical roofs and Renaissance influences.

330 The air of mystery with which Chaumont Castle was rife soon became a legend; the main centers from which this fascination still radiates are the chamber of Queen Catherine de Médicis (bottom right) in her favorite green, that of the sorcerer Ruggieri (top right), and the chapel, with its pointed stained-glass windows (top left).

331 The narrow Gothic-style staircase that runs through the heart of the castle perhaps led to the mysterious laboratory of the occult arts presided over by Ruggieri, the powerful court astrologer who predicted the death of Henri III, which put an end to the reign of the Valois dynasty.

332 and 333 Though it boasts three main buildings, a keep and a court of honor, Villandry Castle does not tell the stories of kings and queens. Spanish magnate Carvallo came to Villandry after the Second World War with the intention of buying the ancient castle to create a special garden.

The rooms, with the original marble checkerboard floor (bottom right), can be visited, and the architectural design of the mighty building admired, but then the visitor will inevitably be drawn to the flower gardens, the avenues lined with lime trees and the unusual vegetable garden (top left).

IN BALZAC'S LOVELY COUNTRYSIDE: VILLANDRY

Nature reigns supreme in the quiet Touraine; meadows and forests play with the silvery ribbon of the river that flows, murmurs and splashes in the royal gardens and penetrates everywhere, constituting the characteristic feature of the gentle, sunny landscape of the Loire Valley. The charm of Villandry Castle revolves around its unique gardens. The history of France has never entered its walls, nor was it ever the home of a king or a courtesan. It was built about 10 miles from Tours by Jean le Breton, prime minister of Francis I, in 1536. He constructed three horseshoe-shaped buildings opening onto the Loire Valley on the foundations of a feudal fortress that was demolished, and of which only the south keep remains. Cross windows, dormer windows with carved pediments and tall, steeply sloping slate roofs form a complex of rare harmony, although the turrets and pinnacles have not survived. A simpler style, which was later to become the Henri IV style, was beginning to predominate in monumental architecture. However, the history of the castle is of little importance at Villandry. It is the square gardens, arranged by color and obsessively well tended, that invite the visitor to roam among terraces, kitchen gardens and flower beds whose colors change from season to season. The layout of the gardens was restored to its original 16th-century design by Spanish millionaire Carvallo, who became the castle's owner after the

Second World War. After discovering the original designs by Androuet du Cerceau, the architect who created the gardens, Carvallo recreated the original structure, with three terraces built on different levels, avenues shaded by lime trees, straight paths along which flowers blossom, box hedges clipped by topiarists and the curious herbariums of the medieval monks; visitors can stroll through the garden of love and the garden of music, amid mallow and chervil, beets, cabbage seedlings and pumpkins.

335 The ornamental gardens dedicated to love are clearly seen from the panoramic terrace. The designer intended the arrangement of the hedges to reflect the symbols of various types of love: hearts and flames represented tender love, deformed hearts delirious love, swords and daggers tragic love, and fans and letters of the alphabet elusive love.

334 Androuet du Cerceau designed the gardens of Villandry, magnificent green spaces that still retain their original appearance, with three terraces built at different levels. The layout of the gardens not only reflects the taste of the period, but also aims to recreate a philosophical symbolism in the arrangement of hedges and floral decorations. Some very rare species, often from distant regions, were cultivated here in the 16th century.

336 *Chenonceau was built for Christine Briçonnet, given to Diane de Poitiers (portrayed as Diana the Huntress by Primaticcio, bottom left) by her lover Henri II (shown in a contemporary portrait, bottom left), reclaimed by Catherine de Médicis, and passed on to Louise of Lorraine, widow of Henri III, who spent 12 years mourning there.*

THE CASTLE OF QUEENS: CHENONCEAU

Just a stone's throw from the flourishing, idyllic rural town of Montrichard stands the most frequently visited and most romantic castle in the Loire Valley: Chenonceau, known as "the castle of six ladies" because of the role played by six chatelaines in its 400-year history. This *caprice des femmes* is famous for its five-span bridge and the two-storey gallery over the Cher, as well as the 15th-century circular keep, the gardens dedicated to Catherine and Diane, the two women who shared the king's favors, and the interior, including Diane de Poitiers' room, Catherine de Médicis' green study, and the queen's chamber, decorated with Gobelin tapestries. At different times the castle was inhabited by Mme. Catherine Briconnet, who built it with her husband, Thomas Bohier, Diane de Poitiers, who was given it by her lover Henri II, Catherine de Médicis, who reclaimed it on her husband's death, and Louise of Lorraine, widow of Henri III, who mourned her husband's death there, dressed in white according to royal protocol; she is said to have murmured nothing but prayers for 12 years.

After Louise of Lorraine, Chenonceau fell into a period of decline until Mme Dupin became its owner in the 18th century, and one of the most famous literary salons of the age devel-

oped around her and Jean-Jacques Rousseau, her son's tutor. In 1864 the castle was bought by Mme Pelouze, who meticulously restored its original design and then sold it to the present owners, the Menier family.

The grace of its design, the airy beauty of the gallery built by Catherine de Médicis and the tidy grounds once provided the romantic setting for the lives of queens and courtesans, which are recreated every summer evening in a sound-and-light show.

337 *So ethereal that it seems to glide through the blue waters of the Cher like a stone galleon, so rich in history that every corner of the expansive grounds and halls evoke the ghosts of the ladies who lived, suffered, rejoiced and intrigued between the walls there, Chenonceau is one of the most famous castles in France.*

338 *The rooms of the castle are richly decorated, as they must have been at the height of its glory: some good examples are the large kitchen (bottom right), the Gothic gallery with its ogival vaults (left) and the chamber of Gabrielle d'Estrée, King Henri IV's mistress (top right).*

338-339 *Pure gold and crimson tapestries decorate Louis XIII's chamber, with its magnificent fireplace and the portrait of Louis XIV attributed to Rigaud and set off by a magnificently carved and gilded frame. On the right can be seen the great fireplace with the symbols of the ermine and the salamander, belonging to Francis I and his bride, Claude de France.*

339 top *The gallery, illuminated by 18 windows ordered by Catherine de Médicis for court banquets, was used as a hospital during the First World War.*

340 top *The Chambre des Reines is a delightful blend of style and luxury; the room is dominated by Diane de Poitiers' bed, which, according to legend, had an "extraordinary" effect on those who reclined in it.*

340 left *Italian furniture appeared in French palaces as early as the 16th century. The item shown in this photo, decorated with ivory and mother-of-pearl, is the work of 15th-century Florentine craftsmen.*

341 *Diane de Poitiers' bedroom, known as the Chambre des Reines, contains two impressive Flemish tapestries of rare beauty (the one in the picture above portrays scenes from court life) and a massive fireplace decorated with the royal symbols in pure gold (right photo).*

340-341 *The chamber of César de Vendôme, son of Henri IV and Gabrielle d'Estrée, who owned the castle in the 17th century, contains a wealth of gold and tapestries.*

342 The graceful
Renaissance design,
the perfection of the
gallery built by order
of Catherine de
Médicis, the round
feudal keep built at
the corner with the
drawbridge and the
huge grounds, with
Diane's garden on one
side, framed by flower
beds, and Catherine
de Médicis' garden
on the other,
surrounded by great
trees, provided the
setting for the opulent
court life lived on
banks of the Loire
(reconstructed on
summer evenings
today in sound-and-
light shows).

343 Chenonceau has inspired generations of painters through the ages; the charm and the tranquil, almost idyllic life of the castle is demonstrated by this 19th-century print, which shows a view of the central building and the bridge connecting it to the keep, with an artist painting the scene below.

344-345 Chenonceau Castle, the most admired and frequently visited castle in the Loire Valley, recounts its history to 800,000 visitors a year.

CRIME, INTRIGUE AND COURTLY LOVE: BLOIS

"Great souls," wrote Victor Hugo, "have left faint traces of their memory at Blois Castle." Its complex history has given the grandiose construction various styles, from the flowery Gothic of the façade to the Renaissance style of the famous staircase and the classical look of the Gaston d'Orléans wing. In the 14th century this medieval building, designed as a bridgehead on the Loire, belonged to the Counts of Châtillon, the last of whom sold it in 1391 to Duke Louis d'Orléans,

brother of Charles VI. When the duke was killed in Paris by the Burgundian John the Fearless, the castle passed into the hands of Charles d'Orléans, the family poet. Taken prisoner at the battle of Azincourt, Charles was incarcerated for 25 years, comforted by poetry and great literature. When he was released at the end of the Hundred Years' War, Charles d'Orléans thought no more of battle. At the age of 50 he fell in love with the 14-year-old Marie de Clèves, married her and went back to live at Blois Castle, surrounded by writers, artists and an army of architects who demolished the old fortress and erected a stone and brick building.

The complex, with its magnificent Renaissance staircase, was embellished by Francis I, who ascended to the throne in 1515, married Claude de France, by whom he had seven children, and built the famous staircase and the splendid fireplaces. Catherine de Médicis gave an aura of mystery to the royal apartments; behind secret

doors in her study she concealed precious documents, her famous pearl necklace and, so it was rumored, bottles of poison. Catherine de Médicis' hideaway, which has remained almost intact, still features 237 carved wooden panels that conceal cupboards that can only be opened by pressing a pedal concealed in a plinth. Francis II, Charles IX and Henri III reigned at Blois between 1547 and 1574, directed by their able mother, Catherine de Médicis. The history of the castle recommenced under Henri III. The States General were convened in the huge hall on the ground floor in 1576 to demand the suppression of the Huguenot religion. The States General were again convened in 1588 by Duke Henri de Guise who, supported by the king of Spain, attempted to depose the king. But before going down to the hall where he was expected, Henri III arranged for his rival to be led into a trap and stabbed. The king watched the murder from his chamber. Eight months later, he was to meet the same fate by the hand of Jacques Clément. Until 1617, when Louis XIII sent his mother, Maria de Médicis, into exile there, Blois played no part in history. However, Maria did not stay long. One night, after two years of boredom, she, despite her bulk, climbed down a rope ladder from the window; her son had no choice but to reconcile with his mother after her adventurous escape. However, by then Louis XIII had discovered that Blois, which was quite

a long way from Paris, made an excellent gilded prison. In 1626 he sent his brother Gaston d'Orléans there, promising him sufficient funds to build a residence worthy of his rank. Gaston, forgetting his love of political conspiracy, had the architect Mansart draw up plans for a castle, which required the demolition of the existing wings. For three years, work on a new wing opposite the main door in the courtyard proceeded apace. Then, after the birth of Louis XIV, the danger that Gaston might inherit the throne of France receded; Cardinal Richelieu cut off the funds and the work came to a halt. Gaston, dissatisfied with the new section he had built, went to live in the Francis I wing, and devoted his time to collecting rare plants.

349 top left The influence exerted in France by the discovery of the Italian Renaissance is due to Francis I, who conducted a military campaign in Italy; this influence is particularly evident in the staircase of the Francis I wing in the inner courtyard of Blois Castle.

349 top right The Gaston d'Orléans wing (the magnificent staircase of which can be seen in this photo) overlooks the inner courtyard. Work on this wing began in 1635 and lasted for three years, until Cardinal Richelieu cut off the funds required.

350 top Visitors can once again follow in the footsteps of Catherine de Médicis at Blois Castle. Her chamber is rich in gold work and luxurious "trifles," such as the four-poster bed and the unusual floor with its gilded tiles framed with the ever-present fleur-de-lys.

350-351 From
Catherine's bedroom,
access is obtained to
her private hideaway,
its walls covered with
fake panels made of
wood and pure gold
that conceal secret
hiding places.

351 top left and
bottom left As at
Chenonceau, the most
luxurious furniture
at Blois came from
Italy. Tuscan
craftsmen, in
particular, were very
popular in the 15th
and 16th centuries,
and were
particularly respected
in France.

351 right Scenes
from court life were
immortalized by
artists of the period,
as in this tondo by
Ulysse Besnard,
known as Ulysse XIX,
which shows
Catherine de Médicis
receiving some
ambassadors.

352 top left and bottom The salamander motif, emblem of Francis I, appears in the friezes on the fireplaces and in the furniture made specially for the king.

352 top right This portrait shows Marguerite of Navarre, known as Queen Margot, the sister of King Henri III of France.

352-353 More halls, chambers and galleries of the grandiose Blois Castle, with fireplaces bearing the initials and symbols of Francis I and Claude de France, Renaissance furniture and portraits; the wall decorations, however, are typical of the late 19th and early 20th centuries.

353 top Another 39 historical portraits from the French royal court, as well as Margot's, crowd the gallery in the Louis XII wing.

353 bottom The busts of Henri II, Henri III, Henri IV and Charles IX have been placed in the Galerie des Loges, among magnificent pieces of ivory-inlaid Italian furniture and tapestries of the Flemish school.

354 top The portrait of Louis XIV attributed to Hyacinthe Rigaud pays homage to one of the most powerful French monarchs in history; however, Louis XIV never spent even a day at Blois Castle.

354-355 The rooms, halls and staircases of Blois Castle present the set patterns of what was once the classic style of castle furnishing: the King's Room, with its four-poster bed, the great fireplaces in every room, coffered ceilings and tapestries hanging from the walls.

355 top This picture shows a detail of the tapestry hanging in the bedroom of Henri III; the three fleurs-de-lys, the king's initial and the royal crown are recognizable.

355 bottom The windows illuminating the Salle des États also bear symbols of the Capetian dynasty's power; on the left is the ermine, the emblem of Anne of Brittany, and on the right the porcupine, emblem of Louis XII.

356 top *The small Beauregard Castle contains a gallery of 327 portraits, unique in the history of the Loire châteaux. The portraits in the long Galerie des Illustres include that of Henry IV on horseback.*

356-357 *Beauregard Castle, nestled in Russy Forest, is cradled by the calm Beuvron Valley.*

THE CHARM OF GREAT MANSIONS: BEAUREGARD AND CHEVERNY

*L*uxuriant, restful countryside leads from Blois to nearby Beauregard Castle, situated at the end of a long drive that cuts through Russy Forest. This small, secluded private castle, its dimensions still as perfect as when it was commissioned in the 16th century by Jean du Thier, secretary of state to Henri II, is worth a visit for its rooms, the large kitchen decorated as in ancient times, and the gallery containing 327 portraits of famous personalities, which is unique in the history of the Loire castles. This Galerie des Illustres was installed by Paul Ardier in the large first-floor gallery that once contained an attractive 16th-century white marble fireplace. The personalities portrayed are prelates, kings, queens, professors and military commanders spanning two centuries. Some pretty delft tiles in the characteristic blue and white colors, laid along the walls in 1628, decorate the austere row of characters hanging side by side, who recount the history of France. At nearby Cheverny Castle, dating from the 17th century, it is the charm of a great mansion, inhabited for 300 years by the family of the marquises of Vibraye and their successor, viscount of Sigelas, that enchants visitors, who can view its magnificent library, painted halls, grandiose weapons room and a collection of 2,000 hunting trophies. The pack of fox-hunting dogs barking excitably from the kennels on one side of the castle recall the great hunting tradition of the castle's owners.

357 top left The 16th-century Cabinet des Grelots is entirely covered with magnificent wood paneling and paintings depicting such subjects as hunting, music and games.

357 top right The great castle kitchen, with its hanging copper pans, is fascinating.

357 bottom right Joan of Arc is portrayed in the Galerie des Illustres.

358 and 359
The family of the
marquises de Vilbraye
lived in Cheverny
Castle for 300 years.
They retained intact
the majestic
proportions of the

rooms, the
magnificent
furnishings of the
king's chamber, as
well as the castle's
Gobelin tapestries
and paintings and
valuable prints.

*360 top Rooms
containing a wealth
of furnishings and
pure gold lead to the
dining room,
containing a rare
carved cabinet, the
Queen's Room, the
well-stocked library
and the orangery (the
photo shows the gaudy
beamed ceiling).*

360-361 Cheverny Castle, made of Bourré stone with slate roofs, is an architectural ensemble with a classical style that marks a development in the evolution of the Loire châteaux.

361 top left The Weapons Room houses part of the castle's extensive collection of military objects.

361 bottom left The large drawing room, in Louis XIII style, contains a wealth of furnishings, from the large red carpet at the foot of the fireplace to the furniture and decorations in blue and pure gold.

361 right The imposing straight Renaissance staircase is flanked by balustrades; the stone it is made of is decorated with reliefs portraying flowers and 18th-century weapons.

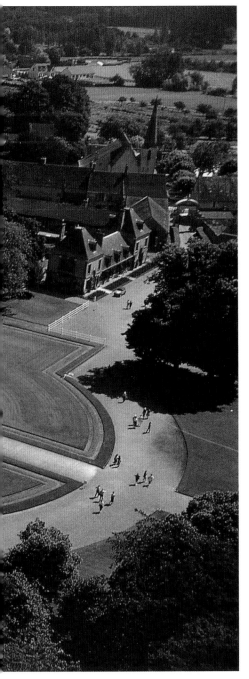

A KING'S DREAM: CHAMBORD

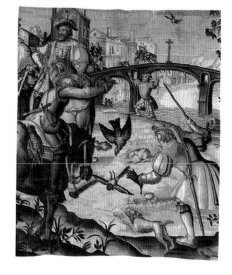

*F*inally, we come to Chambord, a mirage from afar and a labyrinth to visit. Visitors should climb the Renaissance staircase, visit the rooms, go out onto the terraces, look down on the huge grounds and come as close as possible to the forest of pinnacles and turrets. This is how the megalomaniac dream of Francis I appears, in all its splendor. That ambitious king, with his ardent temperament and craving for novelty, glory and splendor, concluded his architectural dreams here. Numbers are not everything, but they give some idea of the scale of this magnificent site: 440 rooms, 80 staircases and 365 fireplaces surrounded by about 13,750 acres of perfectly rectangular grounds (about 3,750 of which are open to the public) crowded with deer and wild boar and surrounded by boundary walls about 20 miles long. Chambord is without doubt the most extravagant, exaggerated and majestic castle in the entire Loire Valley. Plundered during the Revolution, belonged then to Marshal Berthier and to the dukes of Bordeaux, then taken over by the government in 1930, Chambord Castle is the unrivaled star of the Loire Valley. Above all it is a hymn to grandeur; with its tufa and slate roof resembling a hanging garden and a thousand pillars, pinnacles, chimney pots and skylights, it would come as no surprise to see fairies or impudent gnomes gamboling there.

362 and 362-363 The impressive Chambord Castle is the largest in Sologne; it stands not far from Blois, and is surrounded by a huge, ancient park. Its construction was started by order of Francis I, and completed during the reign of Louis XIV, the Sun King. Not all the rooms in Chambord Castle are furnished, but some of them contain a series of late 16th-century Paris tapestries portraying scenes of the king's hunt, woven following cartoons by Laurent Guyot.

363 top *This detail of one of the decorations that frame the tapestries of Chambord recalls motifs with a clearly neoclassical inspiration.*

364 and 364-365
The twin circular
staircase, about 9
yards wide, is the
heart of the great
castle; two people
can go up or down
it without meeting.
The staircase, with
its Renaissance
design, terminates
at the top with a
coffered vault
engraved with a
salamander, the
emblem of Francis I.

365 top left The
rectangular chapel
on the first floor,
situated in a round
tower, is the largest
room in the castle.
It was begun by
Francis I and
finished under Louis
XIV by architect
Harduin-Mansart.

365 top right
The furnishings of
Chambord Castle
are luxurious, and
great attention is
paid to every detail,
as demonstrated by
this radiator covered
with blue and white
majolica in the best
Flemish tradition.

366 and 367 The Queen's Room, the King's Room and the rooms of the Count of Chambord in Chambord Castle are furnished with valuable furniture, Amiens tapestries, four-poster beds and exquisite carpets.

The luxury exuded by these noble chambers is not reflected in all of the more than 400 rooms in the castle; Francis I's somewhat megalomanic dream of creating the most spectacular, majestic, regal castle in France was brought to an end by the revolution of 1789, during which Chambord was stripped of much of its finery. However, what remains clearly shows how magnificent it must have been at the height of its glory.

368 Among the most famous portraits at Chambord are those of the castle's founder, Francis I (top left), Henri IV (top right), Louis XIV (bottom left), who stayed there often, and Stanislaw Leczinski, king of Poland and duke of Bar and Lorraine (bottom right).

368-369 The Salle de Compagnie at Chambord Castle contains a magnificent collection of portraits of outstanding personalities from the reigning French monarchy and illustrious foreign guests.

369 bottom
This young face with an enigmatic smile belongs to Mlle de Blois, one of the most courted and powerful French women of the time.

370 top *Montigny-le-Gannelon Castle, with its alternating brick and stone decoration and tall slate roofs, dates from the late 14th century, when the defensive structure was beginning to be replaced by the castle residence, still grandiose but more worldly than military.*

370-371 *High above the Loir River (not to be confused with the Loire), Châteaudun Castle, with its feudal bulk and slate roofs, overlooks the small town below. A stronghold demolished by the Norman Rollon in 911 already existed on the site in the 5th century.*

CASTLES
AND THE REMEMBRANCE
OF THINGS PAST

T o the north of the Loire River, in the romantic heart of France, the great castles become few and far between. Here, the landscape has the fragrance of harvest time, the charm of deserted horizons and, to the west, already heralds the Normandy countryside, with its boundless greenery and pastures. This area contrasts sharply with the grandiose Loire Valley and its magnificent castles, but here, unspoiled nature and wide-open spaces still lead to lesser known castles, that are no less rich in memories and links with the history of the Loire Valley. The castle of Châteaudun is impressive for the steep crag on which it perches, and the castle of Montigny-le-Gannelon for its magnificent furnishings. Another king's mistress, Mme de Maintenon, leads the tour through the splendors of the castle named after her, while Diane de Poitiers lies in Anet Castle, and the dream of grandeur cherished by the marquis de Laborde sleeps at La Ferté-Vidame. Memories of Proust fill the country footpaths and lanes of Illiers-Combray against the distant background of Chartres and its huge cathedral, reaching for the sky.

371 At the end of a narrow street in the village of Illiers-Combray stands the small 19th-century middle-class home of Proust's aunt and uncle, where the famous author spent his Easter holidays as a boy. Everything has remained as it was recounted in À la Recherche du Temps Perdu – the inner garden with its rosebushes and hydrangeas and the author's bedroom are still there.

MORE HALLS, STAIRCASES
AND FORTIFIED WALLS:
MONTIGNY-LE-GANNELON
AND CHÂTEAUDUN

*H*igh above the Loir (not to be mistaken with the Loire), the castle of Montigny-le-Gannelon, already a fortress in the time of Charlemagne, acquired its present name in the year 1000 and its Renaissance style in the 16th century, under Louis XII, when Jacques de Renty demolished the ancient fortress to build a new residence in the contemporary style. All that remains of that project is the Ladies' Tower and the Clock Tower, which were later connected at the base by a Gothic gallery. The property passed through the hands of various owners, statesmen and princes, such as Adrien, lord of Montmorency, duke of Laval and Louis XVIII's ambassador to Rome, Madrid, London and Vienna, who is often mentioned during the visit. This visit is particularly interesting because it is conducted by a member of the present-day family of the viscounts of Talhouët Boisorhand, who live in the castle and know the history and legends of the area. The building was altered on various occasions; the last and most visible alteration was ordered by Count Sigismond de Lévis, who completely rebuilt the east façade overlooking the Loir in 1886.

*372 top and 373
The rooms in the
castle, decorated in
red, blue and gold,
are full of priceless
antique furniture
and portraits of
illustrious members of
the family. The castle
now belongs to the
descendants of the
family of viscount
of Talhouët, who
personally guide
visitors through the
castle, recounting
its history and
mysterious legends.*

374 left The Gothic-Renaissance staircase leads to the large rooms on the second floor, hung with magnificent tapestries and decorated with coffered ceilings and marble fireplaces.

374 top right The dungeon, dating from the 12th century, has retained the amazing inner framework of exposed beams.

375 Châteaudun Castle belonged to the d'Orléans family, which extended, decorated, fortified and defended it against enemy attack for four centuries (from the 14th to 18th centuries). It was above all Jean d'Orléans (known as "the Bastard" because he was the illegitimate son of Louis I d'Orléans) who undertook the building of the castle as it survives now, incorporating the tall keep.

374 bottom right Three different periods – feudal, Gothic and Renaissance – have given the castle its grandeur. The 12th-century keep is built onto the Sainte-Chapelle, part of the Dunois wing, dating from the 15th century, which is illuminated by large Gothic windows.

The 15 wooden statues in the chapel portray members of the d'Orléans family, carved in the images of saints and beatified personalities, like the tiny Saint Agnes and the Saint Francis, who are none other than Agnès of Savoy and François de Longueville.

Around 6 miles from Montigny-le-Gannelon, the towering bulk of another castle is reflected in the river: this is Châteaudun. The unusual design of the castle, which overlooks the main road to Alençon, is very impressive. However, for visitors arriving from the Chartres direction, the gray walls lose their severe look and acquire the harmony of a Renaissance mansion, with the staircase carved like lace, the great fireplaces, the chapel decorated with magnificent wooden statues, and the tapestries hanging in the reception room.

It was Jean le Dunois who first decided to give his home two faces, representing a compromise between the feudal past and the desire for a more modern residence. The Norman architect Colin du Val, who hailed from Longueville, built the decidedly Renaissance north wing (called the Dunois wing) between the 12th-century tower and the buttress overlooking the Loir. There is a magnificent view from the towers, and as the visit proceeds from room to room the guide tells the stories of Thibault the Trickster, who built the feudal castle (of which nothing now remains), and Jean le Dunois, loyal general of Charles VII and comrade in arms of Joan of Arc at the siege of Orléans, who was the guiding force behind Châteaudun.

*376 top In Aunt
Léonie's famous room
(left) at Illiers-
Combray, Proust
(portrait on right)
was overwhelmed by
the memories evoked
by a little madeleine
dipped into the lime
tea served by his
aunt.*

THE VILLAGE OF THE SWEET MADELEINE

*I*n the huge plain of Beauce, a bell tower pierces the sky like a sharp pencil. "It was the first thing to appear when the train was pulling in to Combray," wrote Proust in *À la Recherche du Temps Perdu*. The pages of his novel seem to turn at every step one takes in the village of Illiers-Combray, which has added the name invented by the author to its own. Here, Proust arrived to spend the Easter holidays at the small house at the bottom of the garden at 4, Rue Docteur-Proust, where many remembrances still remain along with the memory of the sweet, unforgettable madeleine.

Nothing has changed, and on the first floor, Aunt Léonie's room still evokes the atmosphere of that famous page where the author, from the flavor of the morsel of madeleine dipped into the lime tea, recalls past memories. From far off can be seen Chartres Cathedral, which celebrated its 800th anniversary in 1994. At sunset, in the twilit nave, the light sets fire to the reds and blues of the famous 13th-century windows illustrating the lives of the saints, the ancient trades of France, and many Bible stories. The small dark Virgin is venerated at the end of the left-hand aisle. The great statues covering the façade return in the bas-reliefs surrounding the high altar inside, commemorating the art of Jehan de Beauce, who carved the exceptional row of people at prayer in 1514. The still medieval part of the town clusters around the two asymmetrical bell towers in a network of narrow alleys. In the motionless peace of the countryside sleeps Senoches, capital of Perche, the region of good cider. From the small town romantic walks branch off into the nearby forest, around the pond of Lille and La Ferté-Vidame. Nestled in Thymerais Forest, this grandiose patrician residence, now in ruins, still evokes the splendors of the court of the marquis de Laborde, who built his palace in the 18th century on the foundations of the previous castle, where Duke Saint-Simon (author of *Les Mémoires*) lived. The castle was partly destroyed and plundered during the Revolution, and so it has remained until the present day. Fields and meadows protect the abandoned building, which was too large and too magnificent for its bygone splendor to be adequately restored. Maintenon Castle, with its 12th-century keep, the grace of the Renaissance wing and the neoclassical proportions of the side built by Louis XIV, still maintains its royal air. Surrounded by huge grounds, part of which have been sold to the most exclusive golf club in France, the castle was given by Louis XVI to his mistress, Mme de Maintenon, who later became his secret wife. Its drawing rooms and great halls, curtains, velvets, damasks and antique furniture all remain just as they were at the time when the famous lady of the court withdrew with her king to the calm countryside of Eure.

ANET CASTLE: THE TOMB OF BEAUTIFUL DIANE

From Maintenon it is only a short distance to Anet Castle, the last piece in the huge mosaic of residences associated with the history of the Loire. It was built in 1550 by order of King Henri II, who gave it to his mistress, Diane de Poitiers, as their love nest. The message of this residence is apparent right from the entrance portal, a triumphal arch in honor of "Diana the Huntress," with the naked nymph sculpted by Benvenuto Cellini in the lunette; it was a refuge of pleasure, not a theater of war like many other châteaux of the Loire. The most enlightened minds of the time gathered at Anet, and the king and his mistress went hunting or walked in nearby Dreux Forest. The castle, like many others, was damaged and plundered during the Revolution. It was sold, the furniture was scattered, and part of the castle was demolished by unscrupulous purchasers. In 1820 it was bought by the duchess of Orléans and restored for the first time. However, it was to take years, until nearly the end of the century, before M. Moreau and his descendants restored the home so that it was worthy of the history it recounts. Now preciously decorated, each room evokes the memory of the king's lovely mistress. Four tapestries woven especially for her in 1552 decorate the Salle des

Gardes; other Flemish tapestries drape the walls of the room containing a fireplace decorated with an alabaster medallion by Jean Goujon; the four-poster bed with its canopy bears her initials and sentimental souvenirs belonging to Diane are displayed in the Red Room. In the courtyard is the entrance to Saint Thomas' Chapel. Diane's tomb is in the garden, behind the chapel. After the king's death, she took lonely refuge in this castle, where she lived until her death in 1566. Her last residence closes the romantic and dissolute history of the Loire Valley castles.

378 left At the end of the last century the castle was restructured and decorated, and restoration work was carried out on the garden chapel, with its lovely Renaissance dome illuminating an inlaid marble floor that seems to reflect the ornamental motifs of the dome.

*378 top and 378-379
Anet Castle was King
Henri II's gift to his
lovely mistress, Diane
de Poitiers. Here the
king and Diane
retreated for short
periods, far from the
splendors and court
intrigue characteristic
of the castles closest to
the Loire. The
residence, situated on
the edge of Dreux
Forest, is a gem of
secluded Renaissance
beauty.*

*378 bottom right
Diane de Poitiers
(portrayed here as
Diana the Huntress)
retired to Anet after
the death of King
Henri II, when
Catherine de Médicis
took revenge by
confiscating
Chenonceau Castle.*

*379 The spirit of the
beautiful Diane can be
felt in every corner of
the castle, from the
splendid main staircase
(top left) to the
bedroom, with its
decorations, tapestries,
paintings and four-
poster bed (top right),
to the Salle des Gardes
(center right), decorated
with huge Fontainebleau
tapestries, to the
exquisite wood-paneled
Red Room (bottom
right).*

Provence
SECTION FOUR

INTRODUCTION

382 On the Vaucluse plateau around Sault, the village of honey, almonds and nougat, the fields of lavender in bloom seem to be paying a tribute to the wild barrenness of Mt. Ventoux and the mountains of Lure, where aromatic herbs reign supreme.

382-383 The Sault area is a spectacular blend of lavender, kitchen gardens and Saltus oak woods that once covered the entire territory. In fact, this delightful town with mild climate near the Nesque river was named after the oak tree.

383 top left In all of Provence the fields of sunflowers alternate with the olive groves and vineyards. Van Gogh was enchanted by them and painted their glorious yellow with the aim of celebrating a world that fascinated him with its blaze of colors.

A land of scents, sea, mountains and wind. A land exalted by painters and poets. Claude Monet came here to find the light that shines on his water lilies, Pablo Picasso chose Vallauris to be the site of a pottery, Georges Braque adored the countryside of Estaque around Marseilles which was where his ideas that developed into Cubism were inspired, and Mont Sainte-Victoire was made famous around the world by twelve paintings by Paul Cézanne, each of which depicted it in a different light.

With its clear, pure blue sky regularly swept by the mistral, Provence never fails to delight the traveler in search of emotions. From the enchanted clearness of the water in the fountain of Saint-Paul to the pale green of the sea at dawn when sea and coast merge like the colors of Cézanne and Bonnard. In contrast to the infinite shades of the water, there is the dazzling white limestone of the Calanques, the ochre earth at Roussillon, the dark green of the cluster pines, the golden yellow of the sunflowers and the paler yellow of the mimosa. Everywhere in Provence, the subtle smells of thyme, rosemary and mastic trees permeate the air, but it is the intense perfume of lavender that strikes one at the start of summer and blue carpets welcome the visitor to the magnificent abbey of Sénanque and the village of Sault that nestles between Monieux and Lagarde d'Apt. The gentle silver-grey landscapes of olive trees alternate with steep rocky walls, like the Grand Canyon of Verdon, the deepest in Europe and often compared to its namesake in Colorado. Such physical drama is contrasted by the gentle tranquillity of medieval hilltop villages with their twisting, narrow streets lined with cobbles, their houses roofed with round tiles colored with a pale pink that is seen nowhere else, and each with a small central square bordered by centuries-old plane trees where the locals play *pétanque*.

*383 top right
Provence is the
domain of lavender.
In late spring and
summer, the Valensole
plain, between the
Durance river and
the foothills of the
Alps at Digne, is
laden with the scent
of the lovely violet-
mauve lavender
flowers that cover the
earth like a soft,
endless cushion.*

covered with olive trees, lavender and irises were the love of Van Gogh.

For those who prefer bustle and liveliness to the silence of the inland villages, the short trip to the coast is all that is needed to enter the cosmopolitan atmosphere of the crowded port towns. The most famous of all, Saint-Tropez, "a charming and simple daughter of the sea" as defined by Guy de Maupassant in 1888 when he first visited, continues to bewitch the traveler with its famous Tahiti beach and ancient streets.

The worldliness of Saint-Tropez is countered by the simplicity of small ports like Bandol filled with brightly colored fishing boats.

The less well-known coastline between Cassis and Marseilles still has spectacular surprises in store for the first-time traveler: deep, narrow inlets are separated by limestone outcrops

Examples are Gordes, Saint-Paul de Vence, Tourrettes, Biot, Apt, Moustiers and Bormes-les-Mimosas to name but a few. These villages are announced from afar by the tower of a castle or a church with an elegant wrought iron cage in the shape of a prism containing, as if suspended in space, a bell. Its knells echo throughout the local villages whenever the wind blows. At one time they served as a warning to the villagers that the mistral was on its way and that they should shut themselves up in their houses with windows and doors barred. More intimate and retiring is the Lubéron where every Parisian dreams of having a *mas*: its ochre walls and gentle hills

386 top
The charming village of Roussillon is perched on the crest of a hill facing the ochre quarries. Seventeen shades of this earthy iron oxide color the surrounding landscape. In the past the natural ochre pigment extracted here was used for painting houses.

386-387 Les Baux-de-Provence attracts more visitors every year than the Louvre. Tourists are enchanted by the centuries-old streets with old buildings and by the medieval village that was built on the spur of white rock flanked by craggy gorges.

that rise perpendicularly from the sea and are topped by tufts of green. Lovers of unspoiled nature will enjoy the three Hyères islands where cars are forbidden and travel among the thick pinewoods is all on foot or by bicycle: the first, Porquerolles, was the setting for one of Georges Simenon's most famous detective stories, *Mon ami Maigret*, and is a safe shelter for sailors; then there is the national park on Port-Cros and the island of Levant.

The wild, lonely Camargue is a flat wetland of canals and marshes that fan out into the estuary of the Rhône. The Camargue is home to flocks of pink flamingos that suddenly rise up into the air from the marshes, wild horses and dark-colored bulls with lyre-shaped horns that are overseen by the *gardians*, the cowboys of France. At the end of May, gypsies arrive at Saintes-Marie-de-la-Mer from all over Europe to celebrate the festival of Saint Sarah, the black patron saint of the *gitans*.

The visitor in search of antiquities will find extraordinary sites. The roots of great cities like Marseilles, boastful and irreverent, home of Marcel Pagnol and Fernandel, grew out of the Greek civilization but most of all it was the genius of imperial Rome that has left its mark throughout Provence. Orange has one of the best known amphitheaters; Arles (the "merveilleuse petite ville" according to Alphonse Daudet in 1869) boasts a splendid arena, while Saint-Rémy is famous for its Antiques, the french name for the archeological site of the ancient roman town

Glanum. The artistic atmosphere found just about everywhere in Provence is celebrated with superb galleries and museums, large and small, in cities and villages, for example, Arles Antique, the Maeght collection, the Vasarély museum in Gordes, the Petit Palais in Avignon and the Léger museum in Biot. What marks the borders of Provence? As part of the French region Provence-Alpes-Côte d'Azur, the territory strictly only covers the departments of Bouches-du-Rhône, the Var and the Alpes-de-Haute-Provence but its heart beats in Vaucluse and Drôme all the way down to Grasse and Saint-Paul-de-Vence which were owned by the Counts of Provence up till the end of the 15th century.

390-391 At Salin-de-Giraud and west of the Petit Rhône, in the Camargue, lie the geometric salt works. Sea water is pumped onto the evaporation tables and leveled by small dams. At sunset the surface of these basins is covered with fascinating reddish hues.

The ochre earth at Roussillon

View of Les Baux

Ile du Levant, Hyères

Vaucluse

▲
Mount
Ventoux

Rodano

• Orange

Carpentras
•

• Avignon

Luberon

•Saint Rémy-
de Provence

•Arles   Les Alpilles

Durance

Etang de
Vaccarès

Etang
de Berre

Aix
en-Provence
•

Aigues-Mortes
•

Montagne
Sainte-Victoir

Camargue

Bouches-du-
Rhône

• Marseilles

Vineyards in the Barroux area

The Arch of Augustus, St-Rémy-de-Provence

Barcelonnette

Alpes-de-
Haute-Provence

Digne-les-Bains

Var

Alpes Maritimes

Verdon

Vence

Grasse

Massif
de l'Esterel

Argens

Côte d'Azur

Var

Massif
des Maures

Saint Tropez

Hyères

Pelicans at Camargue

Hyères Islands

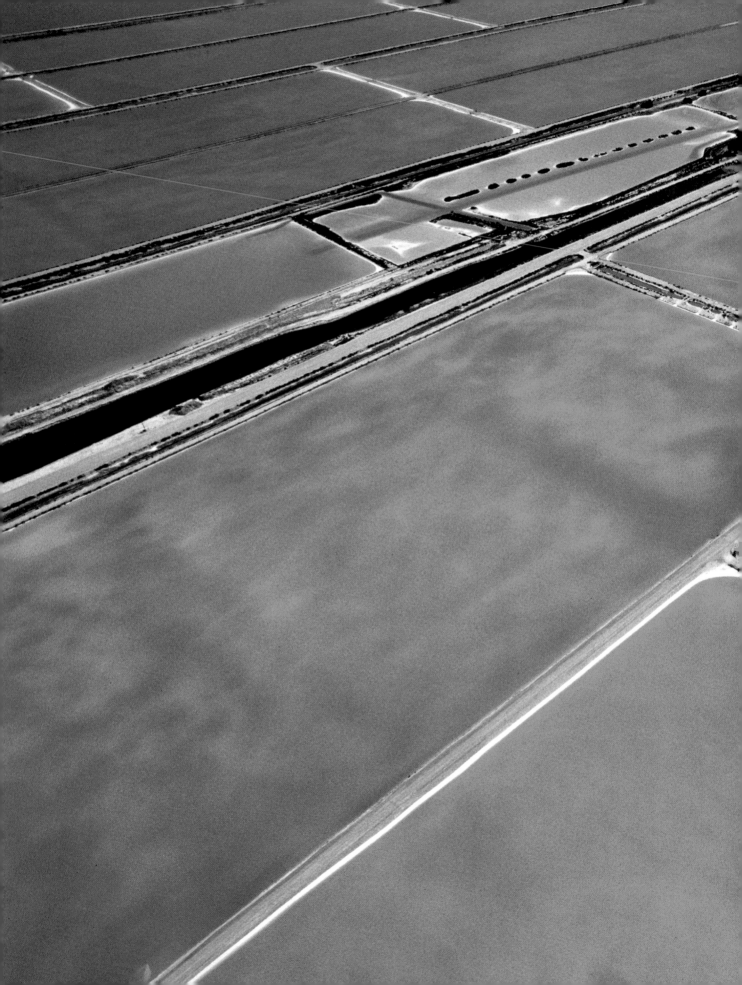

AN ENDURING LAND (THROUGH MILLENNIUMS)

392 top The Avignon Epigraphic Museum, one of the richest and most interesting of its kind in France, has this tablet with inscriptions in Greek and Celtic that bear witness to the contact between these two cultures.

The history of Provence is fascinating. Like a huge stage that opens onto the Mediterranean, the region bears the imprint of every epoch: Roman remains, medieval villages and elegant renaissance palaces. A thin thread connects the various stages of Provence's past, it is the spirit of independence that the region has always shown during the fundamental moments of its history.

The earliest remains worthy of note were immortalized in the fascinating rock-paintings around 2000 BC in the Vallée des Merveilles in the Alpes-Maritimes. The most important event, however, took place in 600 BC when a group of Greek colonizers, the Phocaeans, left the coasts of Asia Minor in search of a Mediterranean port that would allow them to control the tin market. Protected from the winds and supplied with excellent water sources, Massalia (modern day Marseilles) seemed the ideal spot. The new arrivals established solid relations with the local Celtic-Ligurian population to the point of sealing the friendship with the marriage of Protis, leader of the Phocaeans, to Gyptis, a member of a Celtic tribe. Massalia remained independent for five centuries from that time becoming a prosperous and well-known city. The Phocaeans introduced olives, figs, cherries and grapes as well as the concept of money. Able dealers, they instituted trading centers – the famous *comptoirs* – at Hyères, Saint-Tropez, Antibes, Nice and Monaco. From Massalia, Greek culture conquered the Liguri tribe that inhabited the nearby villages. Coins, pottery and Massalian culture spread inland and up the Rhône valley as is evidenced by the statues displayed in the Granet museum in Aix and the Archaeological Museum in Marseilles. The modern inhabitants of Arles still declare that the beauty and grace of their women is derived from their ancient Greek blood.

392 bottom In the Vallée des Merveilles, west of Tende, in the Maritime Alps region, the splendid rock paintings scattered here and there illustrate the primitive life of the people who lived here in 2000 B.C. These paintings, which are not without artistic value, evoke a world that is only apparently remote in time.

392-393 The left wing
of Palais Longchamp in
Marseilles is the home of
the Fine Arts Museum,
the majestic staircase of
which is decorated with
two canvases by Pierre
Puvis de Chavannes:
Marseilles, a Greek
Colony (above) and
Gate to the East. An
exceptional colorist,
Puvis de Chavannes
here recreates a
combination of the
golden age of Greek
civilization and a
vision of an enchanting
Orient that is perhaps
tinged with dream
fantasy.

393 bottom
A two-headed
sculpture of the god
Hermes, who was
worshipped by travelers
and merchants whose
trade often obliged
them to face the
unknown. This Celtic
work of obvious Greek
inspiration betrays an
art that has not yet
found the equanimity
that would distinguish
it in a later age. The
double head symbolizes
the glance of the god
that looks in every
direction to observe a
world that is yet to be
explored.

The wealth of Massalia quickly drew the interest of the Romans who began to create trading relations with the city during the fourth century BC. They were so well developed by the end of the second century BC that the Massalians asked help from the Romans to fight a coalition of Celtic and Liguri tribes that were attempting to take the city. Having arrived as peacemakers, in 122 BC the Romans founded a new city, Aquae Sixtiae, named after the consul Sextius Calvinus, which is today known as Aix-en-Provence. Then the Provincia Narbonese was created which took its name from Narbonne, the important center in the region. Seventy years later, in 49 BC, Julius Caesar inflicted the coup de grace on Massalia, already weakened by trading competition with its neighbors. The city, guilty of having supported Marius in the struggle against Caesar for political supremacy in Rome, fell definitively into ruin. This was instead the fortune of nearby Arles, which from this moment on became the preferred city of the Romans. They built the walls, the splendid arena (still used for bull-fighting), the baths, the forum and the Via Aurelia that connected Spain to Rome. In addition, and most important of all, they built the bridge made of boats across the Rhône which was to remain a means of communication of major importance for almost a thousand years. Arles is the city that mostly fo-

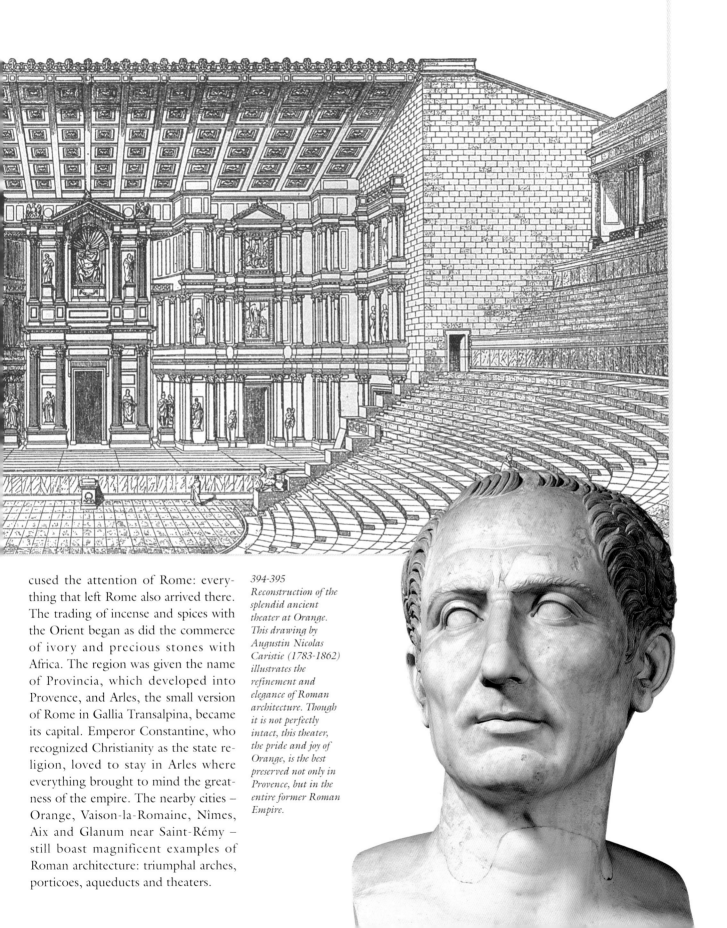

cused the attention of Rome: everything that left Rome also arrived there.
The trading of incense and spices with
the Orient began as did the commerce
of ivory and precious stones with
Africa. The region was given the name
of Provincia, which developed into
Provence, and Arles, the small version
of Rome in Gallia Transalpina, became
its capital. Emperor Constantine, who
recognized Christianity as the state religion, loved to stay in Arles where
everything brought to mind the great-
ness of the empire. The nearby cities –
Orange, Vaison-la-Romaine, Nîmes,
Aix and Glanum near Saint-Rémy –
still boast magnificent examples of
Roman architecture: triumphal arches,
porticoes, aqueducts and theaters.

394-395
Reconstruction of the
splendid ancient
theater at Orange.
This drawing by
Augustin Nicolas
Caristie (1783-1862)
illustrates the
refinement and
elegance of Roman
architecture. Though
it is not perfectly
intact, this theater,
the pride and joy of
Orange, is the best
preserved not only in
Provence, but in the
entire former Roman
Empire.

L'AMPHITÉÂTRE D'ARLES COMME IL EST, A PRÉSE

Était encore en 1824 époque où on en
en 1829 — hommage à Mr Laugier, Baron de
est mort dans le mois de novembre 1843 —

Commença Le déblaiement qu
Chartrouse à qui La ville d'arles recon

A.B

With the fall of the empire and the end of the *Pax Romana* during the fifth century, the future of Provincia also became uncertain. The end of Roman protection opened the floodgates to the Visigoths who destroyed Arles in 471. Provence was by that time known as the land of sun and abundance and as a true garden of Eden so its fortunes made it a desirable target for the greed of many other peoples. By the time the Saracens arrived, incursions were the order of the day. Despite having been sacked, the rich city of Arles continued to enjoy a certain comfort until the eighth century when the Moors destroyed the city's lifeline, its bridge over the Rhône. Only in the year 974, two hundred years after the victory

of Charles Martel at Poitiers, the duke of Arles, Guillaume, chased the Saracens out of Freinet, which had been their final resting place. As liberator, Guillaume was granted the noble title of "Marquis de Provence" and this marked the beginning of the feudal era. Country folk built their houses around the castles and monasteries so creating the first fortified villages perched on hilltops safe from invaders. Religious life during this era was exemplified by the construction of magnificent abbeys like the Benedictine Montmajour near Arles and the Cistercian Sénanque and Sylvacane. The region began to enjoy strong economic development but the

397 left
The statue of
Raymond V of
Tolouse—the last
Catalan count, who
was crowned in Aix-
en-Provence—is in
Rochefort du Gard.

397 right This statue
of a first century
barbarian soldier was
found in Avignon
and is now kept in the
Museum of Roman
Civilization, Rome.

396-397 In order to
defend themselves from
the Saracens, in the
Middle Ages the
citizens of Arles used
the massive walls of the
Roman amphitheater
as ramparts and built
a citadel inside them.

397 bottom In the
ninth and tenth
century the Saracens
invaded and sacked
Marseilles, Arles, as
well as many villages
and monasteries. They
conquered Freinet,
using it as a base to
make raids throughout
France.

lineage of the counts of Provence was weakened by a continuous line of females so that in 1125, the territory was divided into two parts: one went to the Catalan count, Raymond Berengar, while the section north of the river Durance became the property of the count of Toulouse who purchased it as the marquisate of Provence. Regardless of the division of the territory, the feuds between lords for dominion of the province did not cease until 1229 when the *Paix de Paris* gave the dukedom of Narbonne and the viscounty of Carcassonne to the crown of France. All lands to the west of the Rhône remained the property of Raymond Berengar V who established himself at Aix-en-Provence.

Economic development during the 12th and 13th centuries was strong: villages and the population grew and many cities founded by the Romans, such as Vaison, grew considerably. Others along the main paths of communication, like Tarascon and Draguignan, also increased in size. Trade increased at Arles and Avignon and craftsmen grew richer. The port of Marseilles during the Crusades assumed a role of notable importance thanks to Richard Lionheart who departed from the city in 1190 on the Third Crusade. Linen arrived in Marseilles from Flanders and nearby Languedoc for exchange with spices, silk and precious stones arriving from the mysterious East. Despite the struggles with the counts of Provence, the hilltop town of Les Baux that dominated the Val d'enfer was the center of a brilliant and refined court. Here, around 1150, Etienne des Baux, the brilliant wife of Raymond I des Baux, created the *Cours d'Amours*, the first feminist meetings in history. During the meetings, illustrious women of high birth set down the rules of courtly love and discussed the art of loving.

398 top Medieval knights and ladies depicted in a 15th century miniature attributed to Jouvenal des Ursins. It illustrates the famous Roman de la Rose, *which was begun by Guillaume de Lorris and finished by Jean de Meung. A sophisticated poem concerning chivalrous love, this work is rich in allegorical figures.*

Minstrels and troubadours, often great knights, were invited to take part in competitions of singing and poetry. The winners were awarded a kiss from a lady at court and a crown of peacock feathers. This was the era of the explosion of Romanesque art which was manifested in the construction of a huge number of beautifully linear churches, both large and small, using the local pink stone. Examples are Saint-Trophime in Arles

LE.

called the "four queens" – brought new alliances that took Provence into the sphere of French influence. Margherita, with whom the troubadour Rambaud d'Orange fell head over heels in love and for which he was exiled to Porquerolles, married the king of France, Louis IX, St. Louis. The youngest, Béatrix, was awarded Provence and in 1246 married Charles of Anjou, the brother of Louis IX. The new lord of Provence, busy in the Crusades, allowed the large angry cities such as Arles, Marseilles and Avignon to claim independence but the illusion was short-lived. On his return, Charles took the situation in hand and began systematic reconquest of his power. To make his dominion more secure economically, he implemented a tax on salt, which brought him so much it represented half of all his income. Provence was more fortunate under his successors Charles II and Robert who turned out to be good administrators and well-disposed towards the region. They gave the cities the freedom to form their own city councils and the right

398-399 This view of Marseilles in the 16th century in an engraving by Franz Hogenberg, is from Le Théâtre du Monde *by Georg Braun (1599). The leading port town in France at the time, the city was a veritable entranceway for the many pestilences that periodically decimated the population. In the lower left-hand corner is the building where those who seemed to have the plague were confined.*

399 bottom Louis IX, the saint who was king of France in 1226-70, in a miniature. At left he is in front of the baptismal font, while at right he is portrayed together with his wife Margaret of Provence. A monarch who was popular because of his sense of justice and his virtue, Louis died of the plague in Tunis in 1270 after having taken part in the first two Crusades.

398 bottom A 13th century French school miniature shows Pope Clement IV crowning Charles I of Anjou.

with its magnificent portal decorated with scenes from the life of Jesus, and the picturesque chapel of Sainte Blaise in Les Baux, built for the fraternity of weavers and carders that used to meet there. The Benedictine abbeys of Montmajour and Saint-Victor grew ever richer and more important thanks to munificent donations. Raymond Berengar V died without leaving a male heir but the marriages of his four daughters –

to independent administration.

Meanwhile Avignon, the ancient Avenius, "the city of the river and the wind" founded in the second century BC on detritus accumulated during a flood of the river Rhône, revealed itself after decades of ruin to be one of the most open, most cultured and richest attractions in the area, ready to take advantage of an unexpected event. In the 14th century, the Holy See was oppressed by various political factions in Rome and, unable to cope with internal intrigues, Pope Clement V, originally from France and protected by Philippe le Beau, decided to take shelter in France in a Dominican monastery in Avignon. It was the start of the city's fortune, which welcomed seven French popes between 1309 and 1377. Then, as it had no seat worthy of Christ's representative on earth, Benedict XII built the austere Palais Vieux complete with towers and crenellations with the aid of architect Pierre Poisson de Mirepoix. Clement VI completed the construction of the palace and entrusted the building of the Palais Nouveau to Jean de Louvres who produced a

400 Avignon and the Papal Palace in a 14th century miniature. It was Pope Clement V who had the Papal See moved to Avignon and suppressed the Knights Templars order. During the 14th century the papal court at Avignon became a flourishing cultural center that influenced the entire region.

401 top This miniature, part of a 14th century manuscript now kept in Madrid, represents Pope John XXII surrounded by the clergy.

401 bottom Miniature by Pierre Roger from Giovanni Villani's New Chronicle *depicting the coronation of Pope Clement VI.*

magnificent example of Gothic architecture. Moreover, tired of being a perpetual guest in the city, the Pope bought the entire city of Avignon from Queen Joanna, countess of Provence, in 1348.

As can be imagined, in spite of the plague that killed thousands of victims that same year, the stay of the popes made the 14th century the golden age for Avignon. The city was transformed and increased in size. The bishop had a new impressive residence built, the nobles constructed towers and Gothic palaces and religious buildings were renovated. As an artistic and intellectual capital and with the most admired faculty of law in Europe, Avignon had a cultural life of stature dominated by Francesco Petrarch who lived there from 1311. Tradesmen prospered. Pope John XXII (1316-34) encouraged the cultivation of vines – one of the riches of the region – and created the reputation of the vineyards of Châteauneuf-du-Pape.

On the return of the popes to Rome, a long period of internal struggles and raids followed that culminated in the sacking of Marseilles in 1423. A further ten years of disorder continued until peace was restored under King René of Anjou who turned his back on the kingdom of Naples and chose Aix-en-Provence as his seat. Many stories have been told about this king who has gone down in history as "good king René." On the one hand, he loved the arts and culture, wrote poetry and protected artists but, on the other, he was greedy, always in need of money and did not hesitate to tax his subjects hard.

On his death in 1480, Provence was destined to lose its autonomy. The next king, Charles III of Maine, ruled only for a few months before leaving the land to his cousin Louis XI, king of France. Aware of the strong attachment of the Provençal people to their independence, the French instituted a parliament in Provence in 1501 based on the model of the parliament in Paris but with the obligation that the Provençal version should deal with their various problems in the same manner as was done in Paris. The iron

402 top Louis XI portrayed in a miniature by Jean de Valognes in the Chronique de Louis XI, *now kept in the Bibliothèque Nationale, Paris. The king of France in 1461-83, Louis was absolutist, avid and involved in intrigues,*

and was opposed by many feudal lords whose privileges he wanted to curb. On August 20, 1468 Louis decreed the death sentence of the enemy of the Crown, Charles of Melun, the lord of Normanville.

402 bottom Avignon in an old map by Ignazio Danti. Surrounded by a wall and by the Rhône river, the city is here still linked with Villenueve-lès-Avignon by the Saint-Bénézet bridge.

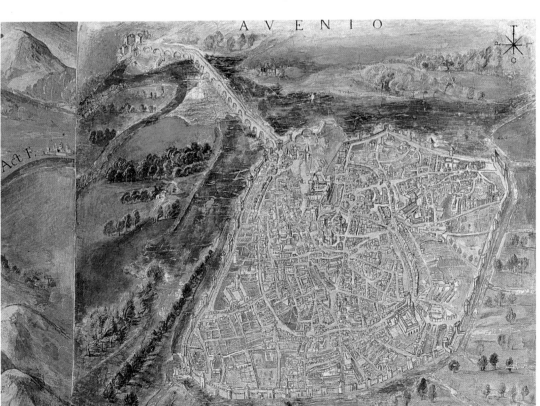

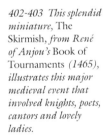

402-403 This splendid miniature, The Skirmish, *from René of Anjou's* Book of Tournaments *(1465), illustrates this major medieval event that involved knights, poets, cantors and lovely ladies.*

403 bottom René of Anjou and his second wife are portrayed in this diptych by Forment (1475). The "Good King" was a poet, musician and man of letters who was loved for his character but hated for the heavy taxes he imposed. He ruled Naples in 1438-42 and later set up his court in Tarascon.

fist of Paris shortly made itself apparent, however. Many Jewish communities lived in southern France at that time with their own schools and synagogues; they also created work for many butchers in requiring their meat to be cut in accordance with the dictates of their religion. At the start of the 16th century, a directive was issued by Paris that gave no choice to the Jews of Provence but to either convert or to emigrate. Some requested asylum in the Comté-Venaisson, the lands belonging to the Papacy, which also welcomed those Jews exiled from Languedoc and the Dauphinate. Only the Jews living in Avignon remained untouched although they were obliged to live in certain closed streets and to wear a yellow cap so that they might be recognized.

At the end of the 15th and start of the 16th centuries, Provence was involved in wars undertaken by the monarchs of France against Italy. Marseilles and Toulon were two strategically important bases from which expeditions set out against the Bel Paese but the French military operation soon backfired on Provence: in 1524, Charles V, the "Holy Roman Emperor," marched on Toulon and Aix and took both cities. It fell to the French king, Francis I, to put the emperor back in his place, which he did in 1536, and to strengthen the borders of the territory that marked the entrance to a powerful kingdom.

The religious wars between Catholics and Protestants that devastated France in the 16th century did not spare Provence. One of the few cities not to be involved was Orange as it had been inherited by the Dutch family, the counts of Nassau, who defended the city's Protestantism.

The same parliament in Aix seemed to follow the directives of the Parisian parliament and prepared itself to condemn the doctrine of the Huguenots. When the abbey of Sénanque was sacked by Protestants in 1544, the reaction of the Catholics was of unparalleled violence: the villages in which Huguenots were known to live were burned to the ground and over 3000 people were killed. Moving against the current of the times, as always, Marseilles allied itself with the Protestants and only yielded when Casaulx, the leader of the city, was assassinated in 1596. When King Henri IV was informed of the fact, he sighed with relief and exclaimed, "Now I am king of France". Two years later, the Edict of Nantes gave the Huguenots freedom of worship and the massacres came to an end.

404 top Pope Clement VII speaking with Francis I in a painting by Giorgio Vasari and his pupils. The French king understood the strategic importance of Provence and reinforced its borders.

404 bottom This work, also by Vasari and pupils, portrays Clement VII and Charles V. The emperor tried to conquer Provence in 1524 but was defeated in 1536.

404-405 A splendid painting of the city of Marseilles by an anonymous 15th-16th century artist.

405 top left The territory of Avignon in a painting by Ignazio Danti kept in the Geographic Maps Gallery, Vatican City.

405 top right The original copy of the Edict of Nantes (1598), which granted religious freedom to the Huguenots (Archives Nationales, Paris).

406 top In the 18th century the city and port of Toulon were expanding rapidly; the local shipyard, enlarged by Colbert in 1664, was the strategic center of the French Navy. This painting by Claude Joseph Vernet is in the Louvre, Paris.

406-407 The port of Marseilles in 1666, with the shipyard where the best ships in France were

built. After conquering the city, Louis XIV set out to make it the gate to the Mediterranean and decided to enlarge it.

407 top This painting by Gordot (Musée Calvet, Avignon) represents the entrance of the Pope's vice legate into Avignon, performed with great pomp, as was the custom in that period.

Yet the rebellious spirit of Provence continued to bother the French crown which was anxious to establish total power over all of the country. In 1664, Louis XIV put a Parisian intendant in charge of the parliament in Aix who was entrusted with dealing with questions of rights, security and finance. The state lackeys, who continued to be sent until the end of the 18th century, fell in love with the region and made Aix into a rich and important city with roads and luxurious houses.

Only Marseilles continued to wor-

ry Louis XIV until, out of patience, he had the city walls breached on March 2, 1660 in a threat of violence to show that all opposition was useless.

The offence caused to Marseilles was repaid by the finance minister, Colbert, who, hoping to increase the state economy, made Marseilles a free port in 1669 so greatly increasing trade. The minister's edict exempted goods arriving from the East from the 20 percent tax that other ports were obliged to pay. As Colbert had forecast, Marseilles became an obligatory stop for goods on their way to

the Caribbean and was able to gain an ever larger foothold in the East where the city sold sugar and coffee from the Antilles. While the port of Marseilles was dedicated to trade, nearby Toulon, where Henri IV had created an arms depot, became the heart of the French navy.

The end of the 17th century saw the creation of a business in the region that is still highly active: the first *Faïenceries* (potteries) were built at Moustiers and Saint-Jean-du-

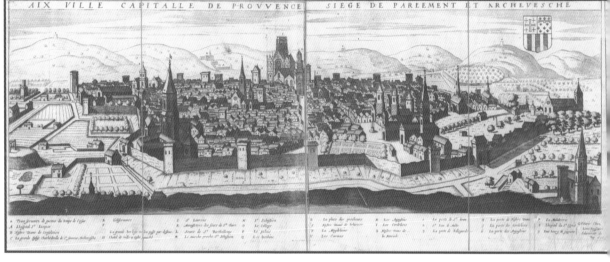

407 center
The old map of Aix-en-Provence in the Civic Museum of Arbaud shows the city surrounded by walls. In the middle is the grandiose Saint-Sauveur Cathedral.

407 bottom Michel Serre's Marseilles During the 1720 Plague *bears witness to the devastation wrought by the epidemic in the city.*

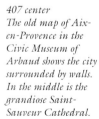

Désert near Marseilles. Initially, manufacture was an extremely simple procedure with the objects then being painted and fired, but firing techniques were perfected in the 18th and 19th centuries by craftsmen who turned out small works of art which are today considered highly desirable objects.

The plague that affected the region for years struck the city particularly hard in 1720 but Marseilles still managed to maintain its role of a rich and commercial city.

The rebel soul of Marseilles showed itself once more with the French Revolution. In 1792, the city sent "missionaries of patriotism" into the deepest countryside with the aim of spreading revolutionary principles. A battalion of more than five hundred volunteer soldiers set off for Paris the same year to support their compatriots in the struggle against the foreign supporters of Louis XVI. To pay tribute to the courage and enthusiasm of the revolutionaries, Rouget de Lisle composed the song of war that has since become the country's national anthem, the "Marseillaise."

The years that followed were characterized by bloody conflict and struggles between the Jacobins and the Royalists. The region remained unquiet and not even Napoleon succeeded in making himself appreciated as the Provençals blamed him for the economic blockade that damaged trade and industry. The region did not flourish again until 1830 with the July monarchy. As a result of the conquest of Algeria, Marseilles became one of France's most important ports and assumed

408 bottom In 1790-91 Avignon was the theater of bloody battles between French patriots and papists. The annexation of the city was sanctioned constitutionally in 1791 and ratified by the National Convention in 1793, but it was accepted by the Papal See only in 1814.

409 top The Marseillaise was the battle song of the Rhine army, which took in thousands of volunteers from all parts of France to support the revolutionary cause.

409 center Napoleon III was accepted grudgingly by the people of Provence. When he ascended the throne in 1851, eastern Provence became one of the centers of resistance against the emperor, who defeated the republicans at Mées.

409 bottom This 1835 print after a drawing by T. Allom shows the Triumphal Arch of Marseilles.

408-409 In 1792 Rouget de l'Isle wrote the Marseillaise, which later became the French national anthem. This composition was written to accompany the battalion of over five hundred volunteers who went north to help the revolutionaries in their struggle against the supporters of Louis XVI.

major significance during the industrial revolution with production of Marseilles soap, oil pressing and ship building. The arsenal at Toulon that employed thousands of people increased in size and became a model city.

With the end of the July monarchy in 1848, Provence once more expressed its hostility to the Bonapartists with its institution of universal suffrage, and when in December 1851 Louis Napoleon Bonaparte seized power, eastern Provence became one of the centers of resistance against the emperor. Consequently Napoleon was forced to send troops that same month to defeat the Republicans at Mées.

410 top In 1879 the Marseillais Clovis Hugues was elected to Parliament, becoming the first socialist deputy in French history.

410 center The Russian troops that landed at Marseilles in 1916 march through the Canebière. The First World War triggered a serious crisis in Provence.

410 bottom German troops enter Marseilles in 1942 through the Triumphal Arch. The following year they destroyed the Vieux-Port quarter, which they considered a hideout for Jews and Resistance fighters. The German occupation lasted almost two years, up to 1944.

Following its opposition to Napoleon III, Marseilles offered unconditional support to the Third Republic (1870-1940) and became a stronghold of socialism. The first congress of the Workers' Party took place here in 1879 and the city sent Clovis Hugues, the first Socialist deputy in history, to the Paris parliament.

Marseilles developed into one of the world's most important commercial ports at the outbreak of World War I, both for goods and for the passengers that set sail for the country's African colonies.

World War II brought a great blow to the industries of Provence. In 1940, France was cut in two with the Germans occupying the Atlantic coast; political refugees from all

around Europe converged on Marseilles, the country's single large unoccupied port, with the hope of sailing from there to the Unites States. Among these were the group of Surrealist painters headed by André Breton and Max Ernst to whom Peggy Guggenheim made a sea-plane available to leave the city. Being a strategic means of passage between the north and south, the region was occupied by the Italians in 1942 and then by the Germans who bombarded the port of Toulon. Marseilles suffered the same treatment but, rebellious as ever, refused to surrender. A Resistance group was created in the city, which was implacably persecuted by the Germans.

410-411 *August 15, 1944: the Allied army lands in Provence. Most of the battles took place in Toulon and Marseilles, and the Germans surrendered after having destroyed the port areas.*

411 bottom left
On November 11, 1942 the German troops invaded Southern France. Two weeks later, the French Navy sank its ships at Toulon rather than hand them over to the enemy.

411 bottom right
On July 29, 1944 young women marched through the streets of Marseilles acclaiming the Liberation. The German occupation was considered a catastrophe for the port city.

The landing of the Allies on the Mediterranean coast on August 15, 1944 marked the liberation of Provence from the Germans. After the end of the war, tourism took hold in the region, both on the coast and inland. As for Marseilles, large petroleum refineries and petrochemical industries sprang up around Etang de Berre and Fons but the damage caused to the port during the war had major repercussions on the city's economy for a long time.

After the glories of Nice, the cinema discovered the enchanting attractions of Saint-Tropez with its narrow, tightly squeezed ochre houses that overlook the ancient port. In 1955, Brigitte Bardot made her film debut here as the main character in the film *Et Dieu Créa la Femme* with her husband Roger Vadim. She built the famous villa *Madrague* where she hides away as soon as her commitments permit her. Intellectuals prefer the ancient villages hidden among the olive trees. Jean Giono praised the charm of Manosque in his novels and the poet René Char settled at Isle-sur-la-Sorgue. Though Saint-Paul de Vence is one of the prime tourist attractions inland, there is no longer any isolated village that has kept its secrets hidden. Ménerbes, Sault, Roussillon and Lourmarin are all villages that have had their old houses rebuilt with taste where famous people, such as Jacques Chirac, come to enjoy the atmosphere that has captivated artists from around

eBretonne

412 bottom In the 1960s Saint-Tropez was the scene of the romance between Jane Fonda and Roger Vadim. When she returned to the United States after her stay in France, Fonda declared that Vadim was a marvelous person.

412-413 During the day, the lively crowd at Saint-Tropez frequents the Crêperie at the port, and in the evening goes to the Pirate, a haunt of actors, film-makers and the international jet set.

413 bottom Saint-Tropez is the undisputed domain of Brigitte Bardot, who made her debut here in the film Et Dieu Créa la Femme. The actress likes to spend her vacation in her villa, La Madrague.

the world for centuries.

The vocation of modern Provence, which makes up part of the region Alpes-Provence-Côte d'Azur, is unquestionably tourism. This has brought exploitation and investment in, not just coastal tourist facilities, but also ancient inland villages as the authorities attempt to preserve the traditional features of this wonderful land. The summer festivals, like those at Avignon and *Chorégies* in Orange, are known around the world as major attractions to the modern traveler.

412 top The love story between Yves Montand and Simone Signoret began in the romantic setting of Saint-Paul-de-Vence. The two actors met at the the famous Colombe d'Or restaurant, which now has a fine collection of works left by artists to pay their bills.

414 left In November-
December 1888,
Vincent Van Gogh
painted this self-portrait
(now the property of
Lehman, New York) in
Arles. This is a half

profile bust facing the
viewer's right,
depicting a thoughtful,
severe Van Gogh. He
dedicated the work to
his friend Laval (lower
right-hand corner).

One gets the impression
that the artist is looking
into the mirror without
seeing himself, absorbed
as he is in his thoughts,
which remove him from
reality.

A cobalt blue sky, bright sunshine, gentle hills, bare mountains, stately rivers, cliffs that
rise vertically from the blue
sea where "the boats rise and
fall" like doves, as Paul Valèry wrote:
this is the Provence loved by artists.

414 top right
In The Sower, which
he painted in June
1888, Van Gogh
celebrates rural
serenity and the
splendor of the sun.
The work betrays a
peaceful state of mind.

Van Gogh arrived in 1888 to glo-
rify these places in his inimitable
manner and with a magical evocative
force. First, he stayed at the Carrel
restaurant in Arles, then he rented a
house in the huge Place Lamartine
(that has since become famous as

414 center right
Van Gogh painted this
landscape in May
1888. The artist was
fascinated by the
environs of Arles: in
this work he painted
the fields of irises, in
the foreground, with
the distant town in
the background.

414 bottom right
There are at least five
canvases of Van Gogh's
bedroom at Arles. The
one reproduced here
with an intimate tone,
was painted in
September 1889 and
gives the impression of
a room that has been
lived in, imbued with
the artist's presence.

415 L'Arlésienne is
the second of the six
portraits Van Gogh
did of Madame
Ginoux. In this
painting,
characterized by
strong contrasting
colors, the woman
seems severe, her face
hardened much like a
stone sculpture.

416-417 Cézanne considered Mount Sainte-Victoire the symbol of Aix-en-Provence and of the land where he was born, and continued to paint it till he died. But he never called it by name, since no one could mistake it, merely writing "viewed from southwest," "from the south," and so on. This was the mountain par excellence, painted with strong brushwork and joyous colors. This work, now in the Hermitage, St. Petersburg, imparts the joy of living in this blessed land.

416 bottom Les Grandes Baigneuses, one of Paul Cézanne's most famous works, is kept in the Musée Granet, Aix-en-Provence. He painted it in his studio in the town center, which is now open to the public.

417 bottom left
Maurice Denis, one
of the first artists and
critics who
appreciated Cézanne,
executed this work,
Paying a Visit to
Cézanne, *as a tribute*
to his friend. The sky
is typically Provençal,
and the hills and
vegetation are
suffused in a light
that seems to radiate
an opalescent powder.
Denis' art, which has
Neo-Classic
overtones, is quite
distant from
Cézanne's
substantial forms.

417 top right
Cézanne painted
many self-portraits.
He loved to depict his
various severe facial
expressions, which at
times he rendered
more detached
by wearing a
bowler hat.

"the yellow house") where he wanted to create a studio for artists: L'atelier du Midi. The first painter to accept his invitation was Gauguin but he did not share Van Gogh's love for Provence to the extent that the two quarreled and separated. On his first arrival in Arles, Van Gogh had been enthused by the explosion of blooms in March and painted as though he found himself in a "Provençal Japan." He painted intensely by both day and night: corn fields, almond trees in blossom, flights of crows, sunflowers, tragic skies, the interiors of houses, squares, portraits, and bridges around Arles similar in composition to Japanese landscapes. The best known of these is *Langlois Bridge* which had attracted him from his arrival. The painter also loved to depict the lights and shadows of night. He would stand at his easel, wearing a broad-brimmed hat on which he had at-

tached candles to throw light onto his palette and canvas. This was how he painted the *Café at Night*. Thirsty for life, for friendship and for the desire to reveal the secret of everything, yet in a constant struggle with himself and tormented by the continual sensation that evil had triumphed over good in the world, he continued until he ended in the psychiatric hospital at Saint-Paul-de-Mausole near Saint-Rémy in 1889, the year before he died and the year before Toulouse Lautrec challenged his friend, painter Henry de Groux, to a duel in response to a denigrating comment made about one of his pictures.

Nor could the painter Paul Cézanne stay away from his birthplace, Aix-en-Provence, for long even if his dissension with his father – who had changed profession from a hatter to a banker and did not like his son's choice – was never resolved. While living in Paris, Cézanne felt physically drawn back to the people and countryside of Mont Sainte-Victoire, which he painted time and again with ceaseless love. He stood at the window of Jas de Bouffan, bought by his father in 1859, and painted the land: the caves of Bibémus that fascinated him for their uninterrupted sequence of geometric shapes, the cubes of the houses, the rocks in the mountains, the farms and the flowers. After the death of his beloved mother, he built

417 top left The
Estaque, *the Gulf of*
Marseilles, is a motif
that Cézanne painted
several times and that
Braque and Picasso
also liked. Cézanne's
Estaque, *which*
anticipated many
modern artists, has
been viewed as a
revolutionary work, a
new way of painting,
in small cubes.

loveliest museums, dedicated to this artist.

Picasso passed several years working in Antibes, close to Biot, and, a little farther away at Vallauris, in 1950 he founded one of France's most important centers for ceramic art with Madoura and Prinnier. His liking for Provence prompted him in 1958 to buy the castle of Vauvenargues that stands in front of Mont Sainte-Victoire near Aix where he worked until 1961. He left the castle to move to Mougins, a few miles north of Cannes, where he died in 1973 but he wanted to be buried in the grounds of the castle in front of the symbol of the *dominus*, in front of the mountain celebrated by Cèzanne, in front of the queen of Provence.

a studio at Chemin des Lauves (today Avenue Paul Cèzanne) in which he never ceased to paint his favorite mountain. He would begin at dawn to capture its awakening, its first breath and its sense of dominion over the whole region. While at Pont-des-Trois Sautets near Aix-en-Provence during the seven-year period from 1898 to 1905, Cézanne painted one of his masterpieces, *Les Grandes Baigneuses*, which inspired *Les Demoiselles d'Avignon* by Picasso in 1907, considered the manifesto of Cubism.

All painters felt at home in Provence. Not even Claude Monet, who in 1872 in his native Le Havre had painted the famous *Impression. Sunrise*, from which the name Impressionism was taken, and loved the cerulean sea of the north and its tempestuous sky, was able to resist the charms of Provence and spent an intense period near Marseilles in 1883 and another in Antibes in 1888.

Matisse and Bonnard moved permanently to Saint-Tropez. Fernand Léger, whose paintings illustrated the dynamism of modern life, established himself at Biot in a studio with an earthen floor, as was common in the houses of farmworkers, and today the village is home to one of France's

418 bottom left
Provençal Landscape *was painted on a wood panel by John Stanton in 1976.*

418 bottom right Signac's Papal Palace in Avignon *is a pointillist work.*

419 top left This *rather disturbing* Provençal Landscape *was painted by Balthus in 1925.*

419 top right Gauguin's *Arles Countryside expresses the artist's joy upon observing the Provençal light.*

419 bottom right *This canvas by Braque represents the landscape at the Estaque.*

418-419 In 1889 Renoir wanted to paint Cèzanne's beloved mountain, Sainte-Victoire, in his own way. As we can see, the celebration of the mountain is secondary compared to the triumphal blaze of colors, with the setting sun imparting a soft light onto the surrounding countryside.

RIVAL SISTERS:
A DIVERSITY OF CHARACTERS

*421 top right
Off the coast of
Marseilles is the
Château d'If, the
tiny cliff-like island
with the castle-prison
that was the setting
for part of Alexandre
Dumas'* Count of
Montecristo.

MARSEILLE,
GATEWAY TO THE EAST

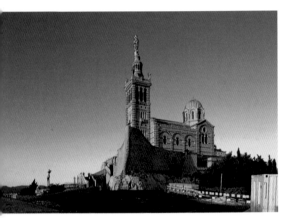

420 Notre-Dame-de-la-Garde, the "Good Mother" as the Marseillais like to call this church, dominates the city. On the top of this gigantic Neo-Byzantine construction designed in the 19th century by the architect Espérandieu, is the monumental statue of the Virgin and Child. On Ascension Day the church is visited by sailors who make a pilgrimage there and offer ex-votos to the Virgin.

420-421 and 421 top left Opening out to the south onto the large Gulf of the Lion and delimited to the northeast by the Provençal Alps, its sky cleared of clouds by the mistral, Marseilles seems to hug the old port between the red walls of the Saint-Jean and Saint-Nicolas forts. Among the few buildings of the old quarter around the port, which was destroyed by the Germans in 1943, is the 17th century Hôtel de Ville, or town hall. The old port is now a huge parking space for sailboats and motorboats.

"Construction and destruction follow one another without cease. No era, no power and no concept is eternal here..." This was how, in 1925, Joseph Roth described the character of the city that is today the capital of the region in his book *The White Cities* after a long trip in the south of France. Very different from other Provençal cities like Arles or Aix, where shady squares and centuries-old streets were built on a human scale, Marseilles, wrapped in the blue of the sea and the white of limestone rocks, is in continual evolution. The "Gateway to the East," in which Greeks, Romans, Jews, French, Lebanese, Italians and natives of the Maghreb have mixed over the centuries, has always been a crossroads of civilizations and still produces surprising contrasts. Officially, North Africans number only 10 percent of the population of 800,000 but in some streets one breaths the atmosphere of the medina, for example, Cours Belsunce where *kaftan* and *tchador* can be glimpsed through the windows.

From whatever direction one arrives in Marseilles, the first view of the city is of Notre-Dame-de-la-Garde. La Bonne Mère, as it is affectionately called by the Marseillais, dominates the city. From its heights, one can see the spectacular *calanques*, inlets surrounded by striking rocky cliffs, and the natural curve of the old port flanked by the forts of St. Jean and St. Nicolas that were built by Louis XIV, not to protect the city but to intimi-

422 top left
*In the old Panier
quarter is the Vieille
Charité, the hospice
built in the second
half of the 17th
century by Louis XIV
and now perfectly
restored. The pink
stone building with
three tiers of galleries
surrounded the
Chapelle de la
Charité, a Baroque
masterpiece by the
architect Pierre
Puget.*

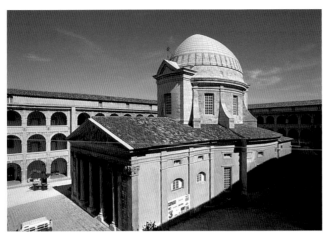

date it. Further north, are the artificial basins of the Joliette and the outline of the small port of Estaque; this was one of Braque's favorite subjects, which he painted for the particular luminosity of the scenery. A little out to sea stands the Chateau d'If made famous by Alexandre Dumas in his novel, *The Count of Montecristo*. In the little port, where the houses were nearly all rebuilt after World War II, a forest of masts appears to grow from the sea and one senses the atmosphere of long trips and far away lands. Each morning, the crews chatter briskly in their strong Marseillais accent as the colored fishing boats return to the quay bearing tuna, sea bass, sea bream, shrimp and scorpion fish. It is the women who are responsible for selling them: wives, mothers and sisters, all strong and well-suited to commerce. In front of the Vieux Port stretches the long and busy Canebière, a street with an incredible number of shops, that takes its name from an old hemp rope-factory. The street is so famous that it was featured in the films and comedies of Marcel Pagnol who based his works on life in Marseilles during the 1920s.

Walking through the city, one realizes that something is changing. *Marseille ça bouge*, Marseilles is moving, someone says, and as it renews itself, it refinds its past. In the old district of Panier, La Vieille Charité, the hospice built during the second half of the 17th century by Louis XIV around the lovely Baroque Chapelle de la Charité designed by Pierre Puget, has been perfectly rebuilt and is now home to a lively cultural center. It stands in the heart of old Marseilles, a maze of dark, narrow streets on the Montée des Accoules which was featured in famous films like *Borsalino* and *The French Connection*. The times of organized crime seem a distant memory now that the city is rebuilding its older districts, creating pedestrian precincts like Rue Saint Ferréol, and replastering old façades. Right in the center, the Cours Estienne d'Orvres had fallen to the level of a parking lot but, today, that has been placed underground and the square has now been given a facelift with fashionable bistros and a charming bookshop whose name, *Les Arcenaulx*, is a reminder of the time when this area used to be a dockyard in which Charles VIII built the ships he sent down to Italy.

Whereas Notre-Dame-de-la-Garde embraces the city from above, the *tour de la corniche* encompasses it from the coast. The *corniche* is the long walkway along the seafront that connects the city to the vallon des Auffes built in 1863. Above the *corniche*, the colline du Roucas-Blanc where luxurious villas were built during the second half of the 19th century recalls a happy period for the city, when the "Porte d'Orient" grew wealthier after the opening of the Suez canal. Examples are the sumptuous Villa Valmer, the Petit Nice, the Talabot castle with its splendid park, and the Borély castle built by the magnate Louis Borély.

AVIGNON, PAPAL DRAMA

A s much as Marseilles is in the throes of change, the compact and harmonious city of Avignon seems to have been kept in a jewel case. Surrounded by a long rectangle of city walls and flanked on two sides by the river Rhône, the City of the Popes is an artistic and cultural pearl, a melting pot of flamboyant Gothic architecture. The golden age of Avignon coincided with the period of the popes' stay, from 1309 to 1377, when the papacy moved its seat to the Midi to avoid the political intrigues that took place in Rome. The result was the construction of a new city with palaces, towers, bell-towers and churches but it was the popes' palace that made Avignon unique. The building of the Palais Vieux with its four imposing and austere corner towers began in 1336 when Pope Benedict XII, the third Avignon pope, ordered the demolition of the old bishop's palace that his predecessor, John XXII, had only just had enlarged. The massive walls hid courtyards, enormous salons and unending suites of rooms. Benedict's successor, Clement VI, had the palace doubled in size and called a troupe of Italian artists headed by Simone Martini and, later, Matteo Giovanetti to his court, who decorated it with such magnificence that it appeared to want to outdo the pomp of the Roman court. This was how the Palais Neuf came into being, a combination of castle, court and fortress with ten large towers to protect it

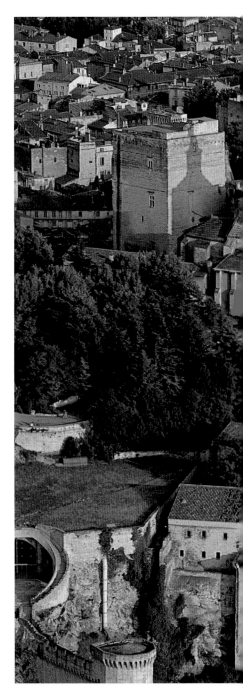

from unexpected attack. The main court, the 19,375 square feet *cours d'honneur*, opens majestically just inside the entrance; this is the site of the Theater Festival, begun in 1947 by Jean Vilar, which still continues to this day with great success.

However, the Popes' Palace is not the only architectural work of art in Avignon. Overlooking the Place du Palais is the 12th century cathedral of Notre-Dames-des-Doms that was once decorated with splendid frescoes now preserved in the Palace, and the 14th century Petit Palais which houses an interesting museum. Its rooms are nearly all dedicated to Italian art apart from the last three, which deal with painting and sculpture from Avignon.

The city is especially enjoyable on foot at sunset when the weak light of the sun reflects off its cream-colored stone. Every corner has curiosities to be discovered, beginning with the Balance district, the ancient gypsy quarter, where restored Gothic palazzi and modern Mediterranean style houses are well blended into the architecture of the past. Centuries ago, King René also fell in love with this city and had a house built here in Rue de Grivolas. The King came here when he preferred a little peace to the luxury and vivacity of the court of Aix or the castle in Tarascon.

428 top left
The wide, tree-lined 17th century Cours Mirabeau, named after the fiery deputy of the Revolution in the 19th century, was once reserved for carriage rides. The locals still love to walk in the shade of the plane trees and sit in the outdoor cafés to watch the world pass by.

428 top right
At the Rotunda, at the beginning of Cours Mirabeau, there is a refreshing fountain decorated with lions and sea lions, built during Napoleon III's reign, that is a spectacular sight indeed.

AIX-EN-PROVENCE,
THE CITY OF FOUNTAINS

A ix, the city of "Good King" René, ancient capital of Provence and homeland of Paul Cèzanne and Count Mirabeau – unyielding representative of the Third Estate during the French revolution – greets the visitor with its many fountains, lovely tree-lined streets and elegant Renaissance and Baroque palaces. Its mild climate enchanted the counts of Provence and the strict financial intendants of Louis XIV who contributed to making it yet lovelier and richer. Reminders of Cèzanne, who spent much of his life in Aix fascinated by the light and colors of the surrounding countryside, are all around the city. A sign-posted route around the city streets takes the visitor to the places where the artist lived: the Collège Mignet in Rue Cardinale where he became friends with Émile Zola, his drawing school next to the Granet museum, the house where he was born and, a few hundred yards from the cathedral, his workshop where he painted one of his most famous paintings, *Les Grandes Baigneuses*.

To its other great citizen, Mirabeau, Aix has dedicated the boulevard that bears his name. The long, wide avenue is shaded by huge plane trees and lined by magnificent palaces that alternate classical simplicity with the ornateness of the Baroque. It is an ideal place to relax, seated in one of its many cafés, like the Café des Garçons where Cèzanne liked to *regarder passer le temps*, watch time pass by.

428-429 The former capital of Provence, Aix-en-Provence, the city of the "Good King" René, Mirabeau and Cézanne, owes its name to the Roman consul Sextius, who in 123 BC set up camp with his troops at the thermal springs.

429 top left Aix is also known as "the city of fountains," as can be seen in this photograph of a detail of the fountain with statues of four dolphins.

429 top right In the old Saint-Sauveur quarter is the cathedral of the same name, built in the fifth century and rebuilt several times up to the 18th century. It conceals a Romanesque cloister with thin columns whose capitals have floral motifs.

429 center and bottom right The flamboyant Gothic façade of the cathedral is decorated with elegant pinnacles and statues. In the interior is the famous triptych of the Burning Bush by Nicolas Froment, as well as splendid Flemish tapestries from the Canterbury Cathedral that decorate the choir.

430 top Place de l'Hotel de Ville, the town hall square, was laid out in the mid-1700s. The fountain in the middle, the work of the sculptor Jean Chastel, is crowned by a Roman column. The flower market animates the square with its myriad colors.

430 center and bottom The shops and market stalls in Aix offer the multi-colored fabrics with characteristic Provençal motifs used to make tablecloths and clothes.

430-431 and 431 top left The Pavillon de Vendôme in the Faubourg des Cordeliers was built in the 17th century on land that the region granted to the Duke of Vendôme, grandson of Henry IV, as a sign of gratitude for having pacified the region. In the 18th century a story was added to the pavilion. The entrance is flanked by two caryatids that support the balcony. Preceded by a delightful French-style garden, the pavilion is now the home of a museum featuring furniture, paintings and ceramics.

431 top right Everywhere in town there are references to Paul Cézanne, who was born here on January 19, 1839 at No. 28 rue de L'Opéra. On Avenue Paul Cézanne, the artist's studio is open to the public; he painted his last works here, including the famous Grandes Baigneuses. The studio also has many memorabilia as well as original drawings and watercolors.

The oldest section of the city is San Salvatore, which stands on the ruins of the imperial city founded by the Romans. It rings the university and the cathedral of San Salvatore that was begun in the fifth century and only completed thirteen hundred years later. The façade, like the rest of the cathedral, shows signs of many architectural styles: Provençal Romanesque, Gothic and flamboyant Gothic reveal the periods during which the building was renovated. Snaking around the cathedral are the old streets of the district, like Rue Gaston Saporta, one of the most elegant with antique and craft shops and aristocratic houses adorned with decorations and columns. A short distance from Saint-Saveur stands the Pavillon de Vendôme, built in the 17th century on land given by Provence to Duke Louis de Vendôme, nephew of Henri IV, for having contributed to the pacification of the region. Facing onto a small French garden, the pavillon today houses a delightful museum dedicated to the life of Provence with portraits of the most important figures in the history of Aix, a series of still-lifes and some attractive majolicas from Moustiers.

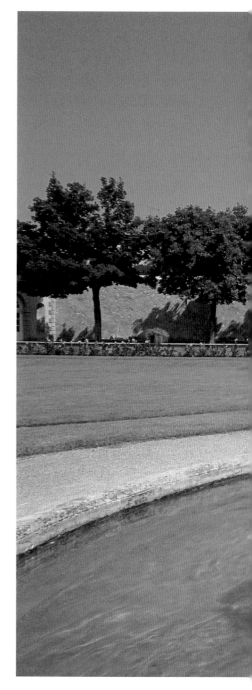

ORANGE, A THEATER FOR ETERNITY

432 top left and top right The Roman theater in Orange, dating from the first century AD, has a stage wall that is so fascinting that Louis XIV called it "the most beautiful wall in my kingdom." The

Romans used the slope of the Saint-Europe hill to build the tiers, which are still intact. The entrance, blind arches, and rows of Corinthian columns are perfectly preserved.

The entrance to the city of Orange from the north offers a majestic welcome through its triumphal Roman arch, the symbolic gateway to Provence, which was built in 20 BC on the ancient Via Agrippa that connected Lyons to Arles. It is seventy-one feet tall with three arcades framed by beautiful

columns, an elegant pediment and two attics, one on top of the other, and is considered one of the loveliest triumphal arches from the Roman era. Bas-reliefs filled with movement and character depict the pacification of Gaul and the victories of Augustus. Founded by the Latin civilization around 35 BC, Orange was a principality belonging to the duchy of Nassau from the 16th century until the Treaty of Utrecht in 1713 when it was returned to France. In addition to the arch, the city is even prouder of its ancient Theater in which the 335 foot long and 120 foot high stage wall still stands: "The most beautiful wall in my kingdom," Louis XIV used to say. The superb construction was built during the reign of Augustus in the lee of a hill as the setting for all kinds of performances: plays, dancing, singing and festivals. The quality of its acoustics and the excellent state of preservation make it the foremost theater remaining from the Roman era. These qualities mean that the theater is still used for public performances of the internationally famous series of operas and musical shows named *Chorégies*. The center of the small city lies a few minutes walk away where its heart, the lovely Place Clemenceau, is overlooked by fine town houses with decorated façades.

432 bottom left The powerful statue of Augustus greeting the audience stands in a niche in the stage wall of the ancient theater.

432 center right Built on the ancient Via Agrippa that connected Lyons and Arles, the triumphal arch in Orange was the first Roman monument in Gaul, and symbolized the power of Rome. Recent research has dated it back to around 20 BC. Fifty years later it was named after the emperor Tiberius.

432 bottom right The triumphal arch is seventy-two feet high and is well preserved, with obvious restoration work on the western side. It has three arches framed by lovely columns and a pediment decorated with low-reliefs depicting scenes of battles between the Romans and Celts.

433 The city of Orange, which has important vestiges of the past, is a must for opera lovers as well. Every year the Chorégies festival features the greatest interpeters of Verdi and Wagner in the ancient theater.

ARLES,
ART AND BULLFIGHTS

Of all the cities in Provence, the most lively is Arles, a true hotbed of initiatives. The Romans were appreciative of its success in commerce and in its ability to establish relations with the whole of the known world of the time. It flourished to the point that everything that civilization had to offer in terms of foodstuffs, fabrics, precious objects, bronze, copper etc. could be found there. Arles was the favorite city of Vincent Van Gogh and where he found inspiration for his paintings of sparkling fields of sunflowers in the surrounding country-

side. Nowadays, it never ceases to amaze for its variety of gatherings and festivals: concerts, shows, bull-fights, the rice festival, an international salon for the *Santonniers* (the sculptors of the figures in representations of the Holy Manger), the festival of the *gardians* of the Camargue, and international photographic meetings that brought the national school of photography into being. Facing onto the Rhône and flooded by the vibrant light of Provence that has proved so popular with painters and poets, the city, wrapped in the strong colors of the surrounding country, continues to inspire every form of creativity; for example, the clothes designer from Arles, Christian Lacroix, used the glittering costumes of the toreadors and the traditional clothes of the women as the inspiration for the collections which made him famous around the world. One comes to Arles to know a city that has a rich artistic and historical tradition into which the Roman remains blend perfectly. Its past continues to live in its ancient monuments: the arena – today used for bull-fights – and the medieval fortified bastion built to defend the city against the raids of the Saracens. From the top of the entrance tower, one's gaze takes in the Romanesque abbey of Montmajour three miles away on a hilltop shaded by pines where Van Gogh often used to paint. Next to the arena stands the theater built in 30 BC framed by large trees that act as a backdrop to the Romanesque bell-tower of Saint-Trophime. Then there are Constantine's baths and the austere parade of sar-

436 top Three miles outside of Arles is the Montmajour Abbey, a Benedictine monastery founded in 949 that lies in an isolated and fascinating place. The Romanesque cloister and crypt hewn out of the rock attract many tourists.

436-437 The Arles amphitheater, built in the first century, was occupied by houses where the citizens took refuge in case of an enemy attack. Only in 1830, when the houses were removed, did the amphitheater begin to be used for bullfights.

437 top Constantine's baths, only part of which remain, are called Palais de la Trouille. In ancient times they probably extended as far as the emperor's palace.

Among the most important remains is a magnificent semi-circular apse covered by a stone vault with brick ribbing that once covered one of the pools.

cophagi of the Alyscamps, the famous Roman and paleo-Christian necropolis. Five years ago, the superb Musée de l'Arles Antique was built in the same place that the immense first century AD Roman circus used to stand on the right bank of the Rhône. It was designed by Henri Cipriani in the shape of a triangle whose sides correspond to the three sections of the museum and is as blue as the Provençal sky. The first side is dedicated to archaeology and contains a spectacular model of how the city used to be during the Roman era; the second houses the museum's scientific activities with a research section and laboratories for the restoration of ceramics and glass; the third is a welcome and information center for the public containing an extensive document center. Now, as in the past, the center of Arles is the Forum square, built on U-shaped crypto-porticoes – grandiose underground galleries – built by the Romans for storing grain and still in fine condition. Looking onto the square is the famous Hôtel Nord-Pinus, described by Jean Cocteau, who used to stay there, as a hotel with a soul. And a lively soul it is too, reflecting the personalities of its past owners, the tightrope walker of the Medrano circus, Nello Bessières, and his wife Germaine, a fiery cabaret dancer, who was a great friend of Edith Piaf. Its guest book contains signatures of some of the great figures of the century: Winston Churchill, Sacha Guitry, King Farouk, Jean-Paul Sartre, Paul Klee and Picasso. On the balcony of room ten, reserved for great toreadors, Luis Dominguin received the ovation of the crowd after a performance in the ring. Lining the walls of the Cintra bar at the Nord-Pinus are bull-fighting posters and photographs of toreadors in glittering costumes and of regular guests at the hotel, such as Yves Montand, Simone Signoret and Picasso in his favorite blue-lined sailor's sweater. Nowadays, the public crowds into the Forum square on bull-fight days and for three days they celebrate with *paella*, sherry and *flamenco* music. Emptied of the corrida crowd, the Forum square returns to being a calm, tranquil place where one goes to sit, in the shade of the huge plane trees protected by the statue of Frédérique Mistral, in the Café de la Nuit that was immortalized in a painting by Vincent Van Gogh and rebuilt a few years ago in the colors that dominate the picture: yellow, green and blue. Van Gogh arrived in Arles in February 1888 and stayed until May of the following year. Reminders of the artist are to be found everywhere in the city although many of the places shown in his paintings no longer exist, for example, the Maison Jaune in Place Lamartine in the north of the city, the famous bridge in the painting *Pont Langlois avec ses Lavandières* was moved 850 yards during work on Arles canal, and the old Hotel Dieu, the hospital to which the artist was taken when he cut off his right ear after an argument with Gauguin, has been turned into the Espace Van Gogh that houses a large library and display area.

437 bottom The Early Christian Alyscamps necropolis, set between the Craponne canal and the houses, is a long avenue flanked by tombs that leads to a church in ruins. This is an evocative site where the citizens of Arles were buried for fifteen centuries.

*438 top left and 439
Saint-Trophime church
was built in the 12th
century of limestone and
is a fabulous example of
Provençal Romanesque
architecture. The
expressive sculptures on
the portal illustrated
passages from the Bible to
the pilgrims on their way
to Santiago de
Compostella. The most
interesting scenes are
The Last Judgement,
Adoration of the Magi
and Massacre of the
Innocents.*

*438 bottom left
The Saint-Trophime
cloister is a
masterpiece for its
balanced,
proportioned volumes
and the artistic
quality of the
sculpture pieces. Two
sides are
Romanesque, while
the other two are
Gothic, with ogee
arches supported by
slender double
columns decorated
with acanthus leaves
and symbolic images.*

*438 top right
Rounding off the
decoration of the
portal of Saint-
Trophime are the
statues of St. Peter,
St. John,
St. Trophime,
St. James and
St. Bartholomew.*

*438 center right
The simple, austere
interior of Saint-
Trophime is one of
the most fascinating
in Provence. Filled
with light from the*

*tall windows, it is
sixty-five feet high.*

*438 bottom right
The interior of the
Arles cathedral is
particularly austere
and draws
inspiration from
ancient motifs: the
vault rests on cornices
decorated with
acanthus leaves,
while the capitals
and small columns
were influenced by
Byzantine
architecture.*

The Fondation Van Gogh, directed by Yolande Clergue, has also been established in Arles. It has its offices in the 18th century de Luppé palace opposite the arena. No paintings by Van Gogh are displayed but there are paintings and sculptures created in homage to the master by contemporary artists. The result is a marvelous variety of themes inspired by Van Gogh: the sculptor Cèsar has displayed an 18th century armchair wrapped in a fishing net, Francis Bacon produced an oil painting showing the shadow of Van Gogh as it appeared in a self-portrait walking through Tarascon, and Fernando Botero painted a picture of a gigantic straw seat with a typical pair of Van Gogh boots lying on it.

Different styles and epochs exist together in Arles. In Place de la République we see the contrast between the solemnity of the City Hall built during the second half of the 18th century by Jules Mansart, the Sun King's architect, and the stirring 12th century Romanesque church and cloister of Saint-Trophime, one of the most beautiful in Provence, that has two sides built in Romanesque style and the other two in Gothic. The outstanding sculptures that decorate the portal provided a lesson in biblical culture to the pilgrims on their way to St. James cathedral in Santiago de Compostella.

In contrast to Arles' cultural side, there is the bustle of the Saturday morning market on Boulevard des

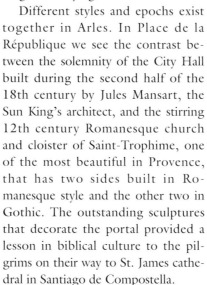

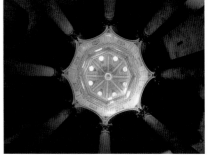

Lices, one of Provence's best. Typical are the stalls selling bull or donkey salami and goat cheese or mountains of fresh oysters and prawns. What makes this market different from others in France is the saddle-makers' section where the sale of bridles, stirrups, creams, boots and saddles remind us that Arles stands at the entrance to the Camargue, the kingdom of wild horses and the *gardians.*

TOULON, MARITIME TRADITIONS

440 top The large Place de la Liberté, in the center of Toulon, is animated by cafés shaded by plane trees. In the middle is the Fountain of the Federation, sculpted in the late 19th century.

440 center A maritime city with an active military port, Toulon has preserved very little of its old town. The cafés facing Place Puget are always bursting with life.

440 bottom Place Puget is the heart of Toulon. Its fascination lies in the thick vegetation that has invaded the three basins of the Fountain of Three Dolphins, a work by sculptor Jean Chastel.

440-441 The bay of Toulon is extraordinarily beautiful when seen from on high. Above the skyscrapers and modern houses in the built-up areas, one can see as far as the Hyères Islands.

441 top Yachts and motorboats rock in the Toulon port, which is surrounded by modern condominiums built after World War II, when the town was destroyed.

Whereas the other cities of Provence have succeeded in maintaining their glorious heritage intact, Toulon suffered the ravages of World War II like no other. Today, the old city has lost its place to modern blocks with vividly colored windows but the invasion of cement has not succeeded in ruining the city's surrounding natural environment. The towers seem smaller from the *corniche* on Mont Faron that bristles with green cluster pines and the distant view stretches from the small and large docks as far as the Giens peninsula. To the traveler, modern Toulon still offers a magnificent setting: surrounded by green hills, it looks onto one of the most beautiful harbors in the Mediterranean, where Vauban, the great military architect of the Sun King, built the largest dockyard in the kingdom to outfit ships for the navy. It was here that on December 19, 1793 Napoleon showed his military genius for the first time when he stormed the city allied to the monarchist party and the English who were obliged to leave. The old dockyard, begun by Cardinal Richelieu and used as a port, has been conserved from Toulon's past while the new docks, built out of Vauban's project, are now a naval base.

443 top
Lying between
Cavalaire and Le
Lavandon, the
Domaine du Rayol
park is a magnificent
oasis open to the
public where an
infinite number of
endemic
Mediterranean
plants are grown.
This botanic garden
also has exotic plants
and palms.

443 center
Carpeted by greenery,
Cap Taillat juts out
into the blue sea
south of Saint-
Tropez.

443 bottom
The white beach of
Escalet, at Saint-
Tropez, lies between
the turquoise sea and
the green maritime
pines and maquis
vegetation.

442 top left
Cap du Dramont,
dominated by the
Esterel cliff, softly
descends to the sea
opposite the Ile d'Or
with its tall medieval
tower.

442 top right
The craggy, barren
coast of Marseilles,
lashed by the mistral,
which clears the sky,
still has a wild look
about it. Every day the
old port is filled with
fishermen who sell their
catch early in the
morning on the quay.

442-443 The rugged
rocks of Esterel fall
headlong into the sea
in a phantasmagoria
of color: from red to
yellow to the purple of
the lichens. All this is
framed by islets and
rocks, and coves and
inlets create
enchanting views.

An unbroken series of light-houses, beaches and deep, well-protected bays with the occasional inlet so small that a sardine could block the entrance, as the Marseillais say. Off the coast lie islands where nature has been left untouched. Lining the seashore are cluster pines, palm trees and the Mediterranean maquis with its smells of rosemary, thyme, mastic tree and marjoram. The promontories on the coast – Cap du Pinet, Cap Camarat, Cap de l'Aigle – offer superb views of the sunrise and sunset. From the delta of the Rhône to the Esterel, the Provençal coast contains an incredible variety of landscapes and colors. In love with Saint-Tropez, Colette, the 20th century writer famous for her novels *Gigi and Claudine*, said, "The blue that rules the sky here is a color only dreamt of elsewhere, but on the Provençal riviera it arcs over everything." The sea too is a light, transparent blue which, at Saint-Tropez, washes up on the famous Pampelonne beach protected on one side by the lush and spectacular Cap Camarat and, on the other, by Cap Escalet. Here the cluster pines and vines grow right down to the beaches of golden sand separated by rocky points. The fame of Saint-Tropez, for many years nourished by the enthusiasm of Brigitte Bardot, has not diminished. During summer, tourists seated in the port cafés play the game of spotting the famous as they come ashore from their yachts moored in the harbor. Yet, even in the heart of the season, the *pétanque* players and lively, colorful market on Wednesdays and Saturdays in the Place des Lices, surrounded by centuries-old plane trees, seem a thousand miles away from the worldliness of the port. The view from the

citadel that guards the gulf covers the whole bay, from the massif des Maures to the Esterel that drops right down to the sea with its bare rock colored red and blue by porphyry and yellow and violet by lichen. The Annonciade Museum housed in an 18th century chapel next to the port holds paintings by such famous artists as Matisse, Derain, Braque and Dufy. Further back, the chapel of Saint Anne, protectress of the town, contains so many offerings that one might think it a small museum of the marina with its silhouettes and models of boats and drawings of the port. Built at an altitude of 675 feet to protect the area from the Saracens, the two villages Ramatuelle and Gassin are picturesque with narrow medieval streets lined with olive trees, eucalyptus and vines. They are ancient sentinels of the sea, like the lovely Grimaud that exudes the spirit of Provence and which is ennobled by Grimaldi castle with its three medieval towers and the small romantic church of Saint-Michel.

Although the peninsula of Saint-Tropez still boasts luxuriant vegetation, the road along the coastline between Cavalaire and Le Lavandou is lined by nothing but houses and hotels except for the botanical gardens named the Domaine du Rayol. They was created by a banker at the beginning of the 20th century to display thousands of plants that grow happily in the Mediterranean climate.

444 top
The regular hexagon of the citadel, with its three round towers and massive ramparts, reminds one of the war-like past of Saint-Tropez. From the top one can see the gulf, the Massif des Maures and the Esterel, as far as the Lérins islands and the offshoots of the Alps.

444 center
The tightly-packed ochre and pink houses with old tile roofs are a lovely background to the old port, which is always vivacious. The summer season opens with the Grand Prix off-shore race, while in August the town is one of the stages in the Tour de France for sailboats.

444 bottom *Le Gorille is a must for anyone landing at Saint-Tropez. Along the quay are small restaurants and cafés that invite you to spend some time watching the sailboats and motorboats come and go.*

444-445 The old port in Saint-Tropez is a favorite with those who have large yachts: the high life, small characteristic restaurants, and the chance to mingle with the international jet set, are an everlasting attraction.

445 top
The oldest houses in Saint-Tropez seem to rise up out of the sea, protected by the bell-tower of the church dedicated to the eponymic saint of the town, Saint-Tropez, who with sword and armor dominates the façade.

In the midst of the green pine trees, the houses of the village of Porquerolles overlook the port: the village area features early 20th century villas that belonged to the owners of the island before the French Government purchased it in the 1970s, a wine-producing estate, bistros, and restaurants.

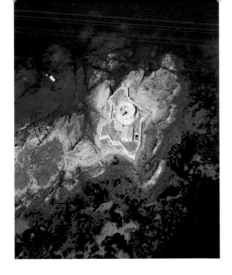

Palm trees are an important feature of the landscape of Hyères, a small town reminiscent of the early 1900s and the oldest resort on the coast. It is the departure point for Hyères archipelago made up of three little islands with lush Provençal gardens, bearing the names Porquerolles, Port-Cros and l'Île du Levant. The three form a veritable oasis where nothing is lacking: in the center of Porquerolles there is a large, perfectly cultivated vineyard that produces a good rosé, which cheers the dining tables of the island. When pirates were at large in the area, they used the island as a refuge and the steps, now worn down by time and weather, that rise out of the sea at Porquerolles were used to carry booty from the boats up to the Pirates Gallery where it was hidden. The small port at Porquerolles filled with sailing boats is lined with houses colored a warm pink.

As always, the song of the cicadas, the smells of rosemary and the mastic trees, and the green of the tamarisks, eucalyptus and umbrella pines seduce anyone who sets foot on the island. The mainland is near but it seems part of another world; here everything is easier. The total absence of cars heightens this sensation – all travel is on foot or by bicycle. In the evening, when the bells fall quiet, silence reigns absolute and the magic of Porquerolles permeates the air even in high summer. Shaded paths and avenues bordered by immense pines with twisted roots invite the visitor to explore in search of charming beaches like the Plage de la Courtade or the Plage de Lequin to the right of the port, or small bays like l'Aiguade or steep rocks like the one that drops into the sea on Oustaou de Diou beach (ancient dialect for the House of God). Then there is the Plage d'Argent that takes its name from the color of the white quartz sand. And the Plage de Notre Dame on the other side of the village, perhaps the loveliest and most secluded of all, which Jean Luc Godard chose for scenes in his film *Pierrot le Fou?* The old Place des Armes is the center of life on the island where games of *pétanque* start each evening at sunset. Is that all there is? Anyone arriving from the mainland might think so at first but soon one realizes that the simplicity of this limited existence has its own fascination. It is easy to chat with the inhabitants of the island: just drop into the Bar de l'Escale for a pastis at aperitif time. This is an obligatory stop-off for the *pétanque* players as they each have a locker in which they keep their balls and the equally important duster to keep them clean.

An hour away by boat lies the smaller island of Port-Cros, a national park, ringed by a glorious sea rich with fish of many different species. The village, arranged around a palm-lined avenue, is small enough to seem like Lilliput; the sea that crashes onto the jagged, rocky coast is a paradise for scuba divers. For those who love underwater exploration, the ideal scuba-diving attraction is a ship that sank at Port-Cros in 1968, which is now the habitat of colonies of sea-eels. Pines, olive trees and maquis with its huge variety of aromatic herbs grow wild inland. Even wilder is the island of the Levant, almost entirely owned by the French navy, just in front of Port-Cros. With its almost inaccessible cliffs, it is a paradise for nudists that arrive here every summer.

450 top left
Precipitous rocks
overlooking the sea
and blooming
meadows are the
features of the zone
between Cassis and
La Ciotat, the town
that witnessed the
birth of cinema. The
coastline from the
Camargue to the
environs of Marseilles
offers a panorama of
uninterrupted
beauty.

450 top right
Celebrated by
Mistral, the greatest
Provençal poet, Cassis
never stops amazing
people with the variety
of its landscape. The
rocks on the western
part of the bay are
every bit as beautiful
as the white cliffs
of Dover.

450-451 The Cassis
cliffs are one of the
most spellbinding
points of the
Provençal coast. The
rust-colored rock
crowned with woods
at Cap Canaille,
which offer a
magnificent view of
the Puget massif and
the islands, is in stark
contrast with the blue
sea, creating a play of
colors that has
inspired many
modern painters.

The winds between the islands in the archipelago of Hyères make this an ideal area for sailing whereas the small port of Bandol on the far side of Toulon – with its fishing boats that arrive either early in the morning or at sunset and its promenade lined with palms and oleanders – is the resort for doing absolutely nothing. Around the village, magnificent vineyards have produced a red wine with a bouquet of vanilla and red fruits since ancient times. There is a strong temptation for the visitor to stop off in one of the many local taverns and sip at a glass of Provençal nectar. The Calanques, steep inlets created out of white limestone, drop into the emerald water between La Ciotat and Marseilles; these form one more spectacular feature among the many examples of natural splendor to be found in Provence. Confronted by such beauty, the enormous cranes in the dockyards at La Ciotat that seem to lift the entire port get forgotten. The name La Ciotat recalls the birth of cinema. Who could forget the first film of the Lumière brothers, *The Arrival of the Train at La Ciotat Station*, presented in Paris on December 28, 1895, that made the spectators at the Grand Café on Boulevard des Capucins jump out of their seats with amazement?

"If you've seen Paris but not seen Cassis, you haven't seen anything" is a local saying. The small town between La Ciotat and Marseilles overlooks a busy fishing port where fishermen unload their wares and has boutiques

dedicated to 19th century Provençal painting; the town's atmosphere is one of cheerfulness and *joie-de-vivre*. This is the departure point for sea trips to the nearby Calanques, a word that calls up thoughts of ancient geological epochs. The cleaves in the rocks extend for over one hundred yards below the water creating grottoes and an ideal habitat for fish. They were formed thousands of years ago by rivers rushing down to the sea which later rose and submerged them.

452 top left and 452-453 *The spectacle of the Calanques in the environs of Marseilles is of incomparable beauty: sheer rock faces precipitating into the sea, and pinnacles that form a barrier for delightful inlets frequented by sailboats and fishing boats.*

The nearest to Cassis is Port-Miou ("safe refuge" in Provençal dialect) that runs inland for nearly a mile and is lined on either side by villas and gardens. Port-Pin is wilder, a half hour further on, with a well-protected, small stone beach and Aleppo pines clinging to the rock walls. At the marvelous En-Vau, where the perpendicular walls are used by rock climbers and a small beach is set between the rock pinnacles, the real Calanques scenery begins: the bright green of the vegetation, the dazzling white of the

452 center left
Quite near the gullies of Sormiou, in the same massif, is the Morgiou fjord. Here rough trails offer panoramic hikes, but even from the sea the view is superb. In July and August this area is inaccessible by land, while in the other months one can get there by car.

452 bottom left
This tiny bay in the middle of Calanques and gorges is a ring of rock surrounding a body of water as transparent as that in a fountain.

452 right
The Calanques at Sormiou are a favorite haunt of the Marsellais, who love to clamber up the rock faces of this fjord, which are furrowed by "trails" suitable for all kinds and levels of climbs.

limestone, and the turquoise of the water. Then there are Sormiou and Morgiou with their *cabanons*, the small huts used by fishermen in the 19th century that have now been transformed into weekend retreats for Marseillais. At Cap Morgiou in 1985, a diver named Cosquer discovered a cave at the end of a tunnel 120 feet below the waterline. 20,000 years ago the cave would have been accessible on foot when it was decorated with wonderful wall paintings, interpreted as ritual signs of the hunt.

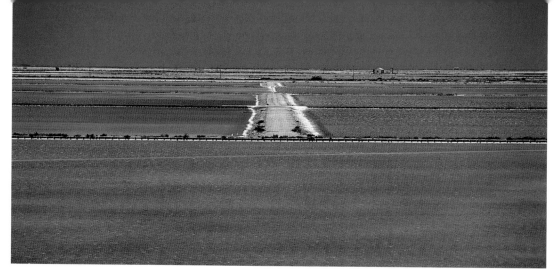

454 top The salt-pans in the Camargue at the borders of the Salin-de-Giraud east of the Grand Rhône, often take on a dreamlike aspect. Large, geometric evaporation basins, and hillocks and heaps of salt welcome the trucks used for transporting this product.

In direct contrast to the vertical Calanques, the horizontal stretch of the Camargue in the province of Arles is enclosed by the delta of the river Rhône. Here can be found salt flats, flower-covered meadows, rarely visited beaches and large lagoons around the Etang de Vaccarès, the home of flocks of flamingos. This is the French Wild West, the kingdom of the Camargue breed of horses, short-horned bulls raised for Spanish bull-rings and bulls with lyre-shaped horns used in the bull-fights that take place in Arles. Overseeing all this are the *gardians*, heirs of ancient traditions, that ride horseback with a trident in hand. They are the custodians of the *manade*, which in Camargue means what you have in hand, i.e. hundreds of hectares of land that are home to animals free to wander and feed at will. Here and there stand the thatch-roofed *cabanes*, the low, oval, traditional white walled homes of the *gardians*. In the center of the *manade* stands the *mas*, the old patriarchal residence with wrought iron balconies. On either side of the property, unpaved roads hidden between the canes run alongside canals down to the huge white beaches where surfers and gourmets gather in the welcoming *cabanons* to eat fresh fish prepared by fishermen-cum-cooks.

456 top and 456-457
*The Camargue lies
between the mouths of
the Petit Rhône and
Grand Rhône:
thousands of hectares
of marshland
populated by
magnificent brightly-
colored birds and
vast prairies that are
the domain of the
famous horses and the*
*bulls with lyre-shaped
horns that are raised
for the bloodless
bullfights held at
Arles. At Giraud the
shallow seawater that
penetrates the ponds
evaporates from
March to September,
leaving a crust of salt
about two inches high
that is gathered from
August to October.*

*457 top right
Excursions on
horseback are one of
the major attractions
in the Camargue.
This area offers riders
the possibility to gallop
through the immense
prairies or follow
paths along ponds and
canals to observe the
flight of numerous
species of birds.*

*457 bottom right The
Camargue horses are
born black or grey
and with time become
white. They are small,
very strong and wild.
They are captured
with lassos, branded
and trained when
they are three years
old. Their job is to
help the gardians lead
the cattle.*

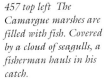

*457 top left The
Camargue marshes are
filled with fish. Covered
by a cloud of seagulls, a
fisherman hauls in his
catch.*

*457 bottom left
On a green headland
surrounded by swamps
and prairies, is this
cabane, a typical house
for the gardians, the
Camargue "cowboys." It
is like a small chapel, low
and oval to resist the
strong wind, and has a
thatched roof that touches
the windows and walls.*

The best days in the Camargue are
24-25 May when the patron saint of
gypsies, Saint Sarah, is commemorated at Saintes-Marie-de-la-Mer, by
gypsies coming from all over Europe.

Saintes-Marie-de-la-Mer is now a
small tourist resort but the nearby
Aigues-Mortes still retains a medieval
atmosphere within its circle of walls
which brings to mind the knights that
set sail from here on the Seventh Crusade. As always in Provence, the past
is an integral part of the land where
nature has created such a variety of
landscapes.

458-459 and 459 top left At dawn and sunset the Camargue marshes, including the vast Etang de Vaccarès, take on fantastic colors: pink, yellow, red, purple. The pink flamingos, immobile on their long legs, seem to be enjoying this magic moment.

459 top right Canals and ponds are flanked by spontaneous vegetation that lends a wild character to this land. There are low shrubs such as saltwort and mock privet, as well as plants adapted to salty earth that are sometimes covered by the water in the winter. Around the marshes, the reeds protect the birds' nests and offer shelter to other animals.

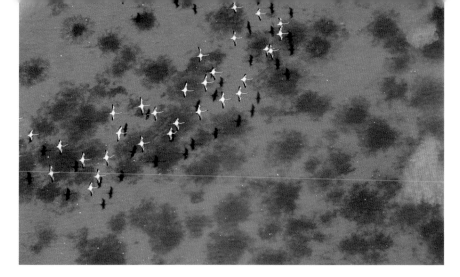

460-461 and 461 bottom right Most of the lagoons in the Camargue, such as the Etang de Vaccarès, are fantastic natural reserves inhabited by over 300 species of birds, many of which winter here. Teals, for example, are among the ducks that live in the marshes. In the Pont de Gau Ornithological Park at Saintes-Maries-de-la-Mer, which is open to the public, visitors can see most of the species that live in the Camargue.

461 top left and top right The coypu, a rodent much like a small beaver, is a habitué here. Boars and red foxes also live in this zone. The small frog perched on a rush seems to be wary, ready to dash away from any creature that might think he is a tasty morsel.

462 top left
Until not long ago, Saintes-Maries-de-la-Mer was a fishermen's village, but in the last few decades it has become a famous tourist locality. Despite the modern restaurants and hotels, the town has preserved some of its characteristic features.

462 top right and 463 top and bottom The solitary homes of the gardians (cow tenders) crop up here and there amid the natural surroundings. These Camargue "cowboys" never move away from the prairies. On the roofs is a cross, the same one the gardians wear around their necks. On holidays the girls wear the traditional red and black costumes of their village.

462-463 Saintes-Maries-de-la-Mer is famous for the huge gypsy festivities held every year on May 24-25. Gypsies come here from all parts of Europe to celebrate their patron saint, Sara. The climax of the ceremonies is the procession, in which the statue of St. Sara, surrounded by the different gypsy clans, is taken on a boat to the beach.

463 center The austere Romanesque church in Saintes-Maries-de-la-Mer, built in the 12th century, looks like a small fortress. Some architectural elements were added in later centuries, such as the clocher peigne *and* the tour haute, *a kind of tower that was used as a lookout for enemies and at the same time was a landmark for sailors.*

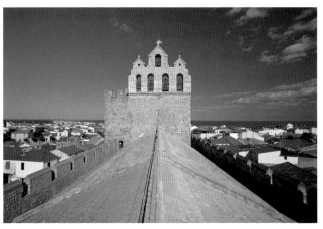

464-465 Aigues Mortes means "still waters," indicating that the region was once a huge swamp. Massive crenellated walls with towers surround the town, which in the past had a fortified port that Louis IX had built to protect the departure of the Crusaders.

STONE VILLAGES AMIDST
OLIVE GROVES AND LAVENDER FIELDS

466 top and 467 top Built along the Durance river, the village of Sisteron has a medieval center with winding alleyways and beautiful old houses with picturesque stairways. The village is dominated by the citadel, which was entirely rebuilt in the late 16th century by order of Henry IV and contains a fascinating 13th century castle and the 14th century Notre-Dame chapel.

466 center The countryside around Sisteron is brightened in the summer with the color of sunflowers. Besides the characteristic small Provençal houses, the village has manor houses such as the Hôtel du Rocher in the de la Baume quarter, and the Domenican church founded in 1248, a splendid example of Cistercian architecture.

466 bottom The Barcelonnette valley, which links Provence and Piedmont in Italy, was isolated and relatively unknown for a long time. The town, at 3609 feet above sea level and blessed with mild, dry climate, is characterized by an area of luxurious villas built in the early 20th century by the inhabitants who had become rich after emigrating to Mexico.

Leaving the coast, one travels inland to find the other Provence, the one loved by writers like Jean Giono and Alphonse Daudet who were born here and explored every corner of it on long walks through its mountains, valleys and canyons.

Everywhere, the changing scenery is dominated by olive trees on the sunny slopes of the hills; the Mediterranean maquis, which has replaced the forests on the limestone slopes of the Alpilles and Mont Sainte-Victoire, consists of bushes, berries and flowers from which the bees make the best honey in France.

First, Haut Provence, which begins with the charming village of Moustiers Sainte-Marie famous for its pottery. In the heart of the hamlet criss-crossed by a maze of alleys and small squares, stands the Musée de la Faïence in the Place du Presbytère where an interesting collection of ceramics from the most important workshops through the ages is displayed. Small 17th century townhouses welcome the visitor in the ancient village of Manosque, many times described with graphic poetry in the books of Jean Giono. To the north, Sisteron is an intact medieval village on the banks of the river Durance, dominated by a fort that overlooks the surrounding mountains and valleys. Traveling upstream, the visitor enters the valley of Barcelonette that connects Piedmont to Provence by way of the Maddalena mountain.

466-467 At the foot of the spectacular de la Baume limestone cliff, the village of Sisteron is divided in two by the Durance river. The historic center lies around the Notre-Dame-des-Pommiers cathedral, built in the 12th century in Provençal Gothic style with Lombard influences.

"Nothing is more romantic than the mixture of these rocks and these chasms, of the green water and these purple shadows, of this sky blue like Homer's sea, and of this wind that speaks with the voice of the dead," wrote Jean Giono about the gorges of Verdon. The rock walls are 2300 feet high and drop sheer into the green water of the river below. A road runs along the top of the ravine with terraces that look down into the abyss while, at the small village of

Rougon, there is a look-out tower that gives a magnificent view over the huge canyon at the point where the river Verdon meets the Baou.

In contrast to the spectacular scenery of this gorge, there are tiny villages all around Provence, perched on rocky hill-tops or nestling in the hollows of valleys filled with cherry blossom, with simple grey stone houses, the inevitable fountain playing in the village square, and shady streets filled with the thousand scents of Provence on market day. Their romantic atmosphere has always made them a perfect setting for love stories, as, for example, for Yves Montand and Simone Signoret who met for the first time in Saint-Paul-de-Vence.

468 At the junction of the Napoleonic and upper Verdon roads, La Castellane, along the Verdon river, is dominated by an incredible rock bluff crowned by the Notre-Dame-du-Roc, which was rebuilt in the 18th century. From here the view of the town is superb.

469 left The Verdon river, whose name derives from its bright green color, is flanked by dizzying rock faces. The most fascinating part of the river, which is 109 miles long, is the gorge known as the Grand Canyon du

Verdon, a fissure in the rock that offers a marvelous landscape: cliffs, ravines, grottoes and suspended terraces.

469 right A road along the gorge affords visitors spectacular views and the chance to see boats going down the tranquil river. In the 1970s, 200 paths were marked out on the rock faces for climbers.

470

Being a meeting point for painters, Saint-Paul naturally attracted the collectors and art dealers whose lives revolved around fashions in art. The most famous of all, Aimé Maeght, created the Collection Maeght in 1964, a museum set amongst olive trees entirely dedicated to 20th century art with internal rooms and a superb open air space where works by Mirò, Kandinsky, Brancusi and others are displayed. The Collection Maeght has made the cobbled village of Saint-Paul, with its small crafts shops, a highly popular tourist attraction. Visitors wishing to enjoy the village's ancient Provençal character that has fascinated so many artists, have to wait until evening when the roads empty of traffic and the silence of the night is only broken by the sound of footsteps and the splash of water in the fountain in the square. Of its historical heritage, Saint-Paul has preserved the defensive walls built by François I in 1536 to protect the village from the attacks of Emperor Charles V.

Another fief of the counts of Provence during the Middle Ages was nearby Biot that sits on top of the hill overlooking the Brague. Its position and simplicity of life made it a great favorite with artist Fernand Léger who moved there from Paris to work on a farm in the middle of the countryside. There he produced paintings, tapestries, pottery and sculptures that today are displayed in the museum that Biot has dedicated

to him where the farm used to stand. Local craftsmen who produce pottery and stained glass exported around the world have taken their inspiration from the dazzling blues and white that predominated in Léger's work. As steadfast as Saint-Paul, Grasse, the medieval capital of east Provence, has been the perfume capital since the 17th century. It is said that Maria de' Medici was responsible. Unable to stand the smell of the washed hides at Grasse, she suggested to the tanners that they perfume their products. The suggestion was taken up as the surrounding countryside, being bathed in sunshine and sheltered from the cold, was highly suitable for the cultivation of the jasmine, orange, rose, lemon and lavender plants from which the perfume could be made. Essence of violet has always been produced at Tourrettes-sur-Loup, a village built on top of a limestone promontory, which seems wrapped in a bright violet mantle in spring. The fame of Tourrettes is also linked to the 15th century castle and to the tiny roads from the houses, which act as a bulwark against potential enemies. Sudden views can be glimpsed between one house and the next and the flower-covered balconies look over a gentle slope covered with olive trees. The olive is such an important tree that should it be necessary to uproot one to build a house, the owner is obliged to replant it elsewhere.

Rivaling Tourrettes as the source of the best olive oil in Provence is the area around Aix-en-Provence. The oldest olive presses are found at the foot of Mount Sainte-Victoire at the gates of Aix.

Arriving in this area, the visitor's thoughts immediately turn to Paul Cézanne who was born here. He had a small house built at Bellevue right in front of the mountain because he liked to paint it at different moments of the day under all the colors and shifts of light. It is the trembling of the leaves of the olive trees that accentuate the particular brilliance of the light in the Alpilles, a series of small mountains with jagged white and grey peaks less than 1640 feet in height. From on high they seem to protect the village of Saint-Rémy, the village that dates back to Roman times and which was painted by Van Gogh many times during his stay there from 1889 to 1890. The meeting point for travelers on this road is Les Antiques at Glanum where one of the oldest triumphal arches from the Gallic and Roman world stands. It was built during the reign of Augustus to celebrate the size of the empire. Standing right beside it in a marvelous state of repair is a mausoleum, said to be of Augustus's grandsons, Caius and Lucius, decorated with splendid bas-reliefs on the four walls and statues of two illustrious persons wearing togas.

Built on the banks of the river Ouvèze, Vaison-la-Romaine also boasts ancient ruins. The addition of "Romaine" to the town's name only occurred in 1924 when wonderful Roman ruins were brought to light by abbot Sautel supported by the Vaison-born industrialist Maurice Burrus, who shared a surname with Sextus Burrus, the prefect of Emperor Nero. The remains were of a similar quality to the House of the Dolphin at La Villasse where large quantities of oyster shells and fish-ponds attest to the prosperity of those times. Then there is the large and beautiful House of the Messii in the district of Puymin where the elegant vestibule leads into the atrium built with a typical central *impluvium*. The Roman theater was built against the hill with the stage cut out of the rock; it is a little smaller than the theater in Orange which is the venue for the international summer performances of song and dance known as *Choralies*. Another of Vaison's Roman attractions is the House of the Silver Bust which boasts mosaics and marbles and takes its name from the statue found there but now kept in the local museum, the Musée Théo-Desplans. Medieval Vaison, the upper city above the river reached by crossing the Roman bridge, was built during the 13th and 14th centuries using stone from the Roman remains. The narrow, twisting streets were almost deserted at the start of the 20th century but began to fill once again when the excavations began to unearth the architectural treasures that have attracted tourists from around the world.

474 top In the heart of the valley, Lourmarin is dominated by the Renaissance castle. Here we see its exterior and the fireplace salon. The complex comprises the old castle, built in the late 15th century, and the new castle, which dates back to the mid-1500s.

474 bottom Les Baux is divided into two areas on a rocky plateau. On the top is the citadel with the ruins of the castle belonging to the Baux, the most powerful liege lords in France until the 15th century; below it is the village proper, rich in Renaissance buildings and small museums, which is a great tourist attraction.

474-475 *Between Château du Bois and Lagarde d'Apt, the lavender covers the countryside with an infinite number of shades of violet. The Romans were the first to cultivate lavender in Provence, as they valued the purifying properties of the scented flower.*

Like the Alpilles hills, the landscape of the Val d'Enfer is colored white and grey but it is harsher and its limestone rock seems to bristle with innumerable pinnacles. This is the valley onto which the fantastic village of Les Baux faces, apparently planted on a rocky plateau surrounded by wild vegetation. The spectacular ruin of the citadel looms over the valley which, during the Middle Ages, used to belong to the lords of Baux, the most powerful vassals in the Midi who claimed to be descended from King Baldassar, one of the three wise men. The village built during the 16th century with the intention of giving Les Baux its ancient splendor stands below the castle in the heart of the citadel. Today the village is invaded by tourists every summer. In order to appreciate its character and the architectural details of the Renaissance buildings, you really have to arrive early in the morning or at sunset. Wan-

dering through streets like Rue des Fours or Rue Trençat, one comes across the Hôtel des Porcelets that is now the home of the modern art museum, the Hôtel de Manville with an exhibition of ancient engravings and prints. More nostalgic and charming is nearby Fontvieille, a tranquil provincial village with a traditional square reserved for games of *pétanque*. Close by stands the famous windmill that inspired Alphonse Daudet in *Lettres de*

mon Moulin written in Paris in 1869. Although he had moved to the capital after a family financial disaster, Daudet always hankered after his homeland and returned there in his heart, as did his boastful hero, Tartarin, to the nearby Tarascon in the book Aventures Prodigieuses de Tartarin de Tarascon read by children around the world. Tartarin's village is ringed by walls with a long central road flanked by a portico. The town also has one of France's loveliest fortified castles with interior in flamboyant Gothic style that was built at the end of the 15th century by King René.

If Tarascon is now a small city, the Lubéron in the heart of upper Provence is a zone where many small typical Provençal villages still exist, with a square protected by plane trees where the locals meet up over a glass of *pastis* and where the flower, fruit and bric-a-brac markets are held. Often, an old manor-house will stand over the village as a reminder of its feudal past, for example, in the enchanting village of Lourmarin with the *chateau vieux*, built between 1495-1525 and the *chateau neuf*, designed after 1540.

475 left The Fontvieille mill, which inspired Alphonse Daudet's Lettres de mon Moulin, *continues to arouse curiosity. In reality this work was written in Paris, where the author's family had moved.*

475 top right Perched on the sides of hill in the heart of the Lubéron mountains is Bonnieux, a rich papal city until the French Revolution whose ascending streets and 16th, 17th and 18th century buildings bear witness to its former splendor.

475 bottom right Saignon, the stronghold that once controlled access to the Pays d'Apt, is one of the most characteristic villages on the northern side of the Lubéron mountain range.

One of Provence's most beautiful roads leads from Lourmarin to Apt where the ochre color of the land signifies Roussillon clay which is extracted pretty much everywhere. This section of Provence is like Colorado for the color of the earth, which changes from yellow, to pink, to orange, to red and to a vivid violet, and for its jagged and contorted limestone towers crowned by a piece of rock like the head on a mushroom that suddenly appear as one turns a bend in the path.

A few miles on lies the village of Ménerbes that became famous after publication of the book *A Year in Provence* by the English author Peter Mayle which was translated into seventeen languages. Ménerbes has been the scene of many important historical events: as a refuge for Protestants, the citadel was besieged innumerable times and has witnessed many massacres. A road through the open countryside takes the visitor to Oppède-le-Vieux, one of the Lubéron's most characteristic villages, which overlooks orchards and fields of sunflowers. After a long period of abandon, it was returned to life during the 1970s thanks to the efforts of Parisians who built holiday homes out of the ruins. Equally lovely is Bonnieux, shaped like a pyramid surrounded by pine trees that stretches up towards the sky at the foot of the Lubéron regional park.

476 top, 476-477 and 477 top right Gorges, cliffs, galleries and panoramic terraces with an overwhelming view: in Roussillon, in the Pays d'Apt, the color of the land ranges from yellow to pink, orange, red, and bright purple. This is the reason why the ravine between Rustrel and Gignac is called the "Provençal Colorado."

477 top left and bottom right Ochre is extracted everywhere around Roussillon. Once it was used to paint walls with, but now it is utilized in the cosmetics industry. Visitors can hike along marked paths in search of the "fairies' hats," incredible conical limestone formations that suddenly crop up amid the vegetation.

Dominated by reddish stone and brick, Gordes seems to appear suddenly from nowhere, surrounded by dozens of small orchards separated from one another by dry-stone walls built with the precision of a watchmaker. The ancient construction technique is demonstrated at neighboring Les Bories, an open-air museum of mysterious huts built in dry-stone at some unknown time. A superb panorama over Vaucluse is visible from the center of Gordes.

479 top left Les Bories, situated in the middle of the countryside southwest of Gordes, can be reached via a path flanked by many low stone walls. The

origin of the dry-masonry houses in this village may even date back to the period when the Ligurians abandoned Vaucluse many centuries before Christ.

479 bottom left The two sackcloth puppets in this photograph seem to be humorously announcing the arrival of Provençal spring.

480 top and center left The yellow of the sunflowers which Van Gogh loved to paint explodes in mid-summer, while the fields among olive and apricot trees are laced with the fiery red of the poppies.

480 bottom left The geometrically patterned fields at the foot of Mount Ventoux are both enchanting and peaceful.

480 right For those who love to hike, there are marked paths among the lovely meadows and woods that lead to Mount Ventoux, on the summit of which are meteorological stations and telecommunication apparatus.

480-481 Near the Sénanques abbey, the village of Gordes, perched on a hill, has revived its former splendor since it was discovered by intellectuals and

artists such as the painter Vasarély. The light-colored and well-restored stone bastides, or country houses, are the dominant architectural feature in this area.

Protecting the valley brightened by the colors of the vegetation – the vivid violet-blue of the lavender, the yellow of the sunflowers, the red of the fields of poppies and the variegated expanses of wild flowers – stands majestic Mont Ventoux with its peak crowned with white stones. Petrarch climbed to the top of this mountain in 1336 with his brother and two servants but wrote laconically, "A mass of rocky, wild and almost inaccessible land."

The green spread that lies at the feet of Mont Ventoux takes its name from the village of Les Barroux, a labyrinth of medieval lanes that faces alone onto the plain of Carpentras.

The best view of the neatly kept vineyards is from the large round towers of the village castle built by the local lords in the 12th century; it stands alone and majestic, proud of its dominant position.

Although Mont Ventoux disappointed the poet, the nearby Fontaine de Vaucluse with its "clear, fresh waters" inspired him to write the most famous of his poems dedicated to Laura, the woman he had met in a church in Avignon on April 6, 1327. The clear spring is the source of the Sorgue, the river that flows around the small town of Isle-sur-la-Sorgue, a true paradise for antique lovers. It all began thirty years ago when Albert Gassier, a *pied-noir* from Algeria, established the first flea market in this enchanting area of France known as the Venice comtadine for the many canals that cross it. Today there are more than two hundred antique shops and dealers that open their shops on the weekends selling paintings, rustic kitchen cupboards, fabrics and garden furniture among other things. On Easter Day and August Bank holiday, the village becomes a tangled mass when stall-holders arrive from all over France to present their antiques along the large Avenue des Quatre Otages. By crossing a small bridge, one can enter Bouigas, the oldest district of the village, with its tiny streets that still go by their ancient names: Rue de l'Orme, Rue de l'Ecrevisse and Rue de l'Anguille. They are all names of fish because the village used to be a center for fishermen after the count of Toulouse gave permission in 1327, confirmed by Pope Julius II in 1508, for the waters of the Sorgue to be fished. The practice, unfortunately, died out at the end of the 19th century when an epidemic killed nearly all the fish.

484 left and bottom right The Pays de Sault is part of the so-called violet triangle on the Albion plateau   *between Sault, Séderon and Banon. In this enchanting valley the period between May and August is a blaze of   colors from flowers that is unrivaled in the rest of France. In the land of lavender, besides the marvelous and   inevitable blue and violet, one can easily see expanses of red poppies and multicolored meadows of alfalfa.*

Mont Ventoux is at the center of the *Triangle Mauve* on the plateau of Albion between Sault, Séderon and Banon, which is covered by a carpet of lavender between June and August in a gorgeous blend of shades of blue and violet.

The local inhabitants are so proud of their production that represents 70 percent of the French lavender market; about fifteen years ago they created a fraternity to protect lavender cultivated to a certain quality. The members of the order wear a mauve cloak and cocked hat. August is spent in a series of festivals dedicated to the valuable violet flower. Sault offers a popular two-day festival that includes parades of carriages, sales of products and a lavender scything competition.

The most spectacular view of lavender is seen by the visitor to the abbey of Sénanque, the Cistercian abbey founded by St. Bernard in the 12th century. Its walls were built from pink stone and the roof is still covered with the original grey flat stones. It stands out against the sky and an unending expanse of perfumed violet. The simplicity and strictness preached by Bernard seem to have found some compensation in the grace of the flower as it gently sways in the wind.

484 top right and 485 Southeast of Mount Ventoux is the Pays de Sault. In July, everything is carpeted with lavender and permeated by its lovely scent. The dry plateau and sandstone-limestone earth are ideal for cultivating this splendid flower. The village of Sault, 2510 feet above sea level, affords a fantastic view of the valley as far as   *Mount Ventoux. On August 15 there is the annual lavender festival.*

486-487 One mile from Gordes, in a narrow valley, the Cistercian abbey of Sénanque stands out among the lavender fields. This is the most beautiful of the three abbeys in this area, the other two being Sylvacane and Thoronet.

488 You will discover old, fascinating villages at the foot of Mount Ventoux. Among these, in the middle of the cultivated hills, is Le Barroux, a tiny village at the foot of a Renaissance castle built by the Baux, the local liege lords. It was rebuilt in the late 16th century and restored in the early 20th century. It is now the home of the Center d'Etudes Historiques et Archéologiques du Comtat.

489 *Around Le Barroux the vineyards alternate with the olive and apricot groves. From the castle in the background there is a* *view of the Carpentras plain and the Alpilles Mountains. A few miles away is another enchanting village at the foot of Mount Ventoux– Malaucène.* 490-491 *The Sault valley is almost circular. Here the green of the olive and almond trees stands out among the blue-violet lavender. The* *best lavender is grown at an altitude of 2000-4600 feet and is distinguished by its leaves and color, which tends to be more violet.*

492 top left The stars of the local fairs are the santons, *the small statues used in the traditional manger scene, handmade by craftsmen who hand down their art from generation to generation.*

492 center and bottom left Christmas is the most solemn holiday for the Provençal. Before going to midnight mass, the family has the gros souper, *Christmas Eve dinner.*

492 top right For Christmas the locals create a tableau vivant *of the manger scene, a very moving event that takes months of preparation.*

493 The santons, *the crèche statuettes, are made of terracotta and are painted and dressed in traditional regional costumes. Representing the most characteristic figures and trades, they evoke life in the old Provençal villages.*

A s a land of legends and folklore, Provence loves to relive its past in magnificent festivals celebrated in costume with traditional dances to the sound of traditional music. Frédéric Mistral, the poet from Arles who was awarded the Nobel prize for literature in 1904, was a great supporter of the Provençal language and helped to create the Arlaten Museum in the city of Arles which offers an admirable cross-section of the region's traditions. The museum displays examples of traditional dress and clothing that are still described by Mistral's own hand-written captions. There are models of the holy manger where Jesus was born with the characters made from glass; this tradition originated when a Venetian noblewoman married a duke of Nevers during the 15th century and brought the art of glass-spinning to the area. Then there are the living amulets that, it was believed, protected one from illnesses, like the snail, the slime of which was supposed to prevent measles. The most interesting room is undoubtedly the one that reproduces the atmosphere of the large Christmas *souper*, the meal eaten on Christmas Eve, which is still celebrated in many families. The table is laden with thirteen desserts, one for each guest at the Last Supper, including almond nougat, hazelnuts, dried figs, grapes, dates and oranges. The rest of the menu comprises baccalà (dried salted cod) cooked with herbs, and different dishes of local vegetables like cauliflower and thistle seasoned with olive oil taken from the first pressing or a white sauce based on anchovies.

Christmas is preceded in Provence by the large *Foire aux Santons*, which is held in Marseilles, along the Canebière, in Arles, in the cloisters of Saint-Trophime, at Les Baux and at Fontvieille, the homeland of Tartarin de Tarascon. The *Santons* (the handmade terracotta statues used in representations of the Holy Manger) are painted and dressed in local costume by *santonniers*, the craftsmen whose art is handed down from father to son. At Aubagne, the center of the santonnier tradition, there is a huge variety of figures: the shepherd offering a lamb, the housewife with a large black hen from which broth is made that, it is said, is excellent for the new-born, and characters that represent figures from the past: the baker selling flat bread, the garlic seller, the fishwife and the fisherman carrying his nets. Around these central figures stands a miniature Provençal village with a well, dovecote, oven and mill. The story goes that these Christmas representations in the houses of Provence date back to the times of the French Revolution when, following the ban on Midnight Mass, the Marseillais decided to celebrate the birth of Jesus in their own homes using terracotta figures. Midnight Mass is still celebrated in some villages as it used to be in ancient times, for example, in the collegiate church of Saint-Martin at Saint-Rémy, where the ceremony of the *pastrage* is renewed each year with the presentation of a lamb by shepherds from nearby villages and the priest tells the story that commemorates the long trip made by the shepherds two thousand years ago to render homage to the Lamb.

The land of Tartarin, Provence relives the dark moments of the Saracen raids with triumph and a lively martial spirit when the procession in honor of the patron saint was accompanied by a military escort of the so-called *Bravades*. That era is commemorated each year at Saint-Tropez on the Sunday before Ascension Day when inhabitants of all ages form a division of troops that recalls those companies of soldiers of fortune. Preceded by music, the modern day soldiers march through the city streets escorting the statue of Saint-Tropez and firing off rifles and pistols. Every self-respecting *Bravade* ends the day singing, drinking and dancing traditional dances.

494 The bravade *is an evocation of the battle-scarred past of Saint-Tropez, which over the centuries defended the gulf against invaders. The celebration on May 16-18, which is particularly dear to* the locals, coincides with the patron saint's feast day. In the past the word bravade *indicated the military escort used during the religious procession to protect it from Saracen raids.*

495 left The participants in the bravade *parade take out their old, brightly colored traditional costumes handed down from father to son, which are fit out by the* Oustau de la Bravade *seamstresses. In June, the second* bravade, the Festival of the Spanish, *commemorates the victory of Saint-Tropez against the Spanish galleys in 1631.*

495 right The bravade *begins with the consignment of the flag to the captain and his senior officers. Then sailors and musketeers accompany the bust of Saint-Tropez in procession through the town, which is decked with red and white flags, while there are cannon-shots and salvoes, which are interrupted by the authorities' salute and the tribute to the French Navy ships.*

In spring, the Camargue celebrates the Ferrade, the day on which one-year-old bulls are branded in a festival that mixes work and fun. The event is of great importance as these are the bulls that will be used in the bullring at Arles at Easter and on the first Sunday of July when the matadors attempt to show their skill in running the bulls through. But there are also bloodless corridas in which the toreadors are required to remove a *coccard* from the lyre-shaped horns of the bull.

498 top left and
498-499 In honor
of their black patron
saint, St. Sara, on
May 24 and 25
gypsies come from
all over Europe
to Saintes-Maries-
de-la-Mer.
The festivities
commemorate
the arrival on this
beach, aboard a
boat without oars or
sails, of a group of
persons exiled from
Jerusalem,
including the Virgin
Mary's sister and the
mother of the apostles
John and James.
According to
tradition, St. Sara,
queen of the gypsies,
was there to welcome
them.

During May, Arles also cele-brates its *gardians*, Provençal cowboys and *guardians* of the herds. The horseback *gardians* are dressed in leather trousers and check shirts and hold a trident in one hand as they parade through the town to the admiration of women dressed in the traditional costume depicted in the paintings of Van Gogh.

The gypsy festival celebrated at Saintes-Marie-de-la-Mer on May 24-25 in honor of St. Sarah is fa-mous around the world. Patron saint of the gypsies, Sarah took in the three Mary's chased out of Ju-daea. On the eve of the festival, the reliquary of the saint is carried in procession to singing and accla-mation. On the following day in a riot of colors and sounds, gypsies from all over Europe carry the statue of the saint right down to the sea to symbolize the welcome offered by Sarah to the three women who miraculously reached the town via the Mediterranean. On the next day, an immense pro-cession of *gitans*, *gardians* and citizens of Arles in traditional cos-tume take the saint's boat to the seashore to be blessed.

498 top right and 499
top left On the eve of
the commemoration,
amid songs and
applause, the
reliquary with the
remains of St. Sara
is taken out of the
chapel with the aid
of a hoist and ropes.
The following day the
statue, accompanied
by the gardians and
women dressed in
costumes, is borne
in procession to
the seashore to
commemorate the
welcome reserved for
the fugitives from the
Holy Land. The next
day St. Sara is
immersed in the sea
and is then taken
back to the church.

499 top right
The gardians take
part in the procession
on horseback and
dressed in traditional
costumes, acclaimed
by the crowd. These
cowboys, who tend
their herds with a
trident in hand, are
the protagonists in
Arles of a festival
in their honor that
takes place in early
May.

499 center right and
bottom right During
the Saintes-Maries-
de-la-Mer festivities
there are also many
events in the
amphitheater, in
which the horsemen
of Camargue proudly
display their skill.

500 top Tartarin and his prodigious adventures is the main character in Alphonse Daudet's best-known work, Tartarin de Tarascon. The author, who hailed from Nimes, spent almost all his life in Paris, but the recollections of his youth were always an important part of his writings.

500-501 The Tarasque, one of the oldest festivities in Provence, takes place in late June. It harks back to the legendary time when the inhabitants of Tarascon were terrorized by a winged monster that looked like a huge turtle, which came out of the Rhône river every year and tore children to pieces.

*501 top and center
On June 1 there is a
wine festival at
Boulbon, a small
village between
Tarascon and the
Durance river. In
keeping with
tradition, the men go
to the St. Marcellin
chapel with a bottle*

*of wine to have this
precious drink
blessed, while the
women stay by the
fireside, ready to
celebrate the return
of their men with a
banquet that is
made merrier by the
newly sanctified
wine.*

*501 bottom Since
remote times, the Nuit
de la Saint-Jean
(night of St. John) has
marked the summer
solstice. To celebrate it,
in many villages huge
bonfires are lit for the
entire night, and the
locals dance and sing
around them.*

Music, songs and a tremendous social atmosphere are also to be found during the bottle procession on June 1st at Boulbon. The main characters are the men that head for the church with a bottle of wine in hand to have it blessed in the chapel of St. Marcelin; the women, meanwhile, prepare a feast at home enlivened by hallowed wine.

One of the oldest festivals is the Tarasque, codified by King René in the 15th century during the last weekend of June at Tarascona. It recalls the time that knights battled heroically to destroy the winged monster of the Rhône that came out of the river each year to tear young men and women to pieces until tamed by Saint Martha. Today, the papier-mâché Tarasque leaves its lair and winds its way along the city streets, to the amazement of children and the entertainment of their parents, whipping its tail from side to side and making the girls scream.

On the night of St. John's day, many villages celebrate the Nuit de la Saint-Jean, which has marked the summer solstice since the distant past. As darkness falls, the night is lit up by fires of all sizes as a hymn of joy that the summer has arrived.

INDEX

Note: c = *caption*
bold = *dedicated chapter*

A

Africa, 210, 395
Agnès of Savoy, 374c
Ahès-Dahud, 206c, 206
Ainay-le-Vieil Castle, 266, **275,**
Aix-en-Provence, 393, 392, 395,
   397, 402, 408, 414c, **429-431**
Aix-la-Chapelle, 32c, 33
Ajaccio, 53
Alain Barbe-Torte, 223
Alain d'Avaugour, 188c
Alain le Roux, 156c
Alençon, 374c
Alexander III, 71, 90, 94c,
Alfred de Musset, 76c
Amasse river, 315
Amboise, 293, 295
Amboise Castle, 266, 293, 312,
   315-324, 325, 326c
Amiens, 366c
Androuet du Cerceau, 333, 334c
Anet Castle, 266, 327, 371, 378,
   379c
Angers Castle, 307, 307c
Angers, 265, 315
Anjou, 303c, **307,**
Anjou, House, 312
Anna of Austria, 111c, 129
Anne de Beaujeu, Countess
   of Gien, 40c, 289
Anne of Brittany, 40c, 237, 275,
   296, 312c, 312, 317, 355c
Apollinaire, 78, 108c
Apremont,
Ardier, Paul, 357
Arles, 11, 85c, 387c, 387, 392,
   393c, 393, 395, 396, 397,
   397c, 398, 399, 414, 432, **434-**
   439, 456, 483c, 492, 497c,
   497, 499, 499c
Armor, **168-226**
Arnon River, 272c, 272
Atlantic Ocean, 8, 10c, 53, 170,
   174, 214, 216c, 249c
Aulenti, Gae, 83

Austerlitz, 57c, 57, 90
Austria, 53
Auxerre, 105
Avignon, 387, 397c, 398, 399,
   401, 401c, 402c, 403c, 406c,
   409c, 413, 424c, 424, 426,
   426c, 483
Azay-le-Rideau Castle, 266, 293,
   293c, **308-311**

B

Balzac, Honoré de,
Baricco, Alessandro, 113
Barnenez, 146
Batz-sur-Mer, 221, 221c
Baudelaire, Charles, 59c, 71,
   76c
Beauharnais, Josephine, 53
Beauregard Castle, 356c, **357-361**
Becker, Roland, 230
Benedict XII, 381c, 401, 424
Berengar, Raymond, 397
Bernard, Emile, 210, 225c
Berry, 286, 290, 291c, 293
Berthelot, Gilles, 308
Berthier, Marshal, 362
Bertrand du Guesclin, 237c, 249,
   251
Besnard, Ulysse, 351c
Betton, 138c
Beuvron Valley, 356c
Biot, 387
Blain Castle, 221c
Blanche of Castille, 35c, 35, 36c,
   307, 307c
Blavet River, 233c, 233, 234
Blois Castle, 266, 283, 293, 295,
   295c, 326c, 327, 327c, **347-**
   356, 357, 362c
Blois, Mademoiselle de, 369c
Bohier, Thomas, 11c, 336
Bonnard, Pierre, 108c
Bordeaux, 83, 151, 168, 362
Botrel, Théodore, 188
Bouges Castle, 272c, 272
Bourges, 38, 284c, 285, 296
Braque, Georges, 108c, 382,
   417c
Brest, 172c, 172, 174, 190c, 203c
Breton, André, 410

Briçonnet, Catherine, 336c, 336
Brittany, 8, 35, **136-261**
Brocéliande, Forest of, 227c,
   228c, 228, 230c
Brousconi, Giullaume, 168

C

Caboche, Simon, 38
Camargue, 384c, 387, 388c, 389c,
   451c, 454c, 455, 455c, 456c,
   457c, 457, 458c, 460c, 461c,
   462c, 497c, 497
Canada, 174, 176c
Caravaggio, 272, 302
Carcassonne, 275, 397
Caristie, Augustin Nicolas, 395c
Carnac, 11, 146, 216c, 216, 260
Cartier, Jaques, 168, 169c, 181
Carvallo, 332c, 333
Casanova, 22
Cassis, 384c, 384, 451c
Castellum, see Loches Castle
Castiglione, Baldassare, 103c
Catherine de Médicis, 42c, 43,
   295, 327c, 327, 330c, 336c,
   336, 338c, 342c, 347, 348,
   350c, 351c, 379c
César de Vendôme, 341c
Cézanne, Paul, 61, 83c, 83, 106,
   120, 382, 416c, 417c, 430c
Chagall, Marc, 120
Chambord Castle, 265c, 266c,
   266, 293, 295, 295c, **362-370**
Chambord, 285
Charlemagne, 32c, 33c, 33, 289,
   373
Charles d'Orléans, 347, 347c
Charles de Blois, 156c
Charles I, 399c
Charles II d'Amboise, 283, 327c,
   399
Charles II, 286
Charles III, 402
Charles V, 36, 37c, 41, 68, 156,
   159, 251c, 404c, 471
Charles VI, 38c, 38, 39c, 265,
   347
Charles VII, 38, 39, 39c, 265,
   285, 286, 289, 293, 296, 299,
   302c, 302, 304c, 308, 315, 374

Charles VIII, 11c, 40c, 41, 158, 159c, 223, 233c, 233, 293, 312c, 312, 315, 317c, 317, 423
Charles IX, 43c, 289, 347, 353c
Charles X, 57c, 57
Charles of Anjou, 399
Charles of Luxembourg, 158
Charles the Bald, 155c, 302, 304c
Charlotte Corday, 51c
Charlotte of Savoy, 315
Charost, Duke of, 283
Chartres, 377c, 377
Chateaubriand, Francois René de 181c, 181
Châteaudun Castle, 266, 370c, 371, **373-376**
Chateauroux, 272
Chatelliers, 315
Châtillon, Counts of, 347
Chaumont Castle, 263c, 265c, 293c, 326c, **327-332**
Chaumont, 283
Chenonceau Castle, 6c, 11c, 266, 293, 327, **336-346**, 351c, 379c
Chenonceaux, village of, 11c
Cher River, 6c, 286
Cher, 272, 285, 336, 336c
Cheverny Castle, 265c, 293, **357-361**
Childebert, 78
Childeric III, 33c, 33
Chinon, 39, 39c, 293, 308
Chinon Castle, 265, 266, **296-298**
Chirac, Jacques, 65
Chopin, Fryderyk, 22
Chrétien de Troyes, 227
Claude of France, 338c, 347, 353c
Claudel, Camille, 83
Clement IV, 399c
Clement V, 401, 401c, 426c
Clement VI, 381c, 401, 401c, 424, 426c
Clement VII, 404c
Clément, Jacques, 348
Clos-Lucé Castle, 295, 324c, 325
Cloux Castle, see Clos-Lucé
Cocteau, Jean, 437
Colbert, Jean-Baptiste, 275

Colin du Val, 374
Colombe, Michel, 223
Combourg, Castle of, 249
Comper Castle, 228c, 228
Conan III, 239c, 239
Concarneau, 210c, 210, 257, 257c
Corbière, Tristan, 163, 203c, 203
Corelleau, Nicole, 210
Cornouaille, 216c, 227c, 239c, 239, 257, 257c, 258c
Corot, Camille, 83, 103c
Costantine I, 393c
Cottereau, Jean, 227
Coudray Castle, 296
Courbet, Gustave, 83
Culan, 266, 272c, 275

D

Dahud, Ahès, 168
Dante Alighieri, 78
Danti, Ignazio, 402c, 404c
Daudet, Alphonse, 387, 475, 475c, 500c
Daudet, Léon, 74
Daumier, Honoré, 83
David, Jaques-Louis, 53c
De Beauvoir, Simone, 116c, 119
De Chirico, Giorgio, 108c
De Gaulle, Charles, 64c, 64, 65c, 73c, 111c
De Vogüé, family, 286
Degas, Edgar, 83, 85c, 114c, 120
Delacroix, Eugène, 83, 103c, 114c, 225c
Desportes, François, 289
Diane de Poitiers, 42c, 266, 327, 336c, 336, 340c, 341c, 371, 378, 379c
Diderot, Denis, 76c
Dinan, 251
Doumergue, Gaston, 172c
Dreux Forest, 378, 379c
Drummond Castle, 205
Dubois, François, 42c
Duchamp, Marcel, 62
Ducos, Roger, 325
Dupin, Madame, 336
Dupuis, Nicolas, 111c
Durance River, 383c
Dürer, Albrecht, 33c

E

Edward II, 38c
Edward III, 38
Egypt, 53
Eiffel, Gustave, 88
Ellé, River, 239c, 239
England, 11, 38, 157c, 168, 194, 272
Ernst, Max, 410
Estienne, Charles, 141
Etienne des Baux, 398
Etienne Marcel, 37c
Europe, 8, 11, 18, 50c, 53, 62, 138, 146, 168, 192c, 216c, 223c, 223, 233c, 249c, 254, 382, 387, 457

F

Fellini, Federico, 88
Ferdinand VII of Spain, 276, 278c
Flaubert, 186
Fleisher, Richard, 184
Fleuriot, Léon, 153c, 154
Fouéré, Yann, 166
Fouesnant, 254c
Fougères, Castle, 249c, 249
Fouquet, Jean, 302c
Fournier, Alain, 284c, 285
Fovault, 74
France, 8, 11, 30, 38c, 38, 39c, 40c, 42c, 43c, 43, 44c, 50, 51c, 55c, 60c, 62c, 65c, 65, 68, 72c, 73c, 74, 87, 94c, 115c, 138, 139c, 141, 156, 157c, 158, 159c, 164, 168, 219, 223c, 223, 237c, 242c, 251, 251c, 252, 265, 272, 285, 289, 295, 296, 302, 304c, 322c, 333, 336c, 347c, 349c, 341c, 357, 366c, 377c, 377, 387, 394c, 397c, 474c
Franchini, Gianfranco, 106
Francis I of Angoulême, 11c, 41, 41c, 42c, 105, 159, 266c, 266, 267c, 289, 293, 295, 308, 310c, 317, 324c, 333, 338c, 347c, 348, 349c, 352c, 353c, 362, 362c, 364c, 366c, 368c, 404, 471c

Francis II, 348
François de Longueville, 374c, 471
Francois II, 158, 159c, 221c, 223, 233c, 237c, 237
Frederick I, 48c

G

G. de Genouillac, 28c, 29c
Garbo, Greta, 88
Gaston d'Orléans, 347, 348, 349c
Gauguin, Paul, 83, 85c, 210, 257, 257c, 417, 437
Georges de la Tour, 225c
Gerard de Nerval, 120c
Germany, 165
Gien, 265, 312, 315
Gien Castle, **289**
Giovanetti, Matteo, 426c
Giscard, Valéry, 65
Glanum, 395
Glot, Claudine, 227
Goldoni, Carlo, 22
Gouézec, 240
Goujon, Jean, 378
Gourin, 258
Gournevece, Alexis, 183c
Grall, Xavier, 181c, 258
Granada, 78
Great Britain, 203c
Gregory XI, 426c
Gris, Juan, 114c
Guérande, 221, 221c, 257c
Guillaume de Lorris, 398c
Guimard, Hector, 63c, 125
Guise, Duke of (Le Balafré)
Guy de Rothschild, 67c
Guyot, Laurent, 289, 362c

H

Haussman, Georges, 59, 59c, 71, 122
Hemingway, Ernest, 120
Henri de Guise, 348
Henri II, 266, 289, 295, 302, 310c, 320c, 327, 336c, 336, 353c, 357, 378, 379c
Henri III, 67, 289, 330c, 336c, 336, 348, 352c, 353c, 355c

Henri IV, 43, 66c, 67, 105, 111, 123c, 219c, 333, 338c, 341c, 353c, 356c, 368c, 404, 406, 430c, 430, 466c
Henry VI, 39c, 68, 73c
Henry VII, 233
Henry IX, 43c
Henry of Orléans, 42c
Henrichemont Forest, 285
Hermine Castle, 219c
Hersat, Théodore, 163
Hettier de Boislambert, Claude, 289
Huelgoat, Forest of, 244
Hugo, Victor, 30, 35, 40, 57, 71, 72c, 74, 111, 141, 251c, 251, 347
Hulm, Thomas, 289
Hundred Years' War, 304c

I

Illiers-Combray, 371, 371c, 376c, 377
Imbert de Bastarnay, 302
Ingre, Jean-Auguste, 83, 225c
Innocent III, 36
Innocent VI, 426c
Ireland, 138, 146c, 156, 166, 168, 203c
Isabella of France, 38c
Italy, 11, 40c, 53, 293, 317c, 317, 349c, 351c, 466c
Ivoy Forest, 286

J

Jacques-Coeur Land, 284c, **285**
Jamet, Cristiane, 240
Jean d'Orléans, 374c
Jean de Meung, 398c
Jean de Monfort, 156, 156c
Jean de Trécesson, 228c
Jean de Valognes, 402c
Jean du Thier, 357
Jean II of Rohan, 234c, 237
Jean III, 156, 237
Jean IV, 156, 181, 197c, 221
Jean V, 156
Jean le Breton, 333
Jean le Dunois, 374

Jeanne de Penthièvre, 156
Joan of Arc, 39, 39c, 73c, 116, 272, 289, 293, 296, 296c, 302c, 304c, 357c, 374
John the Baptist, 36c, 295, 325
John the Fearless, 347
John XXII, 424, 426c
Jouve, Paul, 20c
Julian the Apostate, 36
Julius II, 483

L

La Balue, Cardinal, 304c
La Buissière Castle, 286
La Chapelle d'Angillon Castle, 284c, 285c, 285
La Châtre, 272
La Verrerie Castle, 286, 286c
Lamballe, 138c
Langeais Castle, 40c, 266, 293, 294c, **312-314**
Langlois, Henri, 88
Lann Gough, 234
Largoet, Castle of, 233c, 233
Latona Basin, 127c
Latour, Jean Louis, 167c
Le Braz, Anatole, 206, 260
Le Bris, Michel, 201
Le Brun, Charles, 132, 134c
Le Goff, Daniel, 240
Le Mercier, 74
Le Moyne de la Borderie, Arthur, 138, 163
Le Penven, Jeff, 214c, 214
Le Roux, Francois, 227
Le Vau, Louis, 75c, 126c, 126, 132
Le Viol, Jean-Michel, 257, 258c
Legentiò, Alexandre, 115c
Léger, Fernand, 62, 108c
Leonardo da Vinci, 97, 103c, 293, 295, 317, 322c, 324c, 325
Les Baux, 386c, 388c
Lesbahy, Philippa, 308
Lescot, Pierre, 41
Lévis-Mirepoix, Sigismond de, 372c
Loches, 293
Loches Castle, 293, **302-306**
Locmariaquer, 146

Loir River, 370c, 373, 374
Loire River, 6c, 11, 38, 41, 223c, 265, 266, 272, 284c, 289, 290, 293, 293c, 295c, 296, 302, 306c, 307, 308, 312c, 315c, 315, 317c, 321c, 325, 327, 342c, 347, 356c, 357, 361c, 368c, 371, 372c, 378, 379c
Loire Valley, 8, 11, 265, 266c, 266, 267c, 275, 275c, 293, 295, 295c, 296, 299, 347c, 308, 312, 315, 325, 327, 333, 336, 345c, 362, 371, 372c, 378
Longueville, 374
Lorenzo de' Medici, (the Magnificent), 42c
Lorient, 214c, 214
Lorraine, 50
Louédin, Bernard, 184
Louis d'Orléans, see Louis XII
Louis de Culan, 272
Louis I d'Orléans, 317, 347, 374c
Louis VI "the Large", 35c, 35
Louis VIII, 71
Louis IX, 36c, 36, 68, 72c, 74, 399, 463c
Louis XI, 40c, 158, 159c, 266, 289, 293, 296, 304c, 312, 315, 402, 402c
Louis XII, 11c, 158, 275, 293, 295c, 304c, 317, 325, 327c, 347, 348c, 353c, 373
Louis XIII, 45, 66c, 78, 111c, 111, 126, 131, 338c, 348, 355c, 361c
Louis XIV, 45, 46c, 87, 105, 113c, 113, 126c, 126, 128c, 129, 129c, 131c, 131, 132c, 134c, 212, 252, 266, 286, 289, 308c, 325, 338c, 348, 355c, 362c, 364c, 368c, 406c, 422c, 423, 432c, 432
Louis XV, 46, 47c, 106, 129c, 131c, 132, 252, 272, 289, 325
Louis XVI, 48c, 49, 50, 51c, 57, 68c, 129, 129c, 131, 132c, 160, 377, 409c
Louis XVIII, 56c, 57c, 57, 373
Louis Le Barbier, 45c
Louis Philippe, 76c, 319c

Louis the Pious, 154
Louise de Keroualle, Duchess of Portsmouth, 286
Louise de la Vallière, 126
Louise of Lorraine, 336c, 336
Louise of Savoy, 317
Louis-Napoléon Le Roux, 164
Louppe, Albert, 172c
Luberon, region, 10c
Ludovico il Moro, 304c
Luxor, 8c, 57c, 105c, 105

M

Madeleine d'Auvergne, 42c
Maine, 149
Maintenon Castle, 266, 377c, 377
Maintenon, Madame de, 371, 377c, 377
Malgorn, Theo, 205
Manet, Eduoard, 61, 83c, 83
Mans, 149c
Mansart, Harduin, 132
Manzoni, Alessandro, 22
Marat, Jean-Paul, 74
Margherite de Foix, 223
Marguerite de Rohan, 237c
Marguerite of Navarre, 352c
Maria Amelia of Bourbon, 319c
Maria de Médici, 76, 348, 471
Maria Theresa of Austria, 48c
Marie Antoinette, 48c, 49, 49c, 105, 129, 130c, 131, 132c, 132, 275
Marie de Clèves, 347
Marie, Cristophe, 45c
Marseilles, 11c, 11, 382, 384, 387, 392, 393c, 397c, 398, 399, 402, 404, 406c, 406c, 407, 409, 410, 411c, 412, 417c, 424, 451c, 452c, 492
Martel, Charles, 397
Martray, Joseph, 166
Marx, Karl, 61
Masson, Erwan, 205c, 205
Matisse, Henri, 83, 106, 108c
Maupas Castle, 285, 285c
Maurice de Sully, 35, 71
Maximilian of Austria, 158
Meiffret, Laurence, 188c

Meillant Castle, 266, 272c, 282c, **283-284**
Melzi, Francesco, 325
Mercogliano, Pacello, 317
Michelangelo, 97, 282c, 283
Millet, Jean-François, 83
Millin du Perreux, Alexandre, 302c
Mique, Richard, 130c
Mirabeau, Honoré, 74
Mirò, Joan, 120
Mistral, Frederic, 492
Mitterand, François, 18, 65c, 65, 78, 93c, 97, 101c
Modigliani, Amedeo, 20, 106, 108c, 114c
Molière, (Jean Baptiste Poquelin), 126
Monaco, 392
Monet, Claude, 11, 61, 83c, 83, 106, 114c, 120, 214c, 382
Monroe, Marilin, 88
Montigny-le-Gannelon Castle, 266, 370c, 371, 372c, **373-376**
Montmorency-Laval, Adrien de, 372c
Montmuran, Castle of, 249c
Montrésor, 302
Montrichard, 336
Moreau, 378
Morgan, Michèle, 67c
Morgiou, 11c

N

Nançay, 285
Nançon, River, 249c
Nantes, 83, 149c, 149, 153c, 156, 159c, 165c, 214, 223c, 225c, 252, 404c
Naples, 40c
Napoleon Bonaparte, 53, 53c, 54c, 57c, 57, 60c, 73c, 87c, 87, 90, 104c, 113c, 118c, 119, 160, 276, 278c, 281c, 325
Napoleon III, 58c, 59c, 59, 60c, 71, 83c, 85c, 113c, 122, 302, 409c, 410, 428c
Narbonne, 393, 397
Navarre, 223
New York, 240

Nice, 310c, 392, 412
Nicolas le Grand, 240
Niki de Saint Phalle, 106c
Nimes, 395, 424c
Nini, Battista, 327
Nominoé, 219
Normandy, 35, 64, 149, 174,
    176c, 249, 371
Norway, 203
Nouvel, Jean, 78

O

Odet River, 141c, 212c
Olivier de Clisson, 221c, 237c
Orange, 11, 395, 395c, 413, **432-433**
Orléans, 39c, 272, 289, 293, 296,
    296c, 302c, 319c
Orley, Bernard, 37c
Ott, Carlo, 113
Ouessant, 205c, 205, 206, 208c,
    209c, 234, 244
Oust River, 237c, 237

P

Pagnol, Marcel, 387
Paimpol, 10c
Paris, 6c, 8, **16-135**, 160, 161,
    163, 163d, 197C, 254, 258,
    265, 266, 272, 276, 293, 296,
    296c, 347, 403c, 475, 500c
Pascale, 78
Patay, 272
Pays Bigouden, 141c
Pei, Jeoh Mong, 65c, 97, 98c
Pelouze, Madame, 336
Pepin the Short, 33c, 33
Perrault, Charles, 298c, 299
Philip Augustus, 302
Philip II, 35c
Philippa of Hainault, 38c
Philippe d'Orléans, 290
Piano, Renzo, 106
Picasso, Pablo, 20, 62, 106, 108c, 111,
    114c, 120, 382, 417c, 437, 471c
Pissarro, Camille, 61, 83, 85c
Pius VII, 53c
Plessis-lez-Tours Castle, 293
Poitiers, 397

Pompidou, Georges, 65, 67c
Pontivy, Castle of, 234c
Porhoet, 230c
Proust, Marcel, 111, 371, 371c,
    376c, 377c, 377
Provence, 8, 11, **380-501**
Prud'hon, Pierre Paul, 277c
Puget, Pierre, 422c
Puvis de Chavannes, Pierre, 393c

Q

Queen Margot, see Marguerite
    of Navarre
Quimper, 257, 258c
Quimperlé, 212

R

Rance River, 251c, 251
Raphael Sanzio, 97, 103c, 283,
    302
Raymond I des Baux, 398
Raymond V of Tolouse, 397c
Redon, 230c, 230, 231c
Reims, 32c, 32, 39c, 304c
Renan, Ernest, 197
René d'Anjou,
Rennes, 6c, 149, 156, 158, 163,
    165c, 230c, 233, 234, 239,
    251, 251c, 252c, 252
Renoir, Auguste, 11, 61, 83, 106,
    114c
Rhone River, 387, 388c, 392,
    393, 396, 397, 401, 402c, 424,
    434c, 434, 443, 455c, 500c,
    501
Rias, 254c
Richard the Lionheart, 302
Richelieu, Cardinal, 44, 74, 97,
    101c, 237, 348, 349c, 440
Rieux, 233c, 233
Rigaud, Hyacinthe, 355c
Robert de Boron, 227
Robert de Parme, 267c
Robert de Sorbon, 36, 74c, 74
Rochefort Castle, 230
Rochefort-en-Terre, 230c, 230, 233
Roger the Mortimer, 38c
Rogers, Richard, 106
Rohault de Fleury, 115c

Roi de Bourges, see Charles VII
Rome, 30c, 30, 32c, 33, 57c, 151,
    373, 393, 395, 397c
Roscoff, 203c, 203
Rousseau, Etienne, 308
Rousseau, Jean-Jacques, 74, 111,
    132, 336
Roussillon, 10c, 382, 386c, 387c,
    388c, 412, 477, 477c
Ruggieri, 327c, 327, 330c
Russia, 94c, 146
Russy Forest, 356c, 357

S

Saint Louis, see Louis IX
Saint-Aubin du Cormier, 157c, 158
Saint-Malo, 137c, 165c, 168, 170,
    181c, 181, 183c, 184c, 249,
    251c, 251
Saint-Maries-de-la-Mer, 462c,
    463c, 499c, 499
Saint-Pol-Roux, 141
Saint-Remy, 395
Saint-Sulpice, 78
Saint-Tropez, 384, 392, 412,
    413c, 443, 443c, 444c, 444,
    445c, 495, 495c
Sange River, 290
Sartre, Jean Paul, 116c, 119
Saumur, 312
Saumur Castle, 3, 306c, 307, 307c
Schorr von Carlosfeld, Julius, 32c
Scotland, 138
Seine River, 8, 17c, 18c, 22, 28,
    28c, 30, 31, 32, 32c, 35, 37c,
    40, 41, 45c, 46, 47c, 54c, 67,
    83, 85c, 87, 88, 90, 93c, 116,
    119, 122c, 123c, 293
Sérusier, Paul, 210
Servat, Gilles, 214, 221c
Seurat, Georges, 83
Sienkiewicz, Henryck, 194
Simenon, Georges, 68c, 387
Soissons, 32c, 32
Sologne Forest, 290
Sologne, 290, 291c, 362c
Sorel, Agnès, 285, 293, 296, 299,
    302c, 302, 304c
Sormiou, 11c
Souvestre, Emile, 242, 260

Squiban, Didier, 205
St.Petersburg, 94c, 414c
Stanislaw Leczinski of Poland, Duke of Bar and Lorraine, 368c
Stendhal, (Marie-Henri Beyle), 20
Stivell, Alan, 167, 167c, 214c, 214, 239
Stravinsky, Igor, 106c
Stuart, Mary, 73c, 116
Stuart, James, 286
Sully-sur-Loire Castle, 267c, **290-292**
Suscinio Castle, 216c

T

Tabalry, Eric, 169c
Talleyrand de Périgord, Charles Maurice, 276c, 276, 277c, 278c, 281c
Taureau Castle, 201c, 201
Thibauld the Trickster, 374
Thymerais Forest, 377
Tinguely, Jean, 106c
Toulon, **440-442**
Toulouse, 83, 168, 397, 483
Toulouse-Lautrec, 83, 85c, 114c
Touraine, 293, 312, 333
Tours, 11c, 43, 296, 308, 333
Trécesson, Castle of, 229c

Trèguier, 197, 197c
Tudor, Henry, 233
Tuileries, les, 51c

U

United States, 62c
Urban V, 426c
Ussé Castle, 298c, **299-301**

V

Vaison-la-Romaine, 395
Val de Loire, see Loire Valley
Valençay Castle, 272, **276-282**, 295
Valentino, Rudolph, 88
Valmy, 51
Valois, House, 40c, 330c
Van Blarenberghe, Henri Joseph, 348c
Van Dongen, Kees, 114c
Van Gogh, Vincent, 11, 83, 85c, 114c, 120c, 120, 382c, 384, 414c, 414, 417, 434c, 434, 437, 480c, 499
Vannes, 149, 159, 163, 163d, 174c, 208c, 219c, 219, 233, 234c, 234, 252, 257c, 258c
Vannetais, 216c
Varennes, 50
Vasari, Giorgio, 43c

Venice, 104c, 181
Verdon, 469c
Verdun, 165, 382
Vermeer, Jan, 103c
Vernet, Claude Joseph, 406c
Versailles, 45, 46, 46c, 47c, 49, 49c, 50, 51c, **126-135**, 272
Vibraye, Marquises of,
Vienna, 53, 373
Vienne river, 296c
Vilar, Jean, 426
Villandry Castle, 293, 293c, 332c, 333
Villandry, **333-335**
Vitré, 249
Voltaire, François-Marie Arouet de, 74, 111, 120, 290
Von Spreckelsen, Johan Otto, 93c

W

Wace, Robert, 227
William the Conqueror, 156c

Y

Yann-Ber-Calloc, 214c, 214
Yvonne de Galais, 285

Z

Zola, Emile, 74, 111

PHOTO CREDITS

Antonio Attini/Archivio White Star: pages 10, 14-15, 382, 382-383, 383 top, 384 center right and bottom, 386 top, 387, 388, 389, 392 bottom, 420, 420-421, 422, 423, 424 top and bottom, 425 top right, 429 top right, 429 center and bottom, 430 top, 430-431, 431, 432, 434 top, 435 top left, 436 top left and right, 437 top, 438, 440 center and bottom, 441 top right, 444 center, 445 top left and right, 448, 448-449, 449 top left, 450, 451, 452, 453, 454 top, 457 bottom left, top right and bottom right, 462 top, 463, 466, 467, 468, 469, 470 top left and right, 471 top and bottom, 472, 473, 474 top left and right and bottom, 475 left, 476, 477, 478, 479, 480, 481, 482, 483, 484, 485, 486-487, 488, 489, 499 top right, center right and bottom right.

Marcello Bertinetti/Archivio White Star: pages 24-25, 68-69, 71 left, 72-73, 73 top, 88 bottom, 91 top left, 106 bottom, 106-107, 114 top and bottom, 116 bottom left, 116 top right, 122, 122-123, 124 bottom, 444 bottom, 447 top right.

Livio Bourbon/Archivio White Star: pages 1, 4-5, 10-11, 138, 138-139, 139 top, 170 top, 170 center, 170 bottom, 170-171, 171 top left, 171 top right, 172 bottom, 176 top, 176 bottom, 178 top left, 178 top right, 181 right center top, 181 right center bottom, 181 bottom right, 182 top left, 182 top right, 182-183, 183 top, 184 top, 184 bottom, 185 top left, 185 top right, 186 bottom, 187 top, 189 top, 190 top, 190-191, 191 top, 192 top, 192 center, 192 bottom, 192-193, 196 top left, 196 top right, 196-197, 197 left, 197 top right, 197 bottom right, 210 top, 210 bottom, 210-211, 211 top left, 212 top, 212 bottom, 212-213, 213 top left, 213 top right, 216 top, 218 top left, 218 top right, 218-219, 219 left, 219 top right, 219 bottom right, 221 top, 221 center, 221 bottom, 225 bottom right, 228 top, 228 center, 228 bottom, 229 top, 246 top, 246 bottom, 246-247, 247 top left, 247 top right, 248 top left, 248 top right, 248-249, 249 top, 249 center, 249 bottom, 250 top left, 250 top right, 250-251, 251 top, 252 top left, 252 bottom left, 252 top right, 252 center right, 252 bottom right, 253, 512.

Luciano Ramires/Archivio White Star: pages 7, 78-79, 99, 118 bottom left, 118 right, 178-179, 179 top, 179 bottom, 181 left, 206 bottom, 214 center, 384 top left and center left, 424 center, 425 top left, 426 center, 436-437, 455 top and bottom, 457 top left, 458, 459, 460-461, 461, 464-465.

Giulio Veggi/Archivio White Star: pages 9, 20-21, 67 top, 68 top, 68 left, 69 top, 71 right, 72 left, 74 left, 74 top, 74-75, 76 top, 77, 82, 86, 87, 90, 92 top, 93

right, 104 top, 105, 106 top, 111 bottom, 112-113, 113, 115 top, 116 top and center left, 116 bottom right, 119, 120 top, 123 top, 124 top.

David Ademas/Gamma/Contrasto: pages 167 top, 167 bottom.

Agenzia Stradella, Milan/Costa: pages 398-399.

Aisa: pages 154 bottom, 155, 158-159.

AKG Photo: pages 35 right, 36 bottom right, 45 top and bottom, 47 bottom left and bottom right, 48 bottom left, 49, 51 top and center, 59 bottom, 62 top left, 62-63, 63 top, 64, 336 center left, 368 top left, 394 bottom, 394-395, 399, 402 top, 403 bottom, 408-409, 409 top, 410 top, 411 bottom left, 414 top and bottom left, 416-417, 417 top and center, 419 bottom.

Stefano Amantini/Atlantide: page 426 top.

Kurt Amsler/Dupe: page 449 top right.

Bernard Annebique/Corbis Sygma/Grazia Neri: pages 208 top, 208-209, 209 top, 216-217, 255.

Archivio Scala: pages 33 bottom left, 37 top right, 43 bottom left, 61 bottom, 75 top right, 103 top right, 151, 152, 395, 402 bottom, 404, 405 top left, 406 top, 415, 417 bottom.

The Art Archive: pages 149 top, 154 top, 156.

Bruno Barbey/Magnum Photos/ Contrasto: page 65 center.

Barnaby's Picutre Library: page 62 center right.

J. G. J. G. Berizzi/RMN: pages 146 top.

Jean Bernard: pages 392-393, 393 bottom, 404-405, 407 center and bottom, 408 bottom.

Yann Arthus Bertrand/ Corbis/Contrasto: pages 172-173, 186-187, 198-199, 200-201, 202 top right, 203 bottom, 223.

Yann Arthus Bertrand/Altitude/ The Image Bank: pages 2-3, 67 bottom, 91 top right, 92-93, 96-97, 107 top, 111 top, 113 top left, 126-127.

Bettmann/Corbis/Contrasto: pages 164-165.

Bibliothèque Publique et Universitaire, Geneva/The Bridgeman Art Library: page 398 bottom.

Catherine Bibollet/Agence Top: pages 374, 377, 378-379, 378 top, 378 left, 379 right, 379 top.

Bildarchiv Steffens: pages 290-291, 304 center right, 307 bottom.

Foto BIP/Agenzia Luisa Ricciarini: pages 73 bottom, 113 top right.

Gérard Blot/RMN: page 146 bottom.

Blot/Wallis: pages 434-435.

Yvon Boelle: pages 168 top, 168 bottom, 168-169, 169 top, 174 bottom, 174-175, 175 top right, 186 top, 188 top, 188 center, 188 bottom, 188-189, 190 bottom, 194 left, 198 top, 199 top left, 199 top right, 201 top, 201 center, 201 bottom, 202 top left, 204, 205 top, 205 bottom left, 205 bottom center, 205 bottom right, 206-207, 211 top right, 216 bottom, 217 top right, 226 top left, 226 top right, 226-227, 227, 228-229, 230 bottom, 231 top right, 233 top left, 233 top right, 234, 234-235, 234 top left, 235 top right, 237 top, 238 top left, 238-239, 240, 245 top, 258 left, 258 bottom right.

Christophe Boisvieux: pages 144-145, 230 top, 230-231, 231 top left, 232, 233 bottom, 236, 237 bottom, 238 top right, 239 top, 242 top, 242 bottom, 257 bottom.

Eva Brandecker/Das Fotoarchiv/ Studio B: page 306 top.

The Bridgeman Art Library: pages 153, 156-157.

Henri Cartier-Bresson/ Magnum/Contrasto: pages 166-167.

Castello De Vençay: pages 276 bottom, 278 left, 279 top, 281.

Stefano Cellai/Sie: page 98.

Center Historique des Archives Nationales, Paris: page 405 top right.

Hervé Champollion/Agence Top: pages 262-263, 266 top, 266 left, 267 top, 272 bottom, 272 top right, 276-277, 285 top, 292 top left, 297 right, 297 bottom, 299, 300-301, 315 center left, 315 center right, 316-317, 316 top, 317 top, 317 bottom, 326 top, 327

right, 330 top, 330 bottom left, 332 top, 333 center, 334 center left, 335, 336 bottom, 336 top, 341 right, 347 top, 356 top, 357 top left, 357 bottom, 364, 364-365, 365 top right, 368-369, 375.

Jean Marc Charles/Corbis Sygma/Grazia Neri: pages 224-225.

Jean Marc Charles/Agenzia Franca Speranza: pages 90-91.

J.M. Charles/Rapho/Grazia Neri: page 125 top.

Jean Loup Charmet: pages 31 right, 37 bottom, 50 top, 54, 55, 56-57, 57 center, 58 center, 59 center.

Serge Chirol: pages 265, 272 top left, 272 center, 277 top left, 290, 291 top, 294-295, 295 bottom, 296-297, 297 top right, 300 top, 300 center, 300 bottom, 301 top, 304-305, 315 bottom, 316 left, 323 center and bottom, 331, 333 bottom, 347 center and bottom, 349 top, 350-351, 362, 363 top, 366 top, 370-371, 372 top, 372-373.

Matthieu Colin/Hémisphères: pages 175 top left, 214 top, 214-215.

Collections de la Chambre de Commerce et d'Industrie Marseille - Provence: pages 406-407.

Collezione Privata: pages 28 center and bottom, 32 top and center right, 33 bottom right, 34-35, 37 top left, 39 bottom left, 41 center, 60 top and center, 163.

Giuliano Colliva: pages 12-13, 266-267, 292-293, 306-307, 307 top, 315 top.

Corbis Images: page 401 top.

Gian Carlo Costa/Agenzia Stradella: pages 35 top left, 53 bottom, 60 bottom.

Marco Cristofori/SIE: page 95.

Giovanni Dagli Orti: pages 28 top, 28-29, 30 bottom, 31 left, 32 center left, 32 bottom, 34 top right, 36 left, 38, 40 top, 41 top and bottom, 42 top, 42-43, 43 top, 43 bottom right, 44 left, 44 bottom, 46 top, 48-49, 56 top left, 57 top and bottom, 58-59, 61 top and center, 75 top left, 97, 108 top, 108-109, 126, 127 top, 128, 129, 130, 131, 132, 133, 134-135, 150, 158 bottom, 159, 276 top center, 276 top right, 278-279, 280, 288 top right, 289, 288-289, 292 top right, 294 top, 302 top, 302 bottom, 304 center left, 305 bottom, 308 bottom, 309 top, 310, 311, 312 left, 312 bottom right, 318, 319, 320, 321, 322 bottom, 322-323, 323 top, 324, 325, 327 bottom left, 330 bottom right, 336 center right, 338-339, 340, 340-341, 343, 348-349, 351 center right, 351 top, 352-353, 354-355, 358-359, 360 top, 361, 364 top left, 366 bottom, 366 center left, 366-367, 368 right, 368 bottom left, 369 bottom, 376 top right.

Giovanna Dal Magro: pages 430 center and bottom.

R. De Pardon/Gamma: page 65 bottom center.

Catherine & Bernard Desjeux: pages 334 center right, 334 bottom.

Leonard De Selva/Corbis/Contrasto: page 164 top right.

512 On the corner of a building in the old quarter of Lamballe, a small town on the Cote D'Armor famous for its splendid stables that are open to the public, is the entrance to the little museum that was set up in honour of the local painter Mathurin Méheur (1882-1958).

Cover
The Eiffel Tower at night.
© Giovanni Simeone/Sime

Back cover
Top left - Mont Saint-Michel.
© Livio Bourbon/Archivio White Star

Top right - Fields of lavender near Sault.
© Antonio Attini/Archivio White Star

Bottom - Chenonceau, also known as the "Castle of the Queens".
© Photo Bank